at crazoid you might run into. Don't be
want to live in fear and I wanted my
no weapon. By traveling in this manner
I ...., closer to people, and closer to God.

—from Chapter 5

ENJOY THE EXPERIENCES:

- What happens while crossing a narrow and busy bridge high above the Mississippi River when an eighteen-wheeler passes from behind and blasts its horn?!

- See what happens when the dirty, wet, unannounced stranger knocks on a farmhouse door at nighttime, and asks for a place to stay.

- Relate personally as the boss laughs at the rumor of an employee quitting a good job—while he dreams for the day of his own retirement!

- How do Amish people react to an "Englishman" traveling by horse and buggy—electrified?

- Smile as the playful giant, Carter, gives sleepy horse kisses, noses around for oats inside the buggy, and stalls for a longer break—pretending to drink water.

- Clutch your own arm in pain as Carter accidently kicks the author in the arm and hip full force!

FIND OUT:

- How President Franklin D. Roosevelt enabled all of America to become equal members of the 20th century.

- How housing needs for senior citizens and modern telecommunications in the most remote sections of the United States can be achieved—by systems that are proven, organized, funded, and in place—NOW!

- How democratic organizations in the marketplace can better assure stable local economic development.

- More about the potential roles of solar power.

- How the world's largest monopoly was forced to become democratic and how Americans can have a say in meeting their new and future needs!

NEIGHBORS

Electric Burro on the Road to Bogota

NEIGHBORS

Electric Burro on the Road to Bogota

by Scott Hudson

Breakaw a y Publishing 🌲🌲 Williamsburg

A Breakaw a y Book

Published by Breakaw a y Publishing, Williamsburg

All photographs by Scott Hudson except the following:

Front cover: Rural Wisconsin by Ben Penkivich

Back cover: Kids, Kitty, and Carter by Cindy McCulloch

Other photos: DC-3 over quiet lights, by Richard Woods; Baby Pete, by Frances Hudson; Now what?, by Heather Hemingway; May 11 at capitol, by Mike Buda; Cooling heels in Lake Michigan, by Marijean Stephenson; Downtown Gillett, by Ben Penkivich; Old-timers, by Bob Luce; Soldiers Grove, by Tom Pardee; Carter and friend, by Mary Rueter; Leaving fairgrounds, by Mary Rueter; Climbing bluff, by Bill Foley; Melissa Corbin, by Peggy Corbin; Cooperation in Bogota, by Brenda Epley; Carter nudging goodbye, by Brenda Epley

Map by Robert N. Paxton

Electric Burro Travel Series logo and chapter heads by Trisha Rice

Photo and article from November 8, 1985 *The Commercial Appeal*, Memphis Tennessee

First Breakaw a y Publishing Company edition. All rights reserved.

Manufactured in the United States of America.

Hudson, Scott, 1949–

  Neighbors : electric burro on the road to Bogota.

  1. United States—Description and travel—1981– 2. Middle West—Description and travel. 3. Rural electrification—United States. 4. United States. Rural Electrification Administration. 5. Hudson, Scott, 1949– —Journeys—United States. I. Title.
E169.04.H83   1987   917.7'0433   87-72475
ISBN 0-9619198-1-7
ISBN 0-9619198-0-9 (pbk.)

Dedicated to:

Fifty years of rural electrification in the United States of America,

and to the cooperation between neighbors that allowed it.

"Teacher, which is the great commandment in the Law?"

And He said to him, "You shall love the Lord your God with all your heart, and with all your soul, and with all your mind. This is the great and foremost commandment.

The second is like it, "You shall love your neighbor as yourself. On these two commandments depend the whole Law and the Prophets."

—*Jesus*

CONTENTS

Chapter   Page

Introduction   xi
1 Quiet Lights   1
2 Goal Setting   10
3 The Special Spirit of the REA   21
4 Electric Buggy   27
5 Electric Burro   34
6 A Commemoration   50
7 On the Road Again—Lower Michigan   61
8 A Network of Friends—Upper Michigan   83
9 Rural Values—Wisconsin   104
10 Cooperative Innovation—Iowa   127
   Electric Burro Travel Series #5   134
11 Good Samaritans—Illinois   136
12 An All White Sparrow—Northern Missouri   150
13 Into the Bottoms and Over the Levee—Southern Missouri   170
14 Down in Bogota!—Tennessee   193
15 International Cooperation   207
   Epilogue   217

Acknowledgements

The many people who appear in this book all helped it come to pass. For each one mentioned there have been many that haven't—only because of limited space. I attribute my good fortune to all of these people and to the greater Spirit of Life.

Certainly no one provided greater support than my parents, Leslie and Frances Hudson. Their love has been unfailing and their efforts have bordered on the superhuman, and I'm not exaggerating.

There have been many within the rural electric cooperative family that have been very supportive of the trip. Some have been particularly encouraging. Bob Bergland, J. C. Brown, and the staff of NRECA helped me to believe that such a commemoration could mean more than just an off the wall trip. Farmer and REA pioneer Willard Haenke of Blanchard, Michigan naturally fused his special warmth towards animals and the REA neighbor-to-neighbor program and invited us to stay at his farm, the first destination of the trip. I could always count on cooperators, Ray Kuhl and Mike Buda of Michigan Electric Cooperative Association. Betty and Bud Gordon from my own Cherryland REC did not restrain their youthful enthusiasm and always encouraged.

A special acknowledgement and dedication goes to Bill Matson, president of the statewide Pennsylvania Rural Electric Association. Bill passed away June 16, 1986, but for more than thirty years his voice sang unrestrained about the merits of public power. He was unusually vigorous and eloquent. When the NRECA regional meeting was held in Philadelphia midway during the trip, Bill came to me and encouraged me to continue. He felt that the trip was an opportunity to educate a wider spectrum of people about the merits of non-profit and democratic power systems and he stood up to encourage all state associations and local co-ops to help. Bill has been missed and his shoes cannot be filled.

The family of Eugene and Evelyn Kluesner are mentioned in the book but I would be remiss if I did not thank them again for picking Carter up from Bogota and keeping him while I left the country and began work on writing.

Weldon, Patricia, and Vickie Schramp became family, first when I spent the night with Carter at their place in Perryville, Missouri, again when Weldon picked me and the buggy up in Bogota, and once more when we all brought Carter back to Michigan in the Spring of 1986 from the Kluesner home.

Thanks to Kaye May, Victor Loritz, Art Blagg, and Linda Akin for their efforts at editing.

This list is incomplete and to those who played so many helpful roles, please forgive me for not mentioning you here. Take heart in knowing that even this little mention is inadequate for what you have given me. Thanks.

SRH
July 30, 1987
Williamsburg, Michigan

Introduction

Far removed from flying DC–3's loaded with freight, Carter and I were in Tennessee, healthy, and for the first time in months I was able to let up and relax and just enjoy where I was at. Six months earlier I had bought my first horse and three days later found myself scared to death and totally unqualified, driving a Belgian draft horse and the world's first solar powered and computerized Mennonite-made buggy down a country road outside of Michigan's state capital, Lansing.

Time after time the calls had been too close for comfort. I had been lucky, we had been lucky. But this story is much more than mere survival. It's a story from yesterday and of tomorrow; of people helping themselves by helping their neighbors. I had met hundreds of people who were helpful and kind, many of whose backs were hard pressed against the wall, mostly in rural America, many of them farmers. Yet here we were, not so much by our own doings as by the help of people along the way, neighbors all.

To understand why this trip ever took place at all you have to travel back in time to the depression-riddled 1930's, and out of the city to rural America. Creature comforts and security were missing in those places and times. Much had changed. Much had not. The same elements continued, but now they played a new role in causing this unlikely journey.

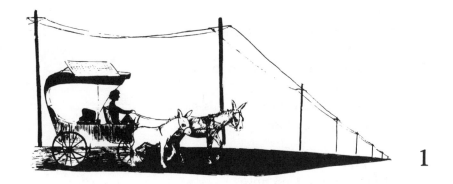

Quiet Lights

Cruising above the silent city
  covered in nightness
The many little lights
  the only evidence that something is there
Quiet lights
  most of them not moving, a few dare to creep along

The mysterious ether, so silent above
  and I am within it
In a ship that pierces the mist
  a mystery unto myself and this creation
And ahead and below
  I see the darkness—it looks even evil
  and the meanness is alive
  and it seems to grow

It grows upward towards me and
  the safety of my ship
And it grows larger—expanding and darker than
  all the rest that surrounds me
The ship remains, I see the blackness reach out
  and I think it
  will touch me.

The lights below remain
  and remain silent
  and unmoving
They offer memories and pathes to who I am
  but they don't offer to help
or to ally themselves with me as this gloom
  continues to come closer

I'm not afraid
  but I jump at the loud noise
  and I feel humbled
Mortal man
  born to die
I remember now
          and as I remember
the dark grey mass
  moving
    living
  swallows me up

I can do nothing
  but feel it around me
moving me

If I liked it
  it wouldn't matter
If I feared it
  it wouldn't matter
I am now inside
  and a part
    with nothing to say
and the silent lights
    speaking of life and friendship
          are gone

    but I continue on . . .

When I wrote this poem it was nighttime and thunderstorms
were everywhere. The old DC-3 was loaded with 2$^1/2$ tons of

hubcaps and the round trip from Detroit, Michigan to Valdosta, Georgia lasted nearly 11 hours, most of them on instruments.

There were two pilots on board this chartered freighter and we alternated the actual flying. When it was my turn away from the flying of the craft I could look out into the darkness and peer down towards the ground.

I thought of what each point of light might represent. Many were streetlights. Some were floodlights lighting the backyard of someone's home. Perhaps that light over there came from someone's bedroom. There were so many stories behind each light, some seemingly irrelevant, others vitally important.

On this night we had to land using the instruments and when we finally broke below the low clouds we were greeted by beautifully brilliant approach lights to the runway—lifesaving sparks of energy. At that moment I didn't care how the light got there, so long as it was there.

The latter part of 1981 found the entire world in the midst of an economic recession. No place in the United States was reeling more than the Motor City. Sales of automobiles were way down. My job as a freight pilot was threatened as auto companies worked to cut their loses. There were few expenses as great as chartering air freight to move needed parts that an entire assembly line awaited.

Our flights became less frequent. The company I flew for was a small one and in December four of the ten pilots were laid off. I joined the ranks of the unemployed.

In August, 1981, President Reagan had fired more than 11,000 air traffic controllers when the union walked out on an illegal strike. The timing couldn't have been better for someone looking for work.

When the Federal Aviation Administration (FAA) called and offered me a job as a controller in Traverse City, Michigan, I did not hesitate in saying yes. The job offered me the chance to get to know the aeronautical world from both sides.

For four grueling months I attended the air traffic control academy in Oklahoma City in order to qualify for the job. Upon graduation I made the long drive to northern Michigan, eager to get established in my new world.

As jobs go it was good—good security, good pay, respect from the community and, as a rule, a job with a professional atmosphere. We truly provided a needed service and I appreciated the responsibility, especially since I was fresh from the cockpit and aware of pilot needs. The job included a room with a good view and I was glad to be working indoors, considering Michigan winters.

I also enjoyed the free flight program. Controllers are allowed eight free flights per year as an effort to promote meaningful communications between the people on both sides of the microphones. It was believed that controller morale would improve by offering this benefit. Since the travel took place in the cockpit, the pilots and controllers could talk with each other and get to know one another's needs and procedures better.

Things progressed well. As I worked towards becoming a journeyman controller, I learned my way around the area and met new friends. I wanted to make my home in the area and spent time looking for a place I might buy.

Five months after moving to Traverse City I found an old barn that was for sale 15 miles out of town. A couple had begun to convert it into a livable sort of building.

I asked them about possible drawbacks, accepting as a given that there would be a lot of work required on my part to make the place genuinely liveable. They replied that the only real drawback was that the area was served by REA.

I hadn't the foggiest idea what they meant. They explained that the electric company that served the area was REA and it was more expensive than the one that served the town. Since I wasn't a big user of electricity anyway, I didn't think too much of it. The deal was made.

I moved into my barn home just as the cold winds of November began to blow. Efforts at learning my way around came to a halt as I worked to winterize the barn before the snow fell. There was plenty to do. You could see daylight through some of the walls. There was no hot water, no shower, little insulation, and no wood for the stove.

I would leave for work at the airport straight from my work at the barn. Eighteen and twenty hour days were common, and it felt good. It was my barn, and it gave me purpose.

Work continued all winter long, alternating between hours at the airport and the barn. Progress was made on both fronts.

At home, life began to include hot water and a shower, a new door here, an insulated wall there. Seemingly endless trips into the woods with my 1948 8N Ford tractor allowed for a wood pile large enough to see me through winter.

At work, I was promoted above the status of trainee and began working the job independent of a trainer. Every two weeks I received a good paycheck and I invested in my new home.

As I gained experience on the job at the airport and began to forget the pass-or-fail environment that carried over from my days at the academy in Oklahoma, I slowly began to realize that the job of an air traffic controller was not what the media portrayed.

I learned to differentiate between slow times and busy times and that the stress of the job was occasional in nature, not a full-time presence. At times I saw evidence of inefficient bureaucracy and personal laziness on the part of some, but I was not a journeyman and deferred judgment. Reality slowly settled in.

One day while working at the barn I interrupted nailing some new flooring long enough to fetch the mail. On this day I received a handful of junk mail and felt slightly depressed that something more meaningful hadn't arrived. I trudged through the snow back to the shelter and warmth of the barn and tossed the junk mail on the table, forgetting about it, and resumed pounding with the hammer.

Later that night, before retiring, I picked through the useless mail and discovered that one of the pieces was a newsletter from the so-called REA, the high cost electric company that the previous owners had told me about. Actually, it wasn't from the REA at all but from the electric cooperative. REA, I learned, stood for the Rural Electrification Administration, a federal agency that had originally provided low cost loans to the "new" cooperatives back in the 1930's and 1940's.

As I looked through the pulp mouthpiece of the utility I found a few articles that kept my attention. There was a piece about how cooperatives represented democratic ideals by allowing people to vote for other "members" and thereby decide who would be in charge of the electric company.

All I knew about cooperatives was a vague memory from history lessons of long ago about some left wing farmers' movement. Was it the Grange, or William Jennings Bryan? Something like that.

Anyhow, as far as I knew . . or cared . . except for some food co-ops on some of the more radical college campuses, co-ops hadn't worked and had died out. I realized that I really didn't know what a cooperative was.

I thought back to a few months earlier when I had to drive 50 miles to the headquarters building of the REA cooperative just so I could sign up as a customer. If it wasn't for the good looking woman who sat down with me and collected my membership fee, I probably wouldn't have remembered anything about the visit, even though she took the time to explain it to me.

I read further and noticed that elections would be held in spring. I couldn't try to become one of those who were in charge of the utility, could I?

"Ah, don't waste your time," I told myself. I tossed the paper down and went to bed.

The next day I got up and poured a cup of coffee. Next to the cup was the co-op newsletter and I picked it up for something to read. I realized that I was qualified to try to get elected.

I thought that as elections go, surely this one would be ignored by most people and just perhaps I could get elected to the co-op's board of directors. I thought about the pros and cons of the idea.

If I actually got elected, I would have to arrange my work days so I could attend the monthly board meetings. I doubted that the people at the airport would have much tolerance for such community involvement, and as a apprentice controller I didn't want to jeopardize my job.

I didn't like meetings. I especially disliked long business meetings. It was a long drive to the co-op building. I tossed the paper back down and decided against the idea.

I poured a second cup of coffee and surveyed the work I wanted to do that day at the barn. As I drank the coffee I glanced out the window at the blowing snow. For some reason I couldn't help but think about the good side of such work within a utility.

It would be a good opportunity to learn and actually try to become a part of my new community. I began to suspect that my job with the FAA might not be fulfilling enough, a little too confining.

I remembered back to my Peace Corps days in Nepal when I worked as a volunteer building water systems in the Himalayan mountains. Usually when I thought of my time on the other side of the world I found myself appreciating how my conviction had grown, believing that the human spirit was the same throughout the world—that a mother looked at her child with the same eyes regardless of language or the name used to address God.

Now as I looked out at the cold Michigan landscape I thought that energy was a common denominator of society, even in Hindu and Buddhist Nepal.

The home of the tallest mountains in the world was a place that had become terribly deforested. It was a third world country with almost no exportable goods, and the cost of oil made fuels other than wood too expensive. But every day the people had to travel further than the day before just to get enough wood to boil water and cook their rice.

While in Nepal I became friends with another volunteer who was working with the development of "go-bar" energy plants. These were nothing more than small, simple containers that utilized cow manure to produce methane gas, which then could be used for cooking. It was a fight against tradition.

As I sipped my coffee, I kept thinking back to earlier days, probably trying to justify any possible attempt at personal involvement in the complex question of energy and society.

When I returned from Nepal I went to work as a restaurant manager and managed to buy a house. Two years later I sold the house, realized a $15,000 profit, and viewed the occasion as an opportunity to pursue my dreams.

It so happened that the U.S. Congress had passed a resolution establishing May 3, 1978 as a day to be known as Sun Day. Its purpose was to acknowledge alternative energy sources.

For the six months leading up to Sun Day I traveled around the state of Michigan trying to learn just what was going on with "new" sources of energy. I learned, and managed to organize an exhibit at the state capital in Michigan.

Sun Day was a success, drawing hundreds of people, fifty exhibitors, a speech by the Governor, and enough legislators and their staff to enable new legislation to be passed to encourage new ways of doing energy business.

Just how successful had my efforts been? The same old utilities still dominated the energy business. Monopolies and big business continued to rule. These democratic electric cooperatives, however, put a new twist to the energy formula, and I pondered the possibility of having a say in my own energy future.

It seemed almost too good to be true. I didn't know what I felt for sure and put down my cold, empty coffee cup and grabbed a hammer. This could wait.

Winter faded and spring was finally born. With it came the elections at Cherryland Rural Electric Cooperative.

I arrived at the stage of becoming a candidate only because I continued to take the various required steps in the process of election. Self doubt and inner conviction dogged me every step of the way and there were numerous occasions when I almost didn't jump through the next hoop, but for some reason, I continued.

Initially, when I qualified as a candidate, I worked very hard at studying the organization and its rules. I learned the area which the electric co-op served and met many of its members, my neighbors. Work on the barn was put off in favor of this new endeavor. When election day arrived, my efforts bore fruit. I took a seat on the co-op's board of directors.

For the next year and a half things went smooth enough. I worked the basic 40 hours at the airport, on occasion working a little overtime. Once or twice a month there would be a meeting at the cooperative which I found interesting and, not counting the financial reports, stimulating. I was enjoying life, making new friends and using some of my free FAA flights to see old friends. The paychecks continued to arrive exactly on schedule and as my time as a federal employee increased, so did the amount on the check.

While doing co-op work I found some degree of satisfaction by helping to develop a low cost loan program. Members could borrow money to finance conservation projects in their homes and businesses. It required cajoling of fellow directors, and plenty of self education along the way, but in the end we figured out a way to implement something that was genuinely a benefit to members of the co-op.

It didn't happen overnight. At times the efforts seemed more frustrating than the program was worth, but there was room for creativity and working with people. I enjoyed the work.

At the airport, the real breadwinner, I gave my best effort. Slowly I realized that the nature of the job was inescapably procedural. Like flying an airplane was procedural. With the co-op comparison so readily apparent, I began to tire of my position with the FAA. Almost always things were done by the book and for most any situation the required action was a learned response. The fact that the first American in space was a chimpanzee only emphasized that aspect of such jobs. It wasn't negative, it was what it was.

One day would turn up as a particularly rewarding day at the airport and I would jump on myself for being so critical and impatient. The following day might be blase and I would begin to slip into a feeling that life was destined to be without passion. The thought of waiting for a retirement 20 or 30 years hence made me think that to live life like that would be wrong.

In the summer of 1983 I had an especially lousy day and I returned home, wishing for better. I walked back to the swimming pond behind the barn and jumped in to cool off. Refreshed, I crawled onto an air mattress to relax.

Just as I was beginning to feel sorry for myself, a breeze blew the air mattress around. The barn came into view and I realized, again, how the FAA job enabled me. My attitude improved and I thought of the many controllers who were sincerely dedicated and very competent.

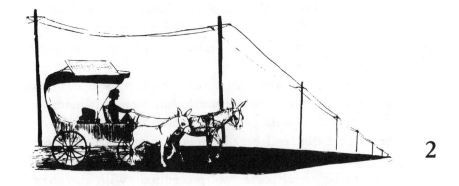

2

Goal Setting

When you have chosen your part, abide by it, and do not weakly try to reconcile yourself with the world . . . Adhere to your own act, and congratulate yourself if you have done something strange and extravagant, and broken the monotony of a decorous age.

—Ralph Waldo Emerson

Slightly more than two years after moving into my barn home I was visiting my next door neighbors, the Hemingways. We talked about the usual things—who won the Detroit-Green Bay football game, the story behind the headlines in the newspaper, Heather getting a "B" in spelling, Norma's car not running right . . . the small and important things in life.

Then it happened. Maybe we were looking through National Geographic, or perhaps a blurb came on TV about Egypt. I started talking about goal setting and dreams. Arguing more with myself than Jeff, I said that if dreams were ever to come true, first there must be a dream.

Jeff was dissatisfied working as a carpenter, much like I was as a government employee. We began talking about the pyramids in Egypt.

"Let's make a date to meet in Cairo two years from today," I suggested. "November 30, 1985, let's have a party in Cairo!"

We talked more about the wonders of Egypt, though he was

more interested in the civilization that had been there while I was searching for a positive direction away from a life that seemed too superficial and tame.

The next day I reminded my good neighbors of our conversation. The best I got was a friendly laugh.

"I was serious," I said. "Two years from yesterday I will be in Cairo."

The amazing thing was that while I had identified a definite goal and a time schedule in which to accomplish it, for the next year I did little towards accomplishing that goal, at least nothing that anyone could see. Mostly I spent the time convincing myself that this thing would come to pass. I was serious about the whole thing and intended that Cairo would mean more than a "trip to Cairo."

It would be pretty quick and easy to go down to the local travel agent and book a week at the Sheraton Cairo. Pay the bucks, apply for vacation time and before I knew it, I'd have "fulfilled" my goal, but found myself back at the airport with a microphone in my hand saying, "Roger six one whiskey, turn left heading zero four zero." In fact, it got to be even easier because the free flight program was expanded to include one international flight per year.

The stage was set. I had given myself two years to get my act together—divorce myself from my good job, somehow continue to make the payments on my barn-home, and get to Cairo. Quite a predicament.

The stage was set, but there was no script, only one actor, and the play itself—Cairo—made little sense.

Six months after making my vow I had made no change in my lifestyle. The only progress towards realizing my dream was purchasing a couple of books on Egypt and considerable thought. One of the people I confided in at the airport was George Hartzell. The two of us worked together as a team about half the time and I mentioned my goal and deadline. He quietly accepted my statement. Occasionally he would question me about how I intended to do it.

"I don't know, George, maybe I'll get a pack burro and make a trip the length of the Nile River," I offered.

"You should talk to Pete Morrison," George replied with a blink of incredulity. "He picked up two burros in Tennessee as part of the federal Adopt-A-Horse program last winter."

The thought of taking a burro the length of the Nile was a hybrid kind of thought. My only exposure to burros was a pet of friends in Washington State. He was named Pancho and was practically a member of the family.

The burro experience tied in with a trip I had made in 1973, two years out of college. I had taken a canoe 630 miles down the Mississippi River. Since then I had an affinity for river life. From that embryonic idea grew the ensuing play.

A few days later Pete happened by. Until this time I had only talked airplane talk with him. I asked if it was true that he was one of the elite burro aficionados and he proudly answered that he was.

I told Pete my intentions. Did he know where I could find one? He replied that one of his jenny's had just given birth the night before and invited me to his farm.

That evening I drove out to Pete's and he met me at the barn. Sure enough—there were five burros—a jack, three jennies, and the newborn jack. When he had bought the original pair for $75 each the jenny was pregnant and he wound up with three for the price of two. It was easy to see why Pete was a respected business-man, he had a keen eye. It hadn't taken long before his herd of three grew to the present five.

We climbed into the corral and fed them handfuls of carrots. Pete explained that after the gold rush in the west the old prospec-tors had died or given up their claims and simply let their pack burros loose. They had prospered in the wild.

The National Park Service decided that in order to preserve the ecosystem at least some of their population had to be reduced. As a result, wild burros were included in the Adopt-A-Horse pro-gram.

These burros of Pete's were so wild that when he first picked them up all they would eat was wood from the side of the barn. Not only that, they wouldn't touch oats!

Fortunately, Pete had a sure touch with animals and they knew he was their friend. At one point the 350 pound jack kicked at Pete's head with his foreleg, missing it by a hair.

The second born jenny was tame enough to be running around, not in the pasture with the other burros, but in Pete's yard at home with his grandchildren and pet St. Bernard. When Pete rode through the cherry and apple orchards the young jenny would gallop after him in his open jeep.

The fact that it was Pete who had these burros encouraged me to pursue an equine tack in this venture. He had flown P–51's and jet trainers in the air force and could easily have continued as a career officer. Instead he chose to take charge of his own destiny and left the employment of the federal government. His laugh was rich and easy and told a lot about his approach to living.

I pestered Pete and visited the young donkey often. Either he got tired of me bothering him or else he felt a closeness to my crazy idea, but it wasn't too long before he agreed to give me the baby burro. It would be several months before the foal would be big enough to move and until then he would stay at Pete's.

I asked Pete if I could name the baby "Pete," but he didn't take to the idea. Pete had called the baby donk Fritz, in good ol' democratic fashion, but he seemed too cute to be named such a partisan name, so I re-named him "Pete." When Pete was around I deferred and called "Pete," Fritz. Except when I forgot and then I swallowed myself in embarrassment because I liked and respected Pete and didn't mean to offend him.

One night, ten months after making the vow, while working alone on the midnight shift at the quiet airport I drew up a list of ten possible trips. My emerging script read:

Burro — Length of Nile
    "   — Kathmandu–Darjeeling
    "   — Mississippi Origin to New Orleans
    "   — Around Michigan
    "   — Cherryland area
    "   — 50th Anniversary REA area
    "   — California
    "   — Mexico
    "   — USA to S. America
    "   — Burro delivery service/message–gifts

The three items that seemed to be constant were that 1) the burro would be included; 2) I would leave my job with the FAA;

and 3) I would be in Cairo, Egypt, on November 30, 1985.

Ignorance is bliss. I hadn't even built a corral for my young burro yet. As the plot thickened, necessitated by the endless march of time, I found myself wanting to do something positive and constructive as an integral part of such a trip. I wanted more than an adventure . . . more than a good time. Somehow I wanted to contribute something honestly constructive. I thought about writing, or filming, or talking about something useful and good.

A few days after making my list of possible burro trips I thought that if the trip were to be self supporting I would have to do something of value. I had clipped an article from the Detroit Free Press months earlier about a Mennonite carriage builder in Elmira, Ontario.

If I had a carriage, I figured, I would be able to carry a computer which I could use as a word processor. As I traveled I could do some freelance writing. Or if I could get a video camera I might put together a travelogue or documentary.

Whatever it was I ended up trying to do I knew I wanted it to be creative. And while I knew that the odds were against the newcomer in any of the ideas I seemed to be leaning towards, my incentive was that my insides cried to think that I might remain at a job where I was not satisfied or happy. I couldn't quit before I had even begun.

As I was thinking of carriages and burro trips, in between working at the airport and attending various cooperative functions, I also made visits to Pete, my baby burro. By this time I was less than a year away from doing a trip and I began to realize that Pete would not be suitable for work as a pack burro or a carriage puller.

I was really on my own. I could talk about my various ideas to my friends and family, but inasmuch as I didn't have a handle on the program myself, they really couldn't contribute much in the form of suggestions or moral support.

I had written a long and detailed letter to two close friends, asking for their ideas and advice. I waited and waited for their reply. Finally one day they called. We talked about this and that but my letter wasn't mentioned. So I asked what they thought about what I had written to them.

"Oh, the letter? We thought you were pulling our legs."

Most reactions were that I was either kidding or that I was genuinely nuts to think about leaving such a good paying job.

I knew that I had to do something if this dream was to come true. I didn't know what to do, but felt that I had to keep on the move. Even if the next steps were totally wrong, it was important that I keep things going. I was under the time gun.

Christmas, 1984, found me in southeast Michigan with my family. The day after Christmas I hopped in my pickup and drove the five hour drive to see what I could about the Mennonite carriage makers. By the time I was halfway to my destination I learned that it was Boxing Day in Canada, a national holiday.

I crossed my fingers and hoped that I would be able to find someone. I arrived in Elmira and found a farm with seven or eight buggies parked in front. I thought that I had arrived but I was wrong. I had found a Mennonite home alright, but they told me that the carriage maker was three farms further down the road. When I found the right building with a tiny twelve by fourteen inch sign reading "Rural Carriage Supplies," not only was I not impressed, but the place looked closed.

I walked up to the cluttered, sheet metal building and found the door open. I went in. After walking through a second pair of doors I saw Edwin Martin. He lived down the road and was doing a little work around the dimly lit shop, getting things ready for the next day when the shop would re-open.

I told him about my idea and he showed me the dozen carriages and sleighs that were scattered around the shop.

"But a burro," Edwin said, "It's too small, isn't it?"

"Oh, no, don't say that," I thought, but I said, "Well, maybe a mule."

The truth was that all my life I had been afraid of horses and the burro was small enough so I wasn't altogether intimidated by the idea. When I said "mule" I thought I was compromising in size, since the mule was a cross between the donkey and the horse, not thinking that a mule might be more of a handful than a horse.

"I can have my burro walk behind the carriage," I added.

Martin called the new owner, Don Buschert, and told him that an American had driven all the way to see about having a carriage made and asked if he could come over to the shop and talk. Don said he would drive over right after lunch.

Edwin was very friendly and invited me to lunch at his home. We returned just as Don drove up in a small pickup, the only person in this group of eleven Mennonite men who belonged to a more "progressive" order allowing for motorized transportation.

Don may have been the only Mennonite at Rural Carriage Supplies who didn't travel via horse and buggy, but that didn't stop him from being very deliberate and soft spoken. He was the obvious new guy around the shop. He asked for Edwin's advice repeatedly and seemed uncertain about how a carriage was constructed. After taking another tour of the various buggies around the shop we went to his office, where Edwin joined us.

Before we got very far a man stopped by to pay for a part for his buggy which he had picked up several months earlier. The two men discussed the debt calmly for about 15 minutes while Don shuffled papers all around the room, which also served as a locker room and a dining room for the workers. There were no files as such. The whole room was a file and it was not organized.

Finally Don asked Edwin what he thought the piece cost and the bill came to less than five dollars Canadian. The man paid and Don gave him a receipt, and then his attention returned to me.

It was a wonder that the business stayed open with such shabby non-procedures. Then again, I was coming from an environment that super stressed procedures. I was becoming aware that part of what I was seeking was the quality of life found in such a pace of life, generally forgotten in the America of the 1980's.

We began to discuss what I would need. Basically I asked for an enclosed carriage suitable for a long trip. We decided that the carriage body would be 42″ wide and eight feet long. At the back would be a shelf as wide as the carriage for carrying bales of hay.

I asked for a maroon color and yellow pinstriping and had to keep requesting this. Don and Edwin seemed to think solid black would be a better color.

I wanted the carriage to be as open as possible for hot weather and yet weatherproof for inclement weather.

One of the custom features I felt I would need was a false bottom of some sort that would be lockable and basically hidden.

In this compartment I would store valuables such as word processor, camera, tools, sound equipment, and money.

I requested hard rubber tires on the rims, an important request, as I was to learn months later. The difference was considerable. Some Mennonite and Amish orders believed that rubber tires made it too tempting to use the carriage for pleasure and so many used only steel rims.

One feature foreign to these men was my request for a design that would allow me to sleep in the buggy. I had in mind a fold down front seat but I didn't go into much detail since I figured these guys were the pros, not me.

I wanted a collapsible and storable desk the width of the buggy which could be used in the rear of the carriage.

Perhaps the highlight of my ignorance was my request for a small desk for the front seat on one side only. I had in mind writing, even typing on a keyboard, as we traveled down the road! In retrospect, this was absolutely absurd. No doubt Don and Edwin are still scratching their heads about this part of the custom buggy.

I requested that the roof be constructed for strength. As my plans evolved and I began to think about actually getting a word processor, I realized I would need a source of electricity. It is an understatement to say that I was considering several options about this time. I was thinking more and more about trying to utilize photovoltaic solar cells as my electrical source. My request for a strong roof was only a guess because I had no idea how heavy solar panels were.

After the three of us had been at this designing and planning business for about three hours, it was time to talk turkey. I have never been blessed with patience and I was doing my best to slow down, trying to ignore the five hour drive I had ahead of me. Worse, a snowstorm was approaching from the west and I would be heading right into it at nighttime.

If Don was slow at designing a carriage, he was worse with money. He figured and refigured again. He never seemed sure of his figures. Finally, after another hour and a half, he came up with an estimated finished cost for this custom buggy of between $2500 and $3000 Canadian. He required a 15% deposit with the balance due on delivery.

I now had the price quote that I needed if I was to do this trip using a buggy. I told him that I would let him know one way or the other by January 15 for sure.

As I left, hurrying to get as far as I could before the storm hit, I saw a carriage coming down the cold December road. The people looked frigid. As I turned up the truck's heater full blast I thought that I may just be crazy. It looked miserable out there on the road in that buggy.

There I was with a decision to make and slightly more than two weeks in which to make it. The buggy was a key to the puzzle I was trying to work out and as I drove into the night, the snow began to fall and my mind was stark alive. I might be crazy, but I sure wasn't bored.

As I drove through some white-out conditions and slippery roads that night coming home from Canada I had plenty to think about. If I did quit my job with the government I would be leaving the best paying job I had ever had. How would I ever make the payments on my barn? The only thing I really had to go on was that I would be receiving about $3,500 from the FAA retirement fund that I had been paying into, but that was the extent of my nest egg. If I said "go" to the carriage, so much for the egg. Reality was setting in.

My return home included mail. In the batch was a Christmas card from good ol' George at work. It was encouraging to find a painting of a fat lady driving a small cart pulled by a burro. Up until that time I was only assuming that burros could pull anything.

A week after I returned home from Canada my neighbor and I took a walk in the woods behind us and watched a 40 pound lynx wildcat stalk his 100 pound Belgian sheepdog. As a result, when Pete Morrison brought little Pete home to the barn on January 12, he decided that he should loan me the mother until the foal could defend himself. With the burros now living in the north end of my barn while I lived "European-like" in the south side, I became convinced that I would have to have some other help in pulling a carriage.

When the deadline came for letting the Mennonites know about whether or not I wanted them to go ahead with my custom built carriage, I still wasn't sure of my plans or my commitment. Nevertheless, on January 15 I mailed a check for $309.37 to Canada. It seems from the time I mailed off that deposit until a year later I was constantly on the go and always busy. I had so much to learn, to organize, to find and borrow and buy; so many fears to overcome.

If I was to outfit this buggy with solar power, I had to locate some solar panels. Even though I had organized the Sun Day exposition years ago and had met many people who were active in the field, and was on the board of directors of an electric utility, I wasn't sure where to go to find them.

I called on my friend, Dick Cookman, who taught a course on solar energy at the local college and owned a store which sold wood stoves and solar hot water panels. They didn't have any of the solar cells that convert light directly into electricity but said they could order the so-called photovoltaic cells.

Dick told me he knew of a discontinued model and if it was still available he could sell it to me for about $400. I had hoped that some enterprising solar company might help sponsor my trip or at least loan me the panels. Cookman's company was just too small.

I left the Cookmans feeling bad that I still hadn't been able to actually see and touch the thing I was after. Photovoltaic cells remained theoretical for me while I had arrived at a stage where I wanted to apply the real thing. I had been theorizing for too long and was eager to grab the ball and run. I felt good, though, because even if I couldn't find a sponsor, I could come up with $400 and make this buggy solar powered.

At no time did I want to find myself in a position that failure or success was in anyone's hands but my own. I wanted the responsibility. Exactly what I was trying to get away from was being in a position where someone else determined if I was doing a good job or not.

Back at the airport, life and work carried on. Somehow when my boss had been visiting the regional headquarters in Chicago he had heard that I was going to take a trip down the Nile River with a donkey. He told me about it and then laughed to my face.

This sort of thing happened a lot and I had to face the ridicule. After that time, however, I found myself possessing resolve that I loved. When negative or unfair things would happen, I was thankful for them because they made me more determined to improve my situation. Even though work as an air traffic controller had its good points, it was a job and not something in which I could believe.

About this period of time things began to acquire a new flavor—neither good nor bad. All my life I had felt good. Physically strong. The world was alive and death was an occasion that came around about as often as the Detroit Tigers winning the World Series.

But in these days my grandfather passed away. My father had a heart attack and was in the hospital. Two friends at the electric co-op died, one during a board meeting. It took time for some of this to sink in, but I began to feel an urgency. Suddenly life seemed short.

I thought of people who put up with jobs they didn't like, even hated, just so they could retire and get their pension. But then what? Live like they'd always wanted to? Ha! Such a cruel joke on themselves because by then the seed had shrivelled and Love had been squelched too long. What a waste! A living death. My life could be just as shallow unless I tried to live as I felt inside. My obligation grew to the spirit of life that was me.

Even though Pete seemed basically useless, the little burro was setting the stage for some kind of trip. It was cooperation that I wanted to represent, along with a sense of constructive adventure.

I decided that I could write about Pete and the cooperative. The rural electric cooperatives could be the actors on the stage. If I wrote a monthly travel column about my travels and focused on what happened to us as we traveled along, then perhaps I would have a start towards doing something of value.

A positive step was taken—Pete became electric and the Electric Burro Travel Series was conceived.

3

The Special Spirit of the REA

Working together to be the best, afterall, isn't that what America is all about?

—Lee Iacocca

When I first got involved with co-ops, it wasn't because I wanted to. It was because if I wanted electricity, I had to join. I got further involved with cooperatives because its democratic nature allowed me to have a voice in my energy future. The more I learned about the role that the rural electric cooperative had played, the deeper my conviction grew in the program.

It was a coincidence that on May 11, 1935, President Franklin Roosevelt had signed Executive Order #7037 which established the Rural Electrification Administration as a government agency, just 50 years before my trip was to take place.

At that time only 10% of America's farms were electrified, and there was little indication that conditions would ever be greatly improved. The reason why there was no electricity in the rural areas was simply that the private companies that had led the way in the development of our electrical system could not make enough money based on their investment and the number of customers per mile of line. The denser the area, the better the profit. Consequently, cities were electrified, but darkness reigned where the people thinned out.

What Roosevelt and the REA did was provide money to anyone—including the private companies—if they would build electric lines to the rural areas. Very few investor owned companies took advantage of the low cost government loans.

The real revolution took place in the country. Neighbors who had dreamed of having electric service for years talked together and organized cooperatives. People went door to door and explained how the REA would loan the needed funds if they got enough people to sign up and pay a membership fee of $5.

The mid-30's were Great Depression days and $5 was genuinely hard to come by. But the farmers of America did come up with the money and the new program took off with near universal support. The spirit that existed in the early days of REA was unlike anything anyone had ever seen.

If the people couldn't get what they needed through the free market system, then in cooperation with the federal government they could do it for themselves—and they did. Constructive adventure.

At stake was more than a question of electricity. The values involved went to the very roots of rural America, and further, to the roots of civilization itself. Roosevelt did not invent barn raisings or quilting bees. It was not the REA that established procedures so that clans of people formed to fight the sabre toothed tiger as one, eons ago. But the principle was the same—cooperation.

It does not go without saying that things were a lot different in 1935 than in 1985 because unless someone has lived without electricity there is no way of understanding the vast difference. Not only that, but most Americans living in 1985 had had electricity all their lives. They expected it to be there.

For a more accurate big picture of REA's role in history, it's interesting to note that while the REA cooperatives represented 50 years of history, it was only an additional fifty years prior to REA when electricity made its public debut. Edison, his light bulb and electric meter, were all new products of the 1880's! Society's adaptation to electricity is a relatively recent phenomenon.

In the beginning (so to speak, and not so very long ago), arguments raged in Congress as to how electricity would be handled.

The same questions are still being debated as private and public interests argue about who owns the rivers of America and who shall benefit from the power derived from them.

While some of the arguments continue to pit private big business interests against public interests, sometimes it is difficult to understand why the same arguments should prevail today. The nature of the waters of the Mississippi and the Colorado has not changed, yet there is no comparison between the technology of the 1880's and the 1980's.

Genius the likes of Thomas Edison demanded to be rewarded for their pioneering efforts in the field of physics (and business), yet the heirs of Edison continue to reap profit long after the death of the original deserving inventors. This in spite of changed circumstances of having an established and understood electric generation system and transmission grid.

When the light bulb was the talk of the town, it was common to place a placard in the same room with the light bulb which read:

> This room is equipped with Edison Electric light. Do not Attempt to Light with Match. Simply turn Key on Wall By the Door. The Use of Electricity for Lighting is in No Way Harmful to Health, nor Does it Affect the Soundness of Sleep.

The early days of electricity were the days when the arguments for private ownership of public power carried their greatest weight. Fifty years later, when FDR blew life into REA, the same arguments were made but times had changed.

The standard of living in the urban areas where electricity was available improved steadily and dramatically. At the same time people brought tales back from the city to the sparsely populated regions of the United States about the "miracles" being performed by the readily available electricity.

Life in the country continued as it had for hundreds of years before electricity. Except now the expectations of rural Americans began to rise.

People continued to take care of farm chores using the flickering and undependable light from the coal-oil lamp. Their eyesight weakened prematurely.

People toiled to draw water by hand. There was no indoor plumbing and the outhouse was a way of life, even in February. Kitchen work was hot and unending.

Hours and hours and still more hours were spent heating and reheating the iron in order to press clothes, and then cleaning the iron of the soot it had accumulated from sitting on the dirty wood stove while it got hot. The examples are endless . . . the REA changed things.

The creation of the Rural Electrification Administration enabled people living in the country to enjoy the same benefits that their urban neighbors did. Without the dispersal of electricity into the countryside, the outcome of the Second World War may well have been different. Rural electrification vastly increased farm productivity and took the place of the young farmers who went off to fight.

Time marched on and REA funded cooperatives reached across the land until 99% of the nation was electrified. By the time the Electric Burro Travel Series was conceived there were more than 1,000 electric cooperatives.

In the 1930's there had been an argument that a bunch of farmers could not run something as complex as an electric utility. By the 50th birthday of the REA the cooperatives were operating with better efficiency and accountability than the mammoth private companies.

There was a weak link, however. The nationwide program that electrified three-fourths of America's land mass and thirty million people was largely still operated by those people who helped give birth to the system fifty years earlier. By and large the people who were running the co-ops had white hair. They were usually male. They were often farmers.

As society approached the ideal of universal electrification, the population aged, electricity began to be taken for granted, and complacency set in. Things changed a lot. Wants and needs changed. Suburbs grew.

Many people moved from the cities to the country and were not aware of what the co-ops had accomplished. Their loyalties were to low cost electricity and they did not know the difference between types of utilities.

While the makeup and nature of the rural areas rapidly changed, the co-ops changed little except for a continual upgrading of the electric system. The democratic organizations often failed to recognize that they were no longer made up of mostly farmers.

When most rural electric cooperatives were started, the areas were almost exclusively farm country. By 1985, there were twice as many retired people on cooperative electric lines as there were farmers. So called blue collar workers now made up more than twice the farmer percentage. There were almost twice as many professional people as there were farmers, and almost as many white collar workers, yet the democratic representation of those who were in charge remained about the same.

The vitality of any organization was only as great as its members and the rule of thumb was that the life expectancy of any organization was one and one-half generations. Unless a group was continually revitalized, the way of the dinosaur could be expected. With such a proud and great history, the degree of complacency on the parts of some sitting directors and members was troubling.

I was troubled as the 50th anniversary of the REA approached. The only plans being made to celebrate and acknowledge the organization were things like "Pioneer Breakfasts," music boxes, stuffed dolls, and napkins emblazoned with 50th anniversary logos—all tokens, all lifeless—and all falling far short of capturing the real spirit that had once served to draw communities closer together.

With survival an issue I wanted to scream because it seemed like a perfect opportunity to reach out and revitalize ourselves was being lost. Nothing was being done out of the ordinary and little imagination was being employed.

My trip could be a commemoration to a wonderful bunch of people and a productive program. My desire grew to be to stimulate the imaginations of those within the REA family and to capture the interest of newer members unaware of their own membership. The buggy could serve to bridge the gap between generations, acknowledging earlier accomplishments and a bygone era, while the photovoltaic solar cells would serve as a connection with new times and a future generation. The co-ops belong to us all, old and young, and it was important that people recognized that we were all neighbors in a community.

4

Electric Buggy

To be first—that is the idea. To do something, say something, see something, before anybody else—these are the things that confer a pleasure compared with which other pleasures are tame and commonplace, other ecstasies cheap and trivial.

—Mark Twain

Days passed. Life consisted of stints at the airport, an occasional co-op meeting, and thought about how and when I would do my journey. Most days I would get off from work or out of a meeting and drive wherever I had to in order to see a computer or a printer or talk to a mule owner or someone who might know how to drive a buggy.

Some days I would skip sleep or drive four or five hundred miles before I was scheduled to be back at the airport. May 11 became the target date to begin my trip and precious time was slipping away.

I still didn't know where the trip would take me, but I read somewhere that the old wagon trains used to average about 100 miles per week. Of course they had to fight off disease and Indians and didn't have established roadways—but they did know a little about mule and buggy travel. On the other hand, they didn't have a tourist season or eighteen-wheelers to contend with. I accepted the figure as a rough measure of how far I might be able to travel. Six months from May 11 seemed reasonable and while November became my initial destination, few people could relate to a date as such, so I looked at the map and began to say "Tennessee by November."

After inadequate research I bought a Radio Shack portable computer which could be used as a word processor. It was my first computer. Since it used almost no electricity it fit in with the idea to demonstrate how technology was advancing at incredible speed, dictating changes in the way electric utilities needed to do business. Its limited electrical requirements were also compatible with my environmentally clean but limited electrical source— photovoltaics.

I hoped to generate some interest along the way from the local media for the sake of telling the story of the REA and what cooperation could do. I also had ideas of trying to sell some freelance articles to various magazines about cross country buggy trips or solar powered computers.

For this I needed a letter quality printer that could operate with my power source and survive the conditions encountered along the way. I opted for another Radio Shack product, mainly because it worked with my new computer, had small power needs, and was on sale. It was big and bulky and not meant to be portable, but I felt I could delay no longer.

I had a logo drawn up and stationery printed for the Electric Burro Travel Series and began to send out "official" correspondence, checking to see if I could gain some sort of sponsorship. The result was not encouraging: no camera, no computer, no photovoltaics, no pre-sold columns or articles. Zero.

While I remained a credible member of society—i.e. employed and with a cash flow—I visited my credit union for a loan to pay for some of the things I needed. The rationale was that even if I didn't make any money and turned up broke at the end of my trip, I wasn't afraid to work and could repay the loan once the trip was completed.

On one of my many trips to everywhere I stopped in at a company located in Troy, Michigan, called ECD. ECD stood for Energy Conversion Devices. I had been slightly aware that there was such a company for several years and that it was doing some work with solar energy.

When I entered the lobby, unannounced, I found myself surrounded with richly paneled walls and a very upbeat decor. Standing in Levis and Adidas I asked the well dressed receptionist who I might talk to about my planned trip.

Surprisingly, I was ushered into the office of vice president Lionel Robbins who patiently listened to my unlikely story. I had stopped with the hope of finding where I might secure some photovoltaics, or PV's, as they were called within the trade. Lionel introduced me to two staff people who listened to my plans in greater detail.

After giving my spiel I was led to a room that contained about two dozen of ECD's inventions. It was astounding.

I learned from marketing men Jim Young and Jack Kondos that ECD was involved in considerably more than photovoltaics. ECD was the parent organization and from it had sprouted numerous other companies, each specializing in one of its founders many inventions. While Jim was employed by ECD, Jack work for Sovonics, the division involved with photovoltaics.

Until I stopped at ECD I knew that solar energy could be categorized into two main applications—direct heating by the sun and the generation of electricity. I knew that the main use of solar energy was for heating buildings and water.

But I thought that photovoltaics were all the same and that the future of electric generation by the sun was condemned to either remote applications where there was no established transmission system—like the middle of a desert, or where cost was not the main consideration—like in space. A third possible application was the future.

My continuing education taught me that there were many types of photovoltaic solar cells and that the two main categories could be broken down into crystalline silicon, and amorphous silicon—also called thin films. This second type was developed by the people at ECD.

Silicon was the magic crystalline material that early photovoltaic cells were made of—common sand. The natural question was that if photovoltaics were made from sand, why were they so expensive?

The answer lay in the time consuming and labor intensive manufacturing process. First the crystals had to be grown in a laboratory. Then they had to be sliced as thin as possible and the cutting process destroyed about half of the hard earned crystals, turning them into dust.

Much progress had been made. When I stopped at ECD the older type crystalline silicon PVs were still the most cost effective PV systems due to automated factories that were continually being improved and the better power to area ratio that they provided.

The energetic and brilliant people at ECD, however, were working to close the gap and had been able to develop a system of mass production whereby they had built a machine that could churn out the newer film PVs, one foot wide and a thousand feet in length! The thin filmed photovoltaics were only seven atoms thick with essentially no waste! With reduced production costs and high reliability the future looked very promising for this new technology.

My interest in photovoltaics was two-fold. For my upcoming trip I wanted the imaginative impact that solar power lent to an old fashioned buggy, and as a director of an electric utility, I wanted to learn how we could improve our business.

Photovoltaics were non-polluting, maintenance free, lightweight, portable and expandable. PV's didn't contribute to the national debt, were relatively free from foreign cartels or acts of terrorism, and the costs were declining. And Sovonics was the only manufacturer of photovoltaics not wholly or majority owned by a major oil company.

After a couple of hours, the people of ECD and Sovonics offered to loan me a solar panel or two and to help me set it up on the buggy which was being completed in Canada. I was to call them as soon as I had the buggy in Michigan and they said they would come up to my barn in northern Michigan to make the necessary measurements. The only drawback was that since amorphous technology was so brand spanking new, the only PV panel they had on hand was the older crystalline type (which they didn't even make) which they had been using as part of their testing program. It suited me fine.

After mailing the deposit in January to get construction started on my carriage, I had called Canada twice to see how things were going and to answer any questions. April 1 was decided as the day I would pick up the completed carriage.

As was becoming the custom, when I left for the eight hour trip from Traverse City to Elmira there was a bad storm approaching right behind me. The return trip would be work.

When I arrived in Elmira, Edwin and Don were there to greet me. The small factory was full of activity. Most of the workers were 60 years old or better. Only two were in their 20's.

I was led into the back room where recently completed rigs were stored. There it was. Was that it? The logo I had drawn up didn't look a thing like this. It was so boxy!

Still, it was pretty close to what I had ordered. The doors were sliding doors in the front and were roll up/batten down in the rear.

I had asked for a maroon velvet type of material for the seats but instead there was black leatherette. It was dull and drab and not soft at all. Nuts! I had wanted some degree of luxury, just for the sake of fun. I should have suspected that black would surface after our first discussion of colors. These guys were into black.

They showed me the different parts of the buggy, sometimes proud at how they had made something work, sometimes very quiet and non-committal. I knew absolutely nothing about carriages and it was difficult to know if the workmanship was good or less than good.

For example, they had made the front seat fold down into a bed but had not thought to make a cushion to fit in-between the front seat and the rear seat. This wasn't right.

Then they showed me the small front desk and the large, storable, rear one. These were pretty nice. The windshield hinged down for rain, wind or mosquitoes, and up for most driving conditions.

The carriage was the main part of the vehicle. The fills were the wishbone shaped "arms" that projected out front of the carriage and the piece that goes on both sides of the animal and to which the animal is hitched. Fills are bolted to the carriage by means of brackets on both the carriage and the fills. When the men tried to bolt the two together, they wouldn't fit. Someone got another bolt and a bigger hammer and beat it in until it fit. Then they couldn't get it out. More beating.

The undercarriage was neither sealed nor painted. Much of the carriage was constructed of hickory wood, the remainder was ply-wood. There were numerous runs in the paint job.

I had asked for the same quality that they had shown me in a sleigh that they had built. This was sub-sleigh quality. I told the gathered men that the carriage didn't appear to be what we had agreed upon.

Feet shuffled. The wind grew louder outside. I knew that Don was slow with figures and the buggy still had to be loaded. I had little choice . . . it was already late in the afternoon.

"Let's see if it'll fit on the truck," I said.

We rolled the carriage through the building and toward the truck. I asked the men how much the carriage weighed. They guessed 600 pounds, empty. I let the tailgate down and four of us lifted first the front end into the truck's bed, and then the rear.

With the tailgate down it fit snugly in the truck with four inches between the place the carriage's rear tires stopped and the end of the tailgate. The carriage's rear wheels extended past the end of the truck's tailgate. On both sides of the buggy was no more than three inches. A perfect fit.

We slid the fills under the carriage. The workers returned to their work while Don and I tied the buggy down. By now the wind was blowing hard.

All was done now except to pay for the rig and drive home. I wrote a check for the balance and Don wrote out the receipt:

> Duplex Carriage with closed top, Body 8′ × 3′6″ L & W, Horse Drawn, Total price $2925, paid by two cheques, U.S. Funds $309.37 and $1900, Total $2209.37.

The strong American dollar was hurting the national trade and destroying many American farmers, but it was a 30% savings for me.

But horse drawn! The words alone intimidated me.

I had thought that the fills looked regular sized, not downsized for a burro or a mule. At this late stage of the game I didn't know what sort of animal I was going to seek to pull the carriage, if I would seek a single animal or a team, or where I would find the beast(s).

I debated about having a shaft made for a team of somethings, but as I left we agreed that they would be able to make the shaft for $100 with a phone call. For now there was a long drive ahead of me, and I could think about it as I drove.

Don walked up to me just as I jumped in the truck to leave. He handed me a spare set of wheel bearings to take with me.

"How nice," I thought. Little did I know.

As the drive began, I thought it was going to be a repeat of my last return drive. I was wrong. It was worse. The wind was gusting to 50 m.p.h. for 8 of the 10 hours, sometimes as a headwind, sometimes a crosswind.

It was a hard drive with white-out conditions too common. Finally, at 4:30 a.m. I drove into my driveway, the drive a fitting April Fool's day joke. Standing at home, surrounded by snow, tired and ready to sleep, I felt there was no turning back. Things were happening, and I began to look to the day when I would be working my last shift.

5

Electric Burro

Don't be afraid to take a big step. You can't cross a chasm in two small jumps.

—David Lloyd George

All my life I had been afraid of horses.

Probably the biggest hurdle I had to climb was fear. I didn't want to actually address my need for an animal to pull the carriage. But now there was a carriage sitting outside my barn serving as a constant reminder of that need.

The burro, little Pete, was shaggy and cute and he served to teach me a little about the nature of the equine. He gave me a critter for my logo and a name for the Electric Burro Travel Series.

But, with five weeks remaining before scheduled takeoff, only now did he have his first halter on. When I put a lead rope on him to see how he would handle it, he freaked out. At this late stage of the game, and at such an early stage of his life, there was no way that he would be able to follow along behind the carriage, let alone pull it.

As a kid, my best friend was C. T. Bryant. C. T. was from Arkansas and his father worked equally as a carpenter and a horse trainer. Naturally, C. T. learned his father's trade and developed

34

into a champion horseman, but the things we had in common when we grew up were things like baseball, marbles, sparrow hunting with our BB guns, and an admiration for the uniforms of the U.S. Marines.

Whenever I visited C. T.'s house, I would follow him around the horses and barns but always kept my distance from the many horses. Even though I saw C. T. handle the giants with authority time after time, I was never convinced that such a large animal would listen to me.

My father and I took a trip to visit C. T.'s father, Harest, and see what he might suggest. Harest knew I was no cowboy. I explained my plans and included the burro, but he responded that a burro was useless. I mentioned a mule.

"Son, you don't want no damn mule. What you need is a good strong horse, like a draft horse," Mr. Bryant said.

One thing was certain—I didn't want anything to do with horses. I had visited Mr. Bryant seeking advice, but I didn't want this kind of advice.

"You see, I've already had stationery drawn up and there is a burro and a mule pulling a carriage on it, so I need a mule," I reasoned with tough, calloused Mr. Bryant.

Mr. Bryant kindly said that he'd keep his eyes open for a mule for me. As my dad and I left he went so far as to say, "I'll find you a mule."

For the next week I sort of relaxed. I had the carriage, a rough idea of a route, and now Mr. Bryant was going to find a mule for me.

A week after my visit I called him to see if he had found a mule yet. I was dismayed when he told me he had made several phone calls on my behalf but had failed to find a suitable animal. He suggested that I begin looking myself, but added that he would keep trying. Oh no! The problem hadn't gone away!

With time continuing to disappear I knew I had no choice and I decided to go to the source. I had heard of an Amish community about 100 miles away and at the first opportunity made the drive to seek an animal from those who still lived their lives with horse and buggy.

Arriving in Gladwin, I began asking around for someone who knew about mules. My questioning led me to 71-year-old Lawrence Riley who claimed to have traveled through 36 of 48 states as a boy in mule driven wagons with his brother, working as a mule trader.

Lawrence wasn't Amish. He knew of a pair of mules that were for sale, however, and we drove 50 miles to where they were located. They were ugly, looking more like fat ponies than mules. Their ears weren't even long. When Lawrence climbed into the corral to bring one of the alleged mules over to me for a closer look, they wouldn't let him get close.

Feeling low, I drove Lawrence back to his one room home and decided to return home myself. Maybe I should cancel the whole thing! I'd only be out the price of one carriage and a little pride.

Before I had gone very far I passed a house with carriages outside. I pulled over, thought about turning around, felt foolish and decided I couldn't be so rude as to intrude on the private Amish. A mile down the road I overruled myself. What choice did I have? I turned around and went back to the Amish house.

I parked the truck by the road and walked up to the house. A bearded young man came to the door and greeted me. I explained that I had just purchased a carriage and intended to make a trip to Tennessee—Did he know where I might find a mule for sale?

The man replied that he didn't know of any mules but that there was an Englishman down the road a couple of miles who had a horse for sale that an Amishman had been driving just that winter. I thanked him and went along on my chase.

I found the home of Ken and Joyce Thurlow and saw the 12-year-old horse that was for sale, Big Daddy. Ken wasn't home but Joyce told me that he was asking $500 and that if I wanted to find Ken I should check at the harness track in town.

As I made the seven mile drive back into town I breathed a sigh of relief at hearing a price that I could handle. I was so ignorant that I had no idea what a horse cost!

When I found the track, Ken wasn't around and I jumped at the excuse to leave. After all, my chicken-sort-of-self rationalized, I had located a horse for sale and had diligently tried to find the owner. I was eager to do this difficult job in stages and on my way home I stopped to tell Joyce that I would call Ken later that evening.

That night I called Ken and told him of my plans, ignorance and fear. I wasn't trying to fool anyone.

Ken told me that Big Daddy was a Standardbred and had been a promising race horse until he had come up lame five years ago. That's when Ken had bought the horse and he harbored hopes of getting Big Daddy back to full health. He told me that the young Amishman had driven him during the past winter and that the Amishman allowed his wife to drive him because of his good nature.

I asked if he thought that my trip would to be too much for him, with his history of lameness and all? Ken answered honestly that it might be, that you never knew for sure since it would depend on so many things, including how he was handled. He invited me to come back to his place and he'd give me a demonstration.

A couple of days later I returned to Gladwin and met Ken. while Ken harnessed black Big Daddy, I did my best to feel kindly towards the beast but was careful not to walk too close. Ken must have enjoyed a few laughs to himself when he asked me to hold Big Daddy while he hitched him to a two wheeled racing sulky.

Ken took him for a trot up and down the road in front of the house. It was a pretty sight. A new world of days gone by opened for me when an Amish neighbor drove past in his surrey and I watched as men in horse drawn vehicles waved to each other. I thought of my intentions to travel in such a manner and to realize values of a way of life largely forgotten.

Ken and his family were easy on me and helped to crack my prison of fear and ignorance. I was invited to dinner and afterward Ken's young kids, Kable and Brenda, took me with them to feed their own horses and to see their newborn foals. Then we all piled into Ken's truck and drove to the harness track. Ken's father met us there and I hung out with the kids and Mr. Thurlow while Ken worked a couple of his horses on the track. It was my first experience at a harness track.

Mr. Thurlow went up to one of the horses in its stall and commiserated, saying, "What are you thinking about son? Huh? What's goin' on in that head of yours?"

The horse didn't move and didn't say a thing so Mr. Thurlow answered for him. "Not much. You don't think too much, do you boy?" and he patted the horse on the neck and walked back to where he had been sitting.

That was it.

Horses were kind, big and strong, and not overly intelligent. It was a simple but valuable lesson.

We finished up with the horses and drove back to the house. The kids went to bed and Ken and I talked until 2 a.m. He invited me to spend the night but I had to be at the airport at 8 a.m., so I thanked him, promised to stay in touch, and began the drive home.

The juggling act continued and I called to tell my photovoltaic friends that the carriage was now at my place.

April 19 brought Jack Kondos of Sovonics and Jim Young of ECD on a day-long mission via airline and rented car out to my barn. I introduced Jack and Jim to Pete and his mother and they fed the two burros some carrots. Next I showed them the idle carriage and they took measurements. We went inside the barn and I brought out my various electric gadgets to be used in the buggy so they could have an idea of what the power requirements would be.

My collection of electric powered implements included the computer and printer, a reading lamp, radio/tape player, crock pot, and a coffeepot. Like most things in my emerging world, I knew little about electric technology or the language that went with it.

They explained to me that when light struck photovoltaic solar cells, DC electricity was generated, the same type of electricity that is used in automobile systems. Basically the solar cells that they would be loaning me would act as battery chargers and I would need to get a deep cycle, 105 ampere, 12 volt battery.

Since all of the electrical goods were designed for household use and AC electricity is the type used in American homes, I also needed to purchase an inverter. An inverter functions to change

DC power into AC power, they explained, and by having an inverter I'd be able to install regular household outlets in the buggy.

Based on the largest user of electricity, the 500 watt coffeepot, they recommended that I get an inverter with at least that much capacity. They told me that they would send two PV's, a couple of brackets to mount the PV's to the roof of the buggy with, and a necessary regulator in time for a May 11 departure. Progress was being made.

The following day I submitted my resignation to the FAA. It gave two weeks notice and my last day of work was to be May 4, 1985.

Eighteen days before I planned to begin my trip, April 23, there was a meeting at the co-op. By now I had been talking about doing this trip as a commemoration of the 50th anniversary of the rural electric cooperatives and the one subject most often brought up to me at the co-op was how I was coming with my preparations.

I explained my various achievements and setbacks and was asked if I had found a mule yet. When I said that I was still looking it was suggested I stop at the Stafford farm a few miles from the co-op and see what he had.

After the meeting I did stop and met Glen Stafford and his stepson, Dale. I told them what I had in mind and asked if they had a suitable horse or mule for such a trip.

Glen pondered out loud, "A horse for a trip like the one you have in mind will need to be strong. It doesn't matter if he is fast or not. You'll need a well mannered horse because of your inexperience. A team would be best. You wouldn't have to use 'em as a team either. You might decide to use one horse for driving the first half of the day and have the other horse walk behind. Switch 'em at noon."

I listened and tried to consider what he had said.

"Well, I don't know but I think I'd just as soon stick to just one horse, Glen. The chance of something going wrong with two horses is twice as great as with one. Plus with only one horse the feeding and medical bills will be half as much."

I thought of 1927 when Lindbergh had become the first to fly non-stop across the Atlantic. He had been successful in large part because he had kept things simple—one pilot, one engine.

"Well, I've got just the horse you need," Glen said and he called to Dale and told him to bring such and such a horse up to the paddock.

As Dale fetched the horse, Glen asked, "What do you plan to do about shoes?"

"I don't know. I thought I'd deal with it as it happened. I'll look for a farrier along the way," I answered.

"What about harness?" he asked.

Harness? I hadn't even thought about that one!

"Come with me," and he led me to one of his outbuildings that was full of tack. There were different kinds of harness everywhere, with leather straps and collars and pads, things called tugs and hames and egg butt snaffle bits—I realized, again, that I had put off this moment for more reasons than having to deal with horses. Learning is not conducive to a nice, warm feeling of security.

Glen understood that I wasn't ready and led me out to the front paddock where Dale was standing with a sorrel horse that I immediately knew was out of the question. Not only was he too big for me but he was beautiful and obviously out of my price range. I had naturally started to use the $500 price tag of Big Daddy as a gauge to what I wanted to spend and surely this horse was way more than that.

I asked Glen what kind of horse he was and he told me he was a four year old Belgian gelding. We walked up to the horse and he opened his mouth to show me his teeth. There was no way I would have known if the horse was four or fourteen. All I saw were a bunch of teeth. For all I knew he could have counted his legs to come up with the figure of four.

I held my breath and asked, "So how much is this guy worth?"

Glen took on the pained look of someone who doesn't want to part with a valuable possession and sucked in his breath and held it, and then said, "I need a thousand fifty."

"A thousand fifty," I thought. I assumed that he had started high, he was a horse trader, wasn't he? At the same time I thought that it would be fantastic to be able to have such a beautiful horse. As I stood there looking at the Belgian, Glen continued working.

"This particular type of horse is a draft horse, like the famous Clydesdale. They're considered to be 'cold blooded' and they're known for their gentle nature and great strength. The other type of horse is 'hot blooded,' like thoroughbreds, and they're considered more temperamental and highly spirited," he explained.

I looked at the huge hooves which had never been trimmed nor shod. The hair was feathered close to the hooves and he looked majestic.

Glen was a very likable kind of guy, about 50 years old with a southern drawl and a voice that sounded a little bit like Willie Nelson. He told me to hop into his truck and we drove to the back portion of his large pasture.

The herd of about 50 horses followed us, aware that he often had corn in the bed of his truck. Glen took the opportunity to point out other Belgians and say that he really didn't care if he sold the horse he had shown me or not because he was going to lease his Belgians to a local dude ranch for the tourist season in just a few weeks. He said he had used the horse he had just shown me on many occasions for hay rides and grand openings, adding that he was a well mannered and road wise horse.

During the following week I visited Glen a couple of different times with different friends who knew something about horses. The first visit brought an assessment that the horse seemed healthy enough but the price was too high. The second visit included a ride on a flat bed wagon. Dale did the driving, sitting on a bale of hay for a seat, while my friend and I sat on the wagon.

I asked Dale what the horse's name was and he replied "Carter." Then he added, "He's got a half sister named Reagan, but she's in Grand Rapids."

Stafford's place is located on a very busy road and as Dale drove, everything seemed to progress just fine. The traffic included many noisy trucks and the horse performed like a champion, according to my friend. We trotted about a mile and by then Carter was sweating profusely.

When we turned around to return, a paper plate suddenly flew up in front of Carter and he bolted! Dale was thrown from his seat and my friend and I both picked up splinters from the wooden bed. Fortunately Dale stayed with the horse and managed to calm him down.

The return trip took place on the shoulder of the road facing traffic. We made it back without further incident, even though some of the approaching semi's had flags on their fenders, flapping in the wind.

Now more than ever I knew that I was qualified to ride on a horse drawn wagon but in no way should I be the one driving.

The following day I drove to Ken's. I told him about the Belgian and he agreed that a solid draft horse would be better than Big Daddy. He thought that his Standardbred could make it all the way to Tennessee, but he wouldn't recommend it because of his lameness five years earlier.

He told me of an Amishman he knew who had a Belgian for sale so we drove deep into the country to see the man and his horse. It was an eight year old mare who was very gentle and a willing worker, the Amishman said. $600.

He harnessed her up and drove her around the yard and then, for the first time in my life, I drove as I walked behind. She was perfect and did as I asked. I was encouraged. Could this be the one?

The old farmer unharnessed the horse and I asked Ken what he thought. Ken wasn't about to be hurried. He asked the man, "How are her feet?" He had told me that one type of horse I definitely didn't want was one that was touchy about having its feet handled because not only would they need shoes but I would have to check them constantly for stones and cuts.

The farmer replied that she was a little touchy about her feet. Ken went to pick up one of the rear feet, speaking gently to her. "Sho-ba-doop-BAM!" She kicked hard, straight back. Ken wasn't a large man but was well known for having more than his share of fight. He didn't try to do it again. We left saying we'd be in touch. We weren't.

We went to the track in Gladwin where Ken's brother was training the pacers and trotters with some other men. Ken got Old Dude harnessed and let me "help" with the two wheeled sulky. It was a cold and windy May day and Ken handed me an extra coat which I gladly accepted.

But then he told me to take Old Dude around the track for

sixteen laps! Oh no! Until that morning I had never driven a horse and now I was supposed to go with one of his race horses? GULP!?!

"Left is left, right is right, don't take it too fast and I'll be watching," Ken said as he led us onto the track and off we went.

Ten days to go until I was to go on my trip and I was doing something for the first time that I expected to do for over a thousand miles. I was scared, but I was also thrilled.

The cold wind made my eyes water and I couldn't see very well, but it was exciting. A few times I thought I was going to be brushed off the sulky by getting too close to the rail. It was close, but there was no problem. We went eight miles on that maiden ride and I crossed my fingers that I'd be able to get Old Dude to stop. Ken and his kids were there to save me.

Little did I know, Ken had another horse ready for me, already harnessed. Before I knew it, we were off for another eight miles! That experience probably did more than any one thing to help me cross a terrible obstacle of fear.

May 4 arrived—my last day at the airport. On that final shift I was feeling nostalgic about having belonged to such a professional group and felt regret to think that when I walked out the door at midnight, it would be over.

The shift began as a normal workday and I signed on as controller-in-charge. At ten o'clock my partner left and I was alone. The weather worsened rapidly.

In addition to talking to airplanes on the radio, part of the job was to make official weather observations, which we sent into the National Weather Service. We also briefed pilots about the weather and other aeronautical data.

Suddenly not one, but two airplanes reported that they were lost and needed help. To have one lost airplane was unusual and to have two at the same time was extremely rare. Three telephones were ringing and two pilots were waiting for weather information! In three-and-a-half years of working for the FAA this last night on the job was the most intense.

It heightened my sense of appreciation for the job and my feelings of loss as I approached my last minutes. Both aircraft managed to find the airport and land safely. The midnight shift controller arrived and my career as an air traffic controller ended. It was sad and scary—what had I got myself into?

It wasn't easy to concentrate on one thing. From horses to airports to Washington, D.C. Life in 1985 found a political reality where the president was trying to do away with the very thing to which I was trying to pay tribute.

The political atmosphere was to improve efficiency by reducing government involvement. To do so the national budget would have to be decreased, which meant that government programs would have to be trimmed or eliminated. The entire Rural Electrification Administration was targeted for total elimination, the reasoning being that government enterprise worked less efficiently than private enterprise.

The premise missed the point. The REA program was efficient citizen enterprise, allowed for by governmental cooperation. The REA program was middle ground and shouldn't have been identified as an ideological enemy.

Most people involved with rural electrification were historically conservative by nature and agreed with the administration in Washington in most cases. The difference was that the rural electric people were aware that the basics had not changed since 1935 when Roosevelt had initiated the REA.

For the most part those areas served by REA funded cooperatives remained the least desirable service areas. In the instances where the population had grown and the rural nature had changed, the electric rates often improved and became competitive with the investor owned companies. In spite of the fact that growth had been made possible because of the original REA program, the arguments were made that there was no longer any need for REA funding.

The majority of the U.S. Congress originate from urban areas, the same areas generally served by private companies. The lobbying done by such major corporations was well organized and practically unlimited.

The giant electric companies supported the move to eliminate the REA because it potentially meant an expanded market for them. Cooperative representatives argued that it wasn't fair or good for the members served by the cooperatives to let the privately owned companies skim the cream off of the co-op's areas.

If the REA were eliminated, who would serve the areas that remained sparsely populated and undeveloped? The administration was ignoring the fact that the remote areas would still need to be served and that non-profit cooperatives offered the people the most efficient and cost effective way to do the job.

The strength of the cooperative lay in its democratic nature and so the national cooperative group organized is own lobbying force of people. Several hundred of us went to Washington to visit our representatives in Congress and help inform them of our rural realities. For three days we visited various Congressional people and their staffs, hoping that they might see the wisdom in continued support for the REA program. It was a never ending battle, a process without end.

Three days before REA's birthday I returned to Michigan, still without something to pull my virgin carriage. I made a final call to Mr. Bryant to see if he had found a mule for me and to ask his advice. He had gone so far as to buy a yearling mule but having gone so far, he decided it was unacceptable for my project.

I told him about Big Daddy and Carter. He told me he thought Glen Stafford was trying to do me a favor and that I should be a gentleman and pay what he asked.

What kind of advice was that?! Nobody in their right mind would pay a horse trader what he asked without so much as a single counter offer. Was Mr. Bryant abandoning me in favor of the world of horse traders?

I called Stafford and asked if I could have a vet look Carter over and he agreed. That afternoon I met the vet at Stafford's. He had Dale hitch Carter to a small drag and after pulling it about 100 yards he took Carter's pulse. It was higher than it should have been.

He asked Glen if the horse was wheezy and Glen indignantly replied that he wouldn't sell a wheezy horse. Glen then said that he would guarantee Carter's good health and went so far as to take me out back to see another Belgian that he said he would trade for

Carter if he didn't make the grade.

The vet showed me how to give a shot and I proceeded to administer my first two shots to Carter. Next I gave the big boy a dose of worming medicine. A blood sample was taken and he said that he would call me later that day and tell me the results.

When he left Glen and I went over the price again—$1,050 for the horse and an additional $250 for a complete harness.

For the next couple of hours Glen and I took a four mile drive that seemed to last forever. I was tense and very unsure of myself. We had only gone about a mile when we came to a store and Glen left me to hold Carter while he went in to get a cigar.

By the time he emerged—about 5 minutes later—I thought I was about to lose control of the horse and was in a sweat. Glen recognized my inadequacy, which he must have suspected all along, and told me that I would need a minimum of two weeks training before I would even marginally be ready for my trip. I replied that I had to leave on May 11 and that there were no two ways about it.

That night I got a call from the vet with the results of the blood sample. Carter was anemic. He repeated that the pulse rate was too high and that he would be leery of the horse, yet he thought that he might work.

The next day I went back to Stafford's and drove Carter around the paddock, this time with Dale. We rode together for an hour or so and then it was my turn to solo. Carter was well behaved and for another hour I practiced driving in a figure eight and circles. Then Glen and I took Carter and the farm wagon back into the pasture. I drove while Glen kicked off bales of hay for the horses.

We drove around for awhile when suddenly about eight big Belgians came galloping past us as fast as they could run. The ground thundered and their beautiful golden manes were flying full behind them. Carter glanced their way and I found myself smiling and laughing at such unbounded power and freedom and beauty.

As we drove back to the paddock I asked if I could bring my carriage over tomorrow and hitch Carter to it and practice some more. After some hesitation because Dale would be working with me and was reluctant about using someone else's equipment, Glen agreed.

Back at the paddock Glen tied Carter to the gate and we went inside. I remembered Mr. Bryant's advice and agreed to pay $1300 for the horse and harness, but would he include transportation to Lansing as part of the purchase price?

Glen was reluctant to do so because his horse club's first outing of the season was scheduled for May 11. He mumbled some more, adding that there wasn't enough time to get the horse shod and that I wasn't ready. Then he said that he would try. I paid him the money and we agreed to meet again at his place with my carriage at ten the next morning.

The appointed day was almost here. The buggy had never been loaded and there was no list of things to pack or set aside. From the first tentative talks with horse people about making such a trip I had met many people who had thought about taking a cross country trip via horse. Occasionally I had actually run into people who had made a trip, not as extensive as the one I had in mind, but still, way more than anything I had ever dreamed of.

One question that always popped up was how I planned to take care of the horse's food and water supply. I approached it simply as something that would happen. I figured that we could carry two bales of hay along with us—a two day supply; 12 gallons of water; and about 100 pounds of oats.

It would be a question of balance. Somedays the distances between "settlements" might necessitate carrying an extra bale of hay. We could take less if the terrain was real hilly, or the weather particularly hot. Many people told me that water was the number one concern and that a three quarter ton working horse would drink 15 gallons or more per day.

An important aspect of the project, central to everything, was the belief that all people are neighbors, not just those living right next door. If Darwin had pointed out the concept of "survival of the fittest," it was others who pointed out the strength of mutual cooperation. Christian love. People helping people.

I loved my next door neighbors and the feeling was mutual, however, their love was expressed on many occasions by imploring me to take a weapon with which I could defend myself.

"Take a gun. You never know what crazoid you might run into. Don't be foolish," they told me.

My life had not been so sheltered that I was unaware that it can pay to be fleet of foot or quick to action. I had learned that it is only prudent to guard your rear.

Still, I didn't want to live in fear and I wanted my faith to be my light. I would carry no weapon. By traveling in this manner I would travel lighter, closer to people, and closer to God.

Another concern of those who had given any thought to something like this was the law. How do the various state laws vary? Could horses travel interstate? Are steel horseshoes legal on all roads? Were health papers required? Was it legal to use the road itself, or would it be necessary to travel on the shoulders?

There was no such thing as a Horse Travel Hotline but everyone seemed to have definite opinions. Certainly in the early days of the automobile similar questions prevailed—only in reverse. Now I would have to blaze an overgrown path, re-learning what had been forgotten as I went.

From my experience in Michigan I expected it would be useless to ask most police or the various offices of the Secretary of State about the regulations that might apply since one referred me to the other, passing the proverbial buck.

On the morning before the scheduled beginning of the trip, my friend, Tom Pardee, met me at my barn and we loaded the carriage onto his truck and drove over to Stafford's. By the time we got there Dale had already left with Carter to have him shod.

My parents also arrived before long and asked what they could do to help. Little preparation had been done to this point and my three helpers helped with some real basics which I had not attended. Basics like packing food for me, applying Velcro for the mosquito netting to the buggy, and buying rope. Dad reattached the orange slow moving vehicle triangle so that it was higher and more visible. Mom glued Velcro to my large 50th Anniversary REA signs that I would carry on the buggy doors.

Dale returned in mid-afternoon with Carter, shod now for the first time in his life. To hear Dale tell the story we were lucky to get him shod on such short notice. Dale harnessed and hitched Carter to the carriage, and we practiced for what I would be doing alone in less than a day. We drove around in the paddock, and then the pasture, and finally graduated to the road.

Glen was visibly apprehensive, certainly hoping that he wouldn't be responsible for a dead greenhorn. He told me countless horror stories of what might happen and what had happened to people and horses that he had known. His favorite concern seemed to focus on the possibility of Carter winding up in a ditch with wire wrapped around his legs, cutting all the while. He recommended that I take along a quality pair of wire cutters and to always have them handy. I did.

We agreed to meet at Glen's at 5 a.m. and to proceed to Lansing so as to be there by 11 a.m. We reloaded the buggy onto Tom's truck and drove back to the barn to meet my parents.

They had picked up a trailer into which we intended to load Pete and his momma. Pete Morrison had offered to keep the donkeys while I was gone, but we couldn't get the stubborn donkeys loaded into the trailer. As a result, they were to stay at home until I could get back and move them. My neighbors offered to take care of the donkeys and my cat, as well as my mail and lawn. Tom loaded the carriage for its first time while my parents packed things like the computer and printer and salt and pepper.

Jim Young and I were on the phone late into the night, many times. The PV's had not yet been shipped as they were supposed to have been. Jim promised that he would somehow get his hands on a panel and bring it the 100 miles to the capitol before 11 a.m. the next morning, even if he had to "borrow" one that ECD had loaned to another party. By the last time I talked with Jim that night, "11 a.m. the next day" was less than ten hours away. Tom and I finished packing the buggy two hours after that.

6

A Commemoration

. . . Bilbo sat down on a seat by his door, crossed his legs, and blew out a beautiful grey ring of smoke that sailed up into the air without breaking and floated away over The Hill.

"Very pretty!" said Gandalf. "But I have no time to blow smoke rings this morning. I am looking for someone to share in an adventure that I am arranging, and it's very difficult to find anyone."

"I should think so—in these parts! We are plain quiet folk and have no use for adventures. Nasty disturbing uncomfortable things! Make you late for dinner! I can't think what anybody sees in them," said our Mr. Baggins.

—J. R. R. Tolkien,
from "The Hobbit"

With eyes scratchy from too little sleep, we arose on May 11 at 4 a.m. Too much was unprepared. The buggy had no brakes. There wasn't enough storage space. The 6 gallon plastic water jugs had to sit on the floor in the rear of the buggy with 100 pounds of oats. There was a battery on board, but no photovoltaics or inverter or regulator or wiring or know-how to hook them all together.

We drove over to Stafford's and had to wake Glen. His group of trailrider friends had been camping and partying until late and while we waited for Glen we drank coffee with two of his friends who were still up from the party.

Before long Glen got up and we went to get Carter. I led him from the barn to the horse trailer, but it was Glen that loaded him into the trailer. Soon we were on our way; Glen and his friends had Carter in front, Tom and I carried the buggy in the middle, and my parents brought up the rear of the convoy.

As we drove along Tom and I talked about the fact that the May 11 anniversary date would apparently be met. That felt good, but by now my main concern was having to actually do it. As we drove south, we also drove towards Michigan's population center and heavy traffic.

My plan was to drive Carter and the buggy back to my Williamsburg home and at that time complete the outfitting of the carriage. Once ready, we would travel north to Michigan's upper peninsula, west to Minnesota, and then follow the Mississippi River south to Tennessee. My rough outline had us traveling for six months, heading south as cold weather approached, with monthly returns home so that I could attend the board meetings of Cherryland Rural Electric Cooperative.

We arrived in Lansing and drove to the capitol building itself. It was a Saturday and the place was almost deserted. We unloaded everything and I brushed Carter for the first time.

Glen harnessed Carter and hitched him to the carriage. About that time Jim drove up with a freshly acquired photovoltaic panel which had to be returned as soon as we took a couple of pictures. Since there were no brackets or anything else with which to hold it up, Tom followed the buggy around the capitol grounds, hiding on the opposite side while reaching up and over the buggy's roof to hold the PV in place.

Eleven o'clock arrived just as Glen and I climbed into the buggy. Glen drove us around the capitol building two times. Not once did I even pretend to do the actual driving.

In less than an hour we had acknowledged the 50th birthday of the REA. Glen unhitched Carter from the buggy, Jim took his PV and ran, and we reloaded everything and left the capital.

A few miles out of town we found a country road that was away from the heavy traffic of town. Again Glen unloaded and rehitched Carter to the carriage. Faster than that Glen said "good luck" and disappeared, eager to get away and back to his party.

Just before he left he again told me that I should wait, and that at least I should recruit someone—anyone—even a child, to go with me. There was no child and I intended just to do it.

Less than two months earlier my father found himself in a Florida hospital, the victim of a heart attack. It was not a particularly severe attack, but when he told me that he was going to come with me, I was against the idea. He insisted that he felt good and that I needed his help. I said no.

He got in the buggy and said "let's go." I got in and we were off. Finally. It began easily enough. No traffic, a slightly traveled road, and the middle of a weekend day. Mom followed at a distance and Tom headed for home.

Dad and I took turns driving, both inexperienced and both driving Carter without conviction and in a zig zag fashion. We had gone about five miles when we came to a narrow bridge at the bottom of a hill. Cars were approaching from both directions and there wasn't much of a shoulder. To our right a little dog was barking like there was no tomorrow. The yipper appeared to be protecting the clothes drying on a clothesline in the breeze. Carter spooked to the left, or maybe I spooked to the left, but we went left anyhow and crossed into a vacant farmyard.

The yard was fairly large and the grass was tall. We drove him around the yard a short while before deciding that the trip had started on the appointed day and that it had been a long day and night and, well, why not seek permission to spend the night here?

I unhitched and unharnessed Carter for the first time and tied him to a log. The thought was to let him graze while I sought permission. It didn't work. Carter spooked as he moved and dragged the rope through the tall grass. I stood there with my new horse, holding the rope while he grazed, and wondered what to do.

Neighbor kids arrived and after talking with them, they fetched their parents. Phone calls were made and permission was granted to spend the night. My parents took their cue and departed. The first day was over. My father and I were forever united and all were healthy and in one piece. I was thankful but I was not having a good time.

That first night in Eagle, Michigan provided for many "firsts." Inexperienced meant that I had never dealt with tying a horse out, sleeping in the buggy, starting out in the morning, or knowing what to expect from ever-changing neighbors.

The first concern was always Carter. Without him the trip didn't exist. Since Carter spooked when tethered as he dragged rope through the tall grass (did he think he saw a snake?) I hurriedly reconnoitered the deserted barnyard.

There was an outbuilding that had only one opening so I led Carter to it and barricaded him inside as much as I could. It was crude, almost desperate, but it worked and that's all I was hoping for. The Belgian wasn't used to being indoors and wasn't content to eat only hay; he was used to being pastured and outdoors. As a result I had to keep checking to make sure he hadn't pushed through the barricade of rope and old lumber, trying to get to the lush grass just feet away. He did try but with nothing else to do I managed to keep on top of things and keep the barricade up.

Kids quickly established themselves as special by not hiding their interest in the horse. The first to greet us were kids—Bob and Peg Brennan. They had seen us traveling down the road and thought that Amish were moving into their neighborhood.

When we stopped they gathered around, wanting to pet and feed Carter. They wanted to see inside the carriage and when I showed them the computer they lit up again, though not as much as they did with Carter.

Hospitality was another early lesson. Across the street from the deserted farm were several suburban types of homes. Peg and Bob's parents, Jim and Pat, visited and invited me over to have dinner with them. Pat suggested I have a shower before supper and she didn't have to offer twice. The Brennans offered me a couch to sleep on but I was too paranoid about losing Carter. Plus I was eager to establish a routine of traveling and camping.

I spent my first night in the buggy and it slept fine. The back of the front seat folded down over my false bottom storage area, and the cover of the storage area slid back to the rear seat, making a 42" wide and 6' long bed. The Canadian Mennonites had failed to provide the missing cushion to this, their first sleeper (or "Minnebago" as some called it). A friend had made the piece for me and had managed to match the existing cushions. All closed up inside the buggy at night, it was especially dark and not suited for anyone inclined toward claustrophobia.

Day dawned and Carter was still in his cage—but only barely.

This was the time I dreaded. Amazingly, I had never put the harness on all by myself and I did not have the hang of it by a long shot. After feeding and watering Carter I timidly went inside his building with the harness. Each time he moved I felt my childhood fears surface. I was careful not to let his rear legs face me and my caution only made the job of harnessing more difficult. Finally, after many attempts and considerable sweat, the harness was on. It looked right—sort of.

Now came perhaps the hardest part of all—hitching the harnessed horse to the carriage. Time after time I would drive Carter to the front of the fills and then try and back him into them, but time after time he would balk at my direction. Finally, somehow, he backed into the fills and I managed to hitch him to the carriage. All was loaded and the only thing remaining was to go.

Day number two—here we go! But no! After a giddy-up and just a few steps, the harness looked cock-eyed. Something wasn't right, but what? I tried to readjust the harness but no matter what I did it came up looking wrong.

What could I do? There were no cowboys around, no farmers. About now I was thinking about the "even a child" that Glen had encouraged me to take for such instances as this, but there were none. Not sure what to do, and ill equipped to hold an impatient horse, I unhitched Carter and led him back to his building. Anxiety and frustration.

After much thought I called Ken Thurlow for advice. He said he would borrow a trailer that could hold a large horse and drive the 150 miles to Eagle that night and pick us up. I could leave Carter with him and figure out what I was going to do. I didn't know what else to do. We had made a start on the appointed historical birthday, but my trip would have to wait.

I called my parents and they returned to rescue the carriage within a few hours. Late that night Ken drove up with his brother's trailer and he loaded Carter. His father-in-law was with him and as we began the trip north he asked me how much experience I had with horses. I told him and he told me he thought as much because horsefolk usually load their own horses, while I had let Ken load Carter. I was down.

It had been a long three days. I spent the night at Ken's and the next day I hitchhiked the 100 miles home. Before I left Ken offered his home to me and said he would work with me and Carter until I was ready. What a friend!

When I got home I thought how foolish I had been to ever leave my job at the airport. In the same instant, I felt repulsed at the thought of trying to get my old job back. That wouldn't help a thing.

The next six weeks were difficult. The first column of the Electric Burro Travel Series was written while in Eagle, and I had sent it out to a number of publications, hoping to get someone to publish it. Now, still without a sponsor, I had to come up with my second monthly article about my trip—without a trip. It was embarrassing.

In some respects things were worse than ever. Before the actual beginning I only imagined how incompetent I was. Now I knew for sure! A week after I left Carter with Ken, Ken brought Carter home to the barn for the first time.

When Ken unloaded the big animal, Carter saw Pete, his first donkey, and went nuts. He snorted so loud the ground shook! He grew a foot taller and circled with Ken holding on tight and me watching in amazement.

Ken had his hands full but was laughing and saying "Ol' Carter don't know what to think about these donks."

I'm glad someone had a sense of humor. Finally Carter settled down. Ken helped me harness him and we took a six mile drive around the local cherry orchards. All went well. That was the longest drive I had ever made with Carter. Fortunately, Ken was a good teacher and had me drive most of the way.

For the first several hours after Carter's arrival, he snorted and ran and threatened to go through the electric fence. The two donkeys weren't afraid at all, only curious. Little Pete especially seemed eager to make friends with the new giant but time was the only answer.

A few days later the three were buddies, and they grazed and ran and rolled in the dirt together. At feeding time Carter protected his own by using a good left jab to keep the donkeys away from his oats. The vet had recommended feeding him plenty of grain to build him up and make his ribs disappear, so things were developing just right.

It seemed to me that there must be thousands of people "out there" who would love to make a trip like this. I thought back to my school days and though I wouldn't have been too keen about an adventure with a horse, I surely had dreamed of being offered a ready-made adventure. So two days after I returned home I took out a classified ad in the Lansing paper which read:

> Experienced horseperson wanted to make cross country trip in horse and buggy. Room and board provided. Phone #

The $107 advertisement brought a total of three phone calls. The first was from a high school girl who loved horses. The second was from a woman who had hitchhiked across the USA several times and whose last job was as a Black Jack dealer in Las Vegas. Neither called back.

A third call came from a woman who was calling on behalf of her husband. He was 67 years old, retired, in good health, had worked with horses as a kid, and she was sure he would like to make a trip of some duration. I told her of my plans and recent history. She said she would relay our discussion to her husband. The next day he called and Bruce Shaw and I made a date to meet at my place and go for a drive with Carter.

It was a matter of days before Bruce arrived with his wife, Laverne. We talked and what Laverne had told me was true. But the truth of the matter seemed to be that as much as Bruce might have desired to come along, Laverne needed his help because of arthritis. She always encouraged.

After talking for awhile we went to the north side of the barn and Bruce proved his adeptness at harnessing and hitching Carter.

We then took a drive of about five miles and Bruce, who had worked as an elevator mechanic, found that the fills were rubbing against the body of the buggy because of an improperly designed mounting bracket.

The Shaws spent the night and the next day we took another drive. When they left for the three hour drive home Bruce told me that he could make the needed bracket, but that he wouldn't be able to come along. Those two drives with Bruce helped to break a paralysis that seemed to be working on me.

There was a constant in the advice I received—I needed to spend more time around horses. Whew! That took serious discipline. I began to harness Carter and drive him in the field behind the barn with me walking behind. We would go in a rectangular pattern, walking, stopping, and trotting. Often he wouldn't walk straight, testing me. I couldn't make him stand. Poor horse. With me being so nervous it's a wonder that he could function at all. Still, I was spending more time with the horse.

The PV's finally arrived and I bought a 500 watt inverter from Sears but the electrics had me baffled. Inertia was with me. Friend Bill Keely came to my rescue and brought his drill press, tools and spirit with him. He drove out to the barn many times in a car that was about to lose its transmission or engine, depending on the trip. With his help the PV's were mounted on adjustable brackets, the inverter was installed and the buggy was wired so that inside the buggy there were four household 110 volt receptacles. He tested the system and we checked to see if the 500 watt inverter would allow the 500 watt coffeemaker to work. Some of the best coffee I ever tasted!

There was inadequate storage space so I worked at building two storage compartments underneath the buggy. These were painted bright yellow to offset the otherwise drab and hearse-like appearance.

A few weeks later Bruce returned with specially made brackets that worked perfectly and allowed the fills to operate without gouging the carriage. Bruce was tireless and his enthusiasm was greater than mine.

Before taking the carriage for a spin, I whimpered about the lack of brakes. Bruce recognized the need and without missing a beat, in his steady and reasoning manner, began to figure out how to build a brake system.

I had started to build a very simple brake system myself, but Bruce had routinely built brakes in the elevator business, so I deferred. We visited automotive stores, hardwares, and junk yards, spending money like I had it. During the three days of Bruce's second visit he made a mechanical brake system, complete with handmade brake shoes, linkages and foot pedal on the front floor.

As important as the brakes were, even more vital was the addition of flashing lights. Bruce had suggested that we put some flashing lights on the buggy during his first visit, but I was more inclined to try not to attract attention. Laverne had taken me to the side and warned me that Bruce was inclined to get carried away with electronic gadgets. She told me that he even had a cigarette lighter on his riding lawnmower. Hmmm–m–m, I saw her point.

When I decided to give in, my main consideration was to have the lights for turn signals in the event some state law along the way required them. When completed they functioned either as turn signals or alternating flashers. Bruce and I took a final drive together and I told him that I suspected that he was an angel. I was at least half serious.

Time kept slipping away and for each day I delayed there would be one less day of warm weather. There were three other things that happened before we got going again. One of those things were half a dozen meetings at the cooperative. Our co-op was party to the $4.5 billion dollar Fermi II nuclear plant in southeast Michigan, and at least our financial survival was at stake. Because of this investment of ours, too many meetings were needed just to keep abreast of events.

A second thing was a visit to Wayne and Jane McCarry's horse farm. I had gotten in touch with them because I heard they gave driving lessons. When I arrived I told them about my plans and my predicament. They were super! Wayne harnessed one of their horses and Jane jumped into the cart with me and talked me through the basics; nothing I hadn't done by that time, but it helped to see it presented in a controlled and orderly fashion. I spent the late afternoon and all evening with them and we talked about everything from picket lines to watering techniques to the Budweiser Clydesdales.

The third deal was a trip to Mackinac Island near the straits where Lake Huron meets Lake Michigan. I rented a Cessna and flew to the island where transportation was carried out by foot, bicycle or horse and buggy, not counting the airstrip. Mainly I wanted to learn what it would take to cross the five mile long Mackinac Bridge to Michigan's upper peninsula (U.P.), but I also wanted to check into the possibility of crossing the straits via the island.

I found out that a few years earlier an Amish family had attempted to drive across Big Mack with a team but had lost control. Ever since then the Bridge Authority had forbidden horses on the bridge.

The logistics and related expense of getting Carter and the buggy across to the island were just too much and I gave up on the idea. I did meet several professional carriage people and was able to come to an understanding so that when Carter and I arrived at the southern edge of the bridge, they would give us a lift across to the U.P.

While on the island I learned that their horses were shod with a rubber coated steel shoe. The shoe had been developed on the island as a means for protecting the roads, however, these people who lived with horses and carriages every day recommended steel shoes tipped with borium for my trip.

Borium was an extremely hard carbide material that extended the life of a horseshoe threefold. They explained that sometimes the rubber didn't bond properly on their shoes but it was no big deal on the island since they were never very far from their stables and a farrier. I would be on the road and wouldn't be doing my own blacksmithing.

Rain began to fall and I decided to head towards the airport. Just as I was about to leave, the owner of a carriage tour company asked, "How many horses are you taking on this trip?"

"Just one."

"Oh yeah? How long's this trip gonna' take?"

"About six months."

"You'll never make it with just one horse."

I felt mixed emotions as I climbed into the airplane and began the one hour flight home. I was happy to have arranged transportation across the bridge and to have learned about horseshoes, but discouraged because people whose livelihood was horse and buggy travel had said that what I intended to do couldn't be done.

7

On the Road Again
—Lower Michigan

If Noah had been truly wise, he would have swatted those two flies.

—Helen Castle

Six weeks passed after the beginning in Lansing and I began to identify with Lincoln's Civil War General-in-Chief, George Mc-Clellen. In the early part of the war McClellen had served as a splendid organizer and strategist. The Union Army was well drilled and appeared to be a formidable fighting force. The troups stood strongly behind their field leader and everything was prepared to attack the rebels, except one thing. McClellen wouldn't fight. Time after time an increasingly exasperated Lincoln would urge McClellen to engage the enemy but there was always an excuse why he couldn't. "You must act," Lincoln wrote, but McClellen continued to procrastinate.

My delays seemed endless. Sometimes the excuses were legitimate, the buggy wasn't ready, or an important meeting was about to happen, but finally Carter's ribs weren't showing and the buggy was completed.

Fear dragged me down. I postponed and remained at home another week. I needed to go and I disliked my thoughts of Mc-Clellen. They were too true.

The often reappointed day returned on June 25 and activity around the barn began before sunrise. My Civil War mentality called for an attack before the enemy forces got strong and the busiest highway around was M–72 and it got busy early.

I had loaded the buggy the day before and it was packed in apparent readiness in front of the barn. I fed Carter as soon as I got up and the butterflies in my stomach were up and at 'em.

"This was it," I felt, and I took a final walk around the buggy to verify that everything was ready.

I climbed underneath the buggy to make sure nothing had changed. But it had! The weight of the now loaded buggy had caused the body of the buggy to sink into its suspension spring and now the brake arm was pressed tight against the floorboard. I would have to redrill the brake arm to allow for free movement. I was sick of delays and didn't want another.

By the time I adjusted the brakes, the traffic was up. It seemed incredible that I could not get going and I was having a terrible time. What I should have done, in retrospect, was to have someone who was qualified come with me for the first three miles which included M–72, and then go. Instead I waited till after the heaviest traffic had died out, around 6 p.m. As I headed out the door to leave, the phone rang. "Remember that . . . Husky Spirit!," our high school cheer, from Tom. On that note I went out and hitched Carter to the buggy and we were gone.

Release! I was scared and happy, and about as excited as I could get. To be on the road, to have overcome the paralysis, and to be following the golden mane of Carter—it was a highlight and the best possible thing I could have done. It was my first solo on the road, my first time on busy M–72, and my first time driving with the buggy completed. Waiting was the worst part. I needed the stimulation of travel to force me to live the dream.

The first mile was on backroads and it was pleasant. It was beautiful. Carter started at a trot and acted superbly. Even when we had traveled three miles and come to the place to get off M–72, with cars backing up on the shoulder and pulling off to take our picture, and where two lanes became three at a scenic turn out— Carter behaved like he wanted to survive.

The strategy was to take it easy on Carter. He had been anemic, though he had filled out considerably since that day a month and a half ago when I had purchased him. Still, he hadn't been worked much at all and I was intent on babying him before pushing him.

That second first day took us only six miles in slightly less than two hours. By the time we reached our pre-arranged stop at Darryl and Esther Amidon's home, Carter was frothing at the mouth and sweating. The Amidon's were expecting us and when we pulled into their drive Darryl led us back to an old unused corral where he had once kept horses himself. Carter was content to graze—I was beside myself.

After months of hurrying, I realized that the time machine effect of horse and buggy existence was in place. The "hurry up" mentality of 20th century western living had no immediate reason to continue.

At least until Carter toughened up we would be limited to the amount of time we could dedicate to travel, and suddenly I had all the time in the world. In view of my attempt at commemorating a fifty year old program, I appreciated the opportunity for such an insight to a way of life generally passed by in the U.S.A. For the rest of the day I simply took it easy.

Jeff and another neighbor followed Carter's trail and we relived the excitement of the day. I brushed Carter and readied the buggy for nighttime. That night I visited with the Amidons, watching a baseball game on TV and talking about the days before electricity.

When I woke up the next morning I slid the front door open and looked out to see how Carter was doing. Nothing could be finer as he happily munched the grass in the corral. There was no hurry to get on the road since I had prearranged the place to stay on the second day out and it was only five miles away.

As the noon hour approached, Darryl drifted down to the buggy and invited me to lunch. We had a leisurely lunch and talked about the early days of REA, and things like the horses and cows that the Amidons used to have in the old days.

With lunch over, Darryl and I walked out the front door in time to see a governmental looking sort of car drive up quickly with the words "Kalkaska Animal Control" on the door.

"Great, someone has already complained and I'm probably not legal for the road," I thought.

I felt some comfort knowing that Darryl was a Kalkaska County Commissioner (Republican) and Esther was township supervisor (Democrat)—at least I had both party bases covered in the event I was involved with this man in green.

"Does anybody here own a draft horse?" he asked, looking at me. "Because if you do, he's trotting down the middle of the road a mile away and has just missed several cars!"

Oh no! I ran down to the buggy and grabbed the lead rope as Darryl grabbed the keys to his van. We drove more than a mile before we saw Carter trotting down the middle of the curving two lane road. He was sweaty and muddy and as we got closer I could see a crazed look in his eyes. I jumped out and he slowed to a nervous walk. Before long I put the lead rope on him and he calmed down enough for me to walk him back to the Amidon's.

When we returned, Darryl was examining the corral. The corral had three rails made out of old lumber, a full 2" × 6", and the top rail was broke in two where Carter had jumped through. He had cleared the bottom two rails which meant a good three foot high jump.

The Amidon property was surrounded by a swamp and enclosed by a barbed wire fence, except for one small opening. We surmised that a horse fly or bee had bitten Carter and he had made his dash. Somehow he had found the one opening through the barbed wire, but not before he had run through the swamp and gotten nice and slimey.

By 3 p.m. he had calmed down and was back to grazing inside the corral. Time to go. Darryl held Carter while I harnessed and hitched him to the buggy. All was ready and I waved to Darryl and Esther and we headed down the flat and straight Rapid City road.

Just as I was beginning to think what had happened was a fluke, two giant, blue-eyed, green flies dive bombed Carter. They were huge! They didn't have a chance to land before Carter suddenly veered sharply into the oncoming traffic lane and across the road, through the ditch.

Luckily there was no traffic. Even if there had been it wouldn't have effected Carter's actions. Carter smoothed out right away and we returned to the right side of the road. If each day was to be as action packed as this we'd never survive and probably never get out of the state of Michigan.

Travel on. that second day lasted only an hour and a half before we arrived at the home of Judy and Dan Vanderwoude. Judy invited us to camp anywhere but since they had a nice yard and a large Belgian horse leaves many large piles of manure, the only place I could keep Carter without destroying their lawn was in the middle of an unfenced and sandy field. I made a stake and drove it three feet into the sandy soil and tied Carter's 23' long rope to it and hoped he would be good and just graze on the skinny grasses without yanking on the impermanent stake. This time I was lucky.

Don and Judy had expected me and I enjoyed supper with the family of four. Everyone was involved with computers and I couldn't help but think how fast society was changing. The Vanderwoudes lived in an area that had been electrified for less than 50 years. They weren't city people yet they weren't what you might think of as country people either. More like "modern rural"— whatever that means.

We were down in Plum Valley and the sun disappeared by 9 p.m. Eleven miles away at my barn sunset was almost an hour later. I retired to bed and the buggy and as I lay there I became aware of a feeling I had experienced before. It was living outdoors and breathing fresh air as opposed to living indoors. It was an awareness achieved by being out and about as opposed to living a regimented sort of life. Life close to fresh air was stronger than life without it. It was a life related to wild and raw while the alternative was related to tame and superficial. My life was gradually changing and the process of becoming seasoned, though scary, led to strength.

The next morning I got up and went to brew some coffee but instead the red warning light on the inverter went on, indicating an insufficient charge. I couldn't understand it since the battery had indicated a full charge just the night before and I hadn't used anything electric. Worse than that—I wanted my morning coffee! A quick fix came by plugging the coffee pot into an outlet in the Vanderwoude's garage. I didn't know it at the time, but the problem was the result of having an inverter rated the same as the coffee maker with no extra capacity.

Another reality presented itself that morning when I shaved and shampooed using the garden hose. Brrr-rr-r. Already I missed the ease of keeping clean by having a shower handy.

Since today would be the first time we traveled without knowing where we would be staying, I aimed for our earliest start yet—10:30 a.m. Of course that wasn't early at all, but the fact remained that my pony was not in particularly good physical shape.

I tried to think of how I might be able to hitch Carter without anyone around to help me hold him or any sort of hitching post. Since Carter was a fool for oats, I decided to hold off giving him his morning oats until it was time to harness and hitch up.

While he was eating, I put the harness on him and pulled the carriage up to him from his rear, neatly inserting the shafts into the harness. I completed the hitching as he finished the remaining oats. It worked!

On this beautiful 80 degree summer day we had a nice breeze and three good sized hills to go up and down. Carter didn't change his pace. The steeper the climb, the more he put his head down and got tough. I was just learning how incredibly strong this Belgian horse was. Going up was one thing but when we had to descend I realized that Bruce's brakes were not all they should be. They couldn't hold the entire weight of the buggy which meant that the weight was transferred to Carter's rear legs via the harness. The hills weren't steep enough to cause a serious problem but if they got much steeper there could be trouble.

The road was paved and lightly traveled. I noticed a pickup behind us and because there was a curve ahead he stayed behind. As we got around the curve the pickup passed on the left. At the same time a car passed on our right on the gravel shoulder!

Whatever was going to happen was totally out of my hands. Carter was startled, but he was cool and continued along straight. After his antics of the previous day, I was certainly pleased.

We had traveled about nine miles when I thought we had better look for someplace to spend the night. The paved road changed to gravel and then sand and the pulling got more difficult as Carter had to work to pull the sinking skinny tires. No one lived along this stretch and since we needed water, we kept going.

After a few miles of this we came to a small house with a couple about 65 years old in the front yard. I pulled into their driveway and said hello. I explained that I lived about 20 miles away and was just starting out on a cross country trip to Tennessee. Did they know of anyplace I might get some water and camp with my horse for the night?

As I was sitting in the carriage trying to explain my situation, Carter decided to keep going. The problem was that the steering radius of the buggy was very limited and there wasn't much room in the clearing of the driveway. I had to steer too tightly, the front wheels hit the wheel stops and the rubber tires dug in. The carriage tipped dangerously.

The people were cool toward me and said little. Carter refused to stand still and I considered myself lucky to be able to head Carter out of the drive. The man and woman stared after us without a word. It wasn't a very promising start to a plan that intended to find a place to stay as we went.

Back on the road, Carter began to zigzag like mad. I blamed it on weariness. It was frustrating. Fortunately, there was almost no traffic.

We came to a farm about half a mile from the old folks and there was a man and woman raking hay by hand in a field. Rather desperately I asked my question again, only this time I mentioned that my horse was very tired. My requesting technique needed work, like my horse and driving.

Jack and Pat Lambeth were busy but they said I was welcome to camp at the back of their property. Still unable to direct Carter with any degree of consistency, I thanked them and headed across the field to a row of pine trees.

I unhitched the horse and tied the 23' long rope to the same stake as the previous night. The ground was the same sand, only this time Carter lost his weariness as soon as he was unhitched and pulled it up like it was a toothpick. I tied him to one of the pine trees, giving Carter 180 degrees of movement. He mellowed out long enough to eat. I got situated for the night, Pat brought me a large plate of hot food and I began to relax. Not for long.

That night was no fun. The Lambeths boarded a mare for a young woman who rented a trailer from them and she kept the horse in Lambeth's corral on the other side of our field. Carter was feeling his oats, and stomped and snorted like he wasn't a gelding all night long. Throughout the night his antics woke me up and I had to get up and see if he was okay several times.

When I got up the next morning Carter was still acting up and the rope was caught behind his rear hoove. The entire area where he could reach was trampled and devoid of anything green. I began to feel like I was babysitting for this horse who insisted on acting like "set me free" a couple of times a day.

I modified the new hitching technique since the ground was sand and it was too hard to push the buggy with sinking tires. Once everything was stowed and ready to go, I positioned the fills so that the shafts were turned to the side as far as they would go. Then I led the harnessed Carter to the open area in front of the buggy, next to the turned fills, and positioned the oats bucket so that while he munched, I could lift the fills over him and straighten them out. By moving the bucket forward or backward I could fine tune Carter's position and easily hitch him. It was an improvement that eased the solo hitching procedure considerably.

The fourth day of travel turned out to be better than the erratic third. Apprehension remained a byword but the roads were good and lightly traveled. Since we had gone a record 12 miles on the third day, I wanted to go less than that. We had traveled about 7 miles and I began to look for a place to stop, but instead we came to a long, steep hill. There was nothing to do but go up.

The hill was over a mile long and the trucks were downshifting to go up or down. At this point I didn't want to test Carter. It took five attempts to get up the hill. We would go for awhile until Carter looked like he might be straining, and then pull to the side and let him catch his wind. After a long climb we reached the top and there was a large field that looked quiet and peaceful. We pulled into the drive of the house across from the field and I asked a boy if he knew who owned it. He said that his family did and that it would be okay if we stayed there. If we needed water, he said, he would bring it to us.

The field was barren of anything but grass except for several trees in the middle, at the bottom of a hill. I climbed two trees and made a picket line.

A picket line is nothing more than a rope strung between two places, higher than the horse's head. From that line a shorter rope is attached, long enough to let the horse's mouth reach the ground to eat or lay down, but short enough so that he couldn't step over the rope and get his legs tangled.

The idea of a picket line is to keep the horse in one place, not to make a "run" where he could travel the length of the line. In this case, the only suitable trees were about 60' apart, and, as I was to learn, the longer the picket line, the more the horse could pull on it and stretch it. Stretched too far, he could get tangled up.

I enjoyed camping alone with Carter. He seemed content to munch while tied to the picket line. I wasn't particularly comfortable around others because I knew I couldn't control the beast, and was tired of being an incompetent. Being alone with my horse in the middle of a large field gave me the opportunity to just relax and quietly reflect on what I was trying to do. It also provided a chance to escape into the fantasy book, "The Hobbit."

Morning arrived and it came time to go. The buggy was packed, Carter was brushed, the picket line was down and stowed and the harness was on. The only thing remaining was to hitch. Carter was eating his beloved oats and standing between the fills, as I began to connect the leather harness straps to the fills. Carter suddenly decided he was scared. At first I thought he was testing me and just didn't want to be worked, but then as he grew taller and began his earth shaking snorts I knew it was more.

Twenty miles to the south of this field was a National Guard base where they play with the big guns. Camp was in session and I realized that Carter was hearing, probably even feeling, the blasts of the cannons. I couldn't get him to stand still, let alone hitched between the fills. When Carter ignored his oats something was wrong!

I got the picket line rope back out of the buggy, climbed the two trees again, and hooked Carter to it. It was obvious that I could not control this horse and four days from home I felt that the trip might well be over.

I got out a donkey magazine and sat on the hill overlooking Carter and the buggy, contemplating what I was going to do. Maybe I could find a trained donkey that was advertised for sale in this magazine and continue without the buggy or Carter. I could do the original idea of a walk. My thought processes were obviously shorted out because I had looked through this magazine for the same thing several times before.

What would happen if I couldn't get underway again with this horse? I thought of getting a three wheeled all terrain vehicle. I could pull the buggy with that. Boy—that would look ridiculous! I could pull the buggy with my truck. No—same problem.

I knew that I would have preferred to be traveling much lighter than I was now trying to do. But I already had Carter and here we were, and maybe he would settle down. Maybe I could struggle to the Mississippi River with him, trade him for a donkey, rent a houseboat, load the buggy and donkey, and float down the river to Tennessee by November.

An hour passed and my gloom grew. Then the cannons quieted as suddenly as they had begun. I doubted that progress would be made but I tried it all again. Up the trees, down with the picket line, and amazingly Carter resumed work on his oats. It worked— he was hitched and we made our way out of the field and back onto the road.

The fifth day of travel was pleasantly uneventful. After about eight hot miles I stopped at a house and asked "the question."

Not only was asking complete strangers for a place to stay a twist for me, but it must have been even more of a shocker for them. To see a horse and buggy traveling along with strange look- ing contraptions on top must have been plenty of surprise to most people by itself. To be asked for a place to stay in addition, no doubt, most people had never had this happen to them.

In Nepal almost every place was rural and remote. Most travel through the Himalayan mountains was accomplished by foot, and as daylight would turn to dusk, with hotels being non-existent, people would stop at the next house and ask if they could spend the night. Almost always the traveler would be welcomed to spend the night and share the food.

In America, 1985, people weren't used to this concept. Still, when I asked the question on this day, the man wasn't as much putting me off as he was trying to adjust to an unusual situation. Instead of inviting me to spend the night in the side yard of his house, not a farm, or directing me to a nearby field, he suggested that I travel another mile to where a friend of his lived. They had cows and a pasture.

We traveled on until we came to the home of the man's friend, Fred and Marge Buhland. The first man had phoned and told them we were coming. They invited me to park the buggy in the 20 acres in front of their house, and keep Carter in the pasture with their 10 head of cattle.

"Does he mind cattle?" Fred asked.

I told him I didn't know. We found out that Carter loved cows and might even have thought of himself as one. A Belgian cow.

That night the Buhlands invited me to supper and I learned that both Fred and Marge held down regular jobs in addition to working as a family, making and selling hydraulic log splitters. They also repaired and rebuilt tractors and had built their own house. After supper we watched a movie on TV together, thanks to their satellite dish.

Cable television was rarely available in rural America for the same reasons that electricity hadn't been available years earlier. Technology allowed the rural people to leapfrog the lack of cable TV and the satellite dishes allowed for quality programming.

The same rapidly advancing technology was beginning to disallow as various programmers began to scramble their signals. Individual networks were beginning to charge for each descrambling unit, erasing any cost effectiveness on the part of the dish owners.

Co-ops weren't fly-by-night operations and there was already talk of forming a new cooperative to begin negotiations with the programmers. If the 1000 electric co-ops joined forces, perhaps a single co-op could offer dish owners a single descrambling unit that could descramble the premium channels at a reasonable fee.

The next morning I was up with the cows and shaved and showered from the neck up with the Buhland's garden hose. Time came to get on the road and Fred and Marge were out to give me a hand. There was a cedar pole about one foot above the ground that appeared to be used as a parking bumper so I decided to use it as a hitching post while I harnessed Carter. Just as I was tightening the belly strap, Carter decided to step over the post. He was ready to go.

He was ready to go alright! Turned out that the bumper post was there to prevent cars and people from stepping on a piece of old plywood over the well pit! When Carter stepped over the pole, his foot landed on the plywood and it began to go through!

Fred and I strained to move him back but the short lead rope prevented him from going anywhere in his new position. We kept trying and finally were able to unsnap the lead rope. It was sheer luck that Carter moved to the left and not the right. If he had gone right he could have gone through the plywood and broken his leg!

Luck stayed with us and the hitching was completed. We had run out of hay so Fred brought a bale out for me to take with us. This began a pattern that was to continue for the duration of the trip.

City and suburban living in the USA dictated that for many goods received or services rendered, you paid. In rural USA the reality was often exactly the opposite. After strapping the bale of hay to the rear of the buggy, goodbyes and good lucks were given and off we went.

The set of county maps I carried with me were very detailed. Unfortunately, they were often less than accurate. Many times a road would be shown that didn't exist, or was misnamed, so that sometimes I would have to stop and ask directions.

On this day the people I asked directions from told me of a shortcut that would save three miles. The map didn't show the shortcut they spoke of but at 3 miles per hour, such a shortcut would save us an hour. I was skeptical since it had been my experience that when people are asked directions they will sooner give directions than say, "I don't know."

Nevertheless, off the main road we went and down an ever narrowing side road. A mile later the small, paved road turned to dirt, and then sand. We continued as the wheels kept sinking and I debated whether it was wise to continue.

"Oh well, give it a shot," I told myself and on we went.

After another mile of quiet, pleasant surroundings the sandy road turned into a two track trail and I thought a mistake had been made. The small hills grew big and on one extremely steep downhill Carter couldn't hold the buggy and broke into a trot. It was a scary and potentially dangerous predicament since the next step would be for the harness to take his legs out from under him. This was all in spite of the deep sand and fully applied brakes.

After another half mile I saw the main road ahead of us. The shortcut had worked! According to my maps we could cross the busy main road and stick to the quieter back roads and not add any distance to our journey.

Two miles later found us on dirt roads with "No Trespassing" signs everywhere. By now Carter had walked more in one day than ever before. It was hot and he was having to work. The land was heavily wooded and where the land wasn't posted, it was unsuitable for camping. The main incentive to push on was the fact that we were out of water. We had been traveling for six hours and finally I told myself that within 15 minutes I would declare us to be officially desperate and we would stop, trespassing or not. Carter was acting great and I was not going to abuse him.

It was here that I began a tradition of telling Carter to "cross your fingers" whenever we needed some serious luck. The tradition continued because it always worked, and it was fun to tell a horse to do something so stupid as to cross something he didn't have.

Literally fourteen minutes later we came to the first house in hours and further along I could see some horses. We pulled up to the "horse house." Three women were standing outside. I met Pat Yuill and her friends and told her that we had traveled 15 miles and that my horse was tired.

She said she had a corral we could use. Her husband was a traveling salesman and was gone but she was a member of the Michigan Trailriders, the same group which the McCarrys and Stafford belonged to. She understood my plight.

Before the trip began I had hoped to spend a night at Tom and Sheila Pardee's house when we passed through Gaylord. Now that we were at Pat's house, which was in Gaylord, I realized that their place was 15 miles further east and we really needed to head north.

I tried calling but there was no answer. It so happened that Tom and Sheila were scouring the area roads till late that night looking for traces of Carter, which was usually easy to do. Pat was kind and I spent the night in the buggy next to Carter's corral as he cooed to Pat's pretty mare.

The next day I got in touch with the Pardees. With Pat saying it would be fine to leave Carter where he was for another day, I ended our first week on the road. It had been action and terror packed. We had covered all of 57 miles and the obstacles we had met were never more omnipresent. It was disturbing that I was so preoccupied with Carter. I had intended to stop and talk with people along the way, to write, and to enjoy the travel. The after-thought of a horse had become the number one thing in my life.

Tom picked me up and I said goodbye to Carter for a day and I basked in survival. The Pardees and I hung out at their home, water skiing, weeding a very steep hill in their yard, and basically taking things slow and easy. A nice summer day with friends.

The second week on the road began with incredibly more gusto than the prior two starts. Tom drove me back to Yuill's place and we proceeded to give Carter a bath and a good brushing. My confidence level was way higher than before and while I remained apprehensive, the feeling was no longer desperate. We were far from being home free, but after a week on the road, the hitching and harnessing chores were going fairly smooth. Carter still didn't stop and stand like I wanted, but there was little comparison be-tween now and a week earlier.

Tom and I parted with the understanding that later in the trip he would use some vacation time on the road with me. Carter and I had some big hills to deal with soon after leaving Tom and thoughts of friendship turned to more immediate concerns as my hands became often and suddenly very full again. There was plenty to learn.

One of the early tricks I learned was that if murderous horse-flies began to show their ugly faces, or if Carter began to get threateningly spooky, I could break him into a trot and he would stop thinking about what had been about to spook him and begin to concentrate on the fact that he was now being urged to a faster pace. I began to use the trick for approaching dogs or bleating sheep or anything that might upset ol' Carter.

It worked, but I found out it wasn't the way to handle a horse for any extended period. I was reminded by various horsepeople that Carter was a large horse and that Tennessee was a long way away. By trotting him on hard surfaces he would be jarring his big legs too much and could come up lame; he'd never make it. I became judicious in the use of the trot.

Two days later we approached the northern Michigan town of Wolverine, population 384. Carter's rear legs began to shake and after only 11 miles he was in a heavy sweat. The days of early July were hot and the hills steep and numerous. I looked hard for a place to stop.

To our right a sign said "Circle M Ranch" but it looked like a trailer park. I hesitated. It was hard to see because of the trees but whatever the Circle M Ranch was, I sure didn't want to be camping next to a trailer park. Carter's legs began to twitch again and I stopped thinking about it and reined right.

It was near quitting time at the Circle M ranch and the ranch turned out to be a slaughter and packing house, as well as a pheasant farm. As we entered the gates two men came out and I told them our predicament, including my amateur status. They had me continue on and climb a steep hill while they sought permission for us. At the top of the hill a man came out to show us a large corral that we could use. This was the beginning of the 4th of July weekend and he said that there would be no cattle kept here for awhile.

Another man sauntered up and noticed Carter's twitching hindquarters and commented; "Tired, huh?"

I was glad to hear a prognosis since even though I thought that, I didn't know and was afraid of heat stroke or something equally radical.

We talked for awhile and I noticed the tattoo on this guy's right arm—"Horse Poor." Danny Sloan introduced himself and told me that he had some Percheron draft horses at home and invited me to ride with him to see them, but first, how about a trip to a nearby lake for a quick bath? Heaven! As we were about to leave, Dan noticed a rivet that had come loose on the bridle and he took it with us to see if he could fix it. I closed up the buggy and Carter proceeded to investigate his new home.

The lake bath was super. Afterwards we went over to Danny's home and saw his ten head of Percherons. We talked horses and Danny bragged about Percherons and I let him because maybe he was right and his voice carried only good fun.

Dan and I sat in the backyard as his wife, Marva, fed their baby goats with a bottle. Their nine-year-old twin daughters playfully took turns fetching the next little goat to be fed.

I was included in the supper plans and afterward Danny mended the bridle while I watched. As bedtime approached we took a ride into downtown Wolverine to see how Carter was doing. He was fine, grazing alone within the large corral. The Sloans invited me to spend the night, and Danny's sister, Nancy, vacated her bed so I would have a comfortable place to sleep.

The next day was July 4 and Marva drove me into the Circle M. Carter was soaked and prancing around like the race was about to begin. It was still early and no hotter than 75 degrees. What was wrong?

We called Danny and asked him to stop by to see what he thought. Soon Danny came and immediately pointed to the churned up earth where Carter had been trampling. Then he pointed to a pasture down the hill where the owner kept two big black Percherons. Carter was excited and was wanting to be with them—thus, his sweaty excitement. Of course!

Since we were at the ranch, Danny fed the pheasants. As he finished, his father drove up. Mr. Sloan had worked with the Army mules in Burma during World War II and carried a reputation as a horseman with a special touch. We talked, and the suggestion emerged that Carter take the day off.

"After only two days on the road?" I thought.

Then again, it was a holiday and the roads would be really busy. A day off fit in with taking it easy on Carter until he got in shape, plus it was getting hotter and more humid by the minute. I took my horse gurus where I found them and we stayed another night.

That night we watched the fireworks and later generated a few more at a packed Torry's Bar in downtown Wolverine. A good time was had by all and the man with the gitfiddle sang my request of "On the Road Again" by Willie Nelson.

The next day we only traveled 7 miles, keeping with the plan. Danny met us at the end of the driving day and put Carter through some paces for fifteen minutes. This was what Carter and I both needed. Danny was making Carter work like he should, using only the bridle and long reins; stopping on command, trotting on command, backing up—everything but sommersaults. I tried my hand and suddenly felt competent enough to do what I was doing!

Along these lines came a surprise the next morning. I was hitching Carter right next to a main highway, M–27. As I maneuvered Carter with the black bucket of oats, a car with two men drove up. They got out and watched, and began to talk. They had seen us the day before and wanted to know if we would be going by their houses so they could alert their kids. I said that we would.

Next they commented that I obviously knew what I was doing since I was hitching up such a large horse so easily (!), but wouldn't all the traffic on this busy holiday weekend be dangerous? The one man had had two horses and on two separate occasions they had gotten out of the pasture and been killed by cars on the highway. We talked some about the definition of faith before I asked if they knew any place down the road about ten or twelve miles where we could camp that night. They knew of a KOA campground about that far away. I thanked them and we hit the road.

With no place in mind except "not the KOA campground," we crossed the pavement of M–27 to the northbound dirt shoulder. The sky was overcast, and we clip-clopped along in 55 degree temperatures and drizzle all day long. Carter was perfect and seemed to enjoy the coolness and the rain. I left the buggy's rear doors down and slid the front doors shut to keep out the same cool wet breeze.

One thing that never failed to happen throughout the trip was that as we traveled along I would see people outdoors, and as we approached and they saw us, they would disappear into their houses. Invariably they would reappear with their camera and come down the road for a closer shot.

On this occasion seven people filed out of one house, and three of them had cameras. Since we were approaching 14 miles, I asked if they knew of a place where we might spend the night. They replied that they had just moved to the area but just ahead was a real nice couple who owned the local country store. Why not ask them?

We passed a young, grey donkey and Carter perked up his ears. He was unpredictable when it came to those long eared critters, but he remained cool. Ahead I could see a small store with some gas pumps in front.

A little girl came out, followed by a woman. One of the seven people I had just spoken with had called ahead to let them know that a stage coach was heading their way and was looking for a place to spend the night.

As we pulled up in front of "The Corner Store," owners Gary and Denise Drolshagen with five year old Dawn, invited us to spend the night. Dawn was excited. They told me they had previously kept a pet bear and her cub in their fenced backyard, which was complete with a playground slide, garden hose, and a young turkey named Christmas. But it was a small yard and big Carter would have totally messed it up.

Gary called his neighbors, the Howells, who worked a riding stable down the road and also owned the pasture right next door. The way it worked out was that I held Carter while Jackie Howell and Gary mended the fence. Carter spent the night in the pasture, the buggy was kept in the backyard with Christmas, and Danny fetched me for another night in Wolverine.

When I returned the following morning, the Howell sisters were there and Thelma harnessed Carter while I observed her style. Even though there were people waiting at their stables to go riding, Thelma rode along with Denise and Dawn and myself.

Thelma drove and revealed horse secrets. She added that I should keep an eye on Carter's left rear foot because he seemed to be favoring it. After a couple of miles Thelma left to return to the stables and the Drolshagens went back to their life at the country store. Thelma said that she would give Sally Gordon a call for us. Sally was a horseperson who lived about five miles away and she'd probably be able to give us a place to stay.

We arrived at a place where there was a swamp on both sides of the road. Mosquito country. Before reaching the shade and water of the swamp, the temperature was close to 90 degrees. Unfortunately the shade was so nice on the dirt road that the temperature cooled just enough to bring the skeeters out in force.

We came to a lady who had stopped her pickup to say hi, but we couldn't stop or it would have been serious dinner time for the bugs. The lady was Sally. Fortunately, Sally stopped again further down the road and invited us to her place. It wasn't much, she said, but she loved animals and we were welcome.

It took about an hour to get to Sally's. She lived in a trailer on top of a big hill, overlooking miles of state forest and farm country. Three miles away, beautiful Mullett Lake could be seen. Next to her trailer was a barn large enough for about ten horses, and acres and acres of pasture.

Sally was a well educated woman with long, dark hair. She was about five feet tall, and dressed according to the weather or what clothes happened to be clean, not according to Vogue magazine. She told me that she had a major birthday coming up but her spirit was the sort that was forever young and I couldn't guess if she was about to turn 40 or 50.

It would be inaccurate to say that Sally lived alone. In addition to about 8 horses and one pony that were kept in the barn and pasture area, she had geese and rabbits and dogs and cats and goats. She couldn't and didn't say no to an animal in need. At times she shared her trailer with a pet rabbit, an orphan deer, and a dog and cat. She had always wanted to be a veterinarian. Her mother had been the state's first female licensed vet, but had given up practice when she married Sally's father. Sally practiced medicine on her own animals when they needed it, and her friends sought her advice.

Sally showed me a good place to park the buggy and then helped unhitch my steed. She led Carter to a paddock next to her stallion's but soon had to move her stallion since he was being too intolerant of the new horse. We had only traveled six miles and Carter was feeling good. Sally and I watched as Carter dipped his head with a sweeping turn, his mane flying, and ran and kicked within the paddock as if to say to the world, "I feel good."

Sally was alert and noticed that Carter might be feeling good but that he had two rope burns behind his rear hooves. She told me that injuries on the feet were very hard to treat since they were always flexing, and that those burns had occurred some time earlier. I thought back and—of course! That fourth night out when Carter had been tethered to the pine trees and had stomped all night long. After that he had gotten touchy about me cleaning his rear feet. Sally brought some ointment and began her treatment. While she was applying the curative salve to the affected joints, she also noticed that the borium tips on the shoes were in need of attention.

One thing which I had had to decide as the trip took form was whether or not to try and continue as a member of the board of directors at the co-op. To do so would mean that I would have to interrupt the trip at least once a month, just so I could return home and attend meetings. I didn't want the hassle, or the loss of "purity" of the nature of slow horse and buggy travel, but I viewed the co-op work as my blinders.

The story went that there were plenty of fast horses out there on the range but unless that energy was channeled along useful paths, the energy was really good for nothing. The horse that wore blinders undeniably lost some freedom but it was by wearing blinders that they were able to direct their energies and accomplish things of value.

A series of meetings were coming up and I needed to get out my third "Electric Burro" column soon. Sally volunteered to keep and doctor Carter and call her farrier while I returned home for the first time. Luck stayed with me and I found a ride going my way the same day, so I left, promising to return soon, and to call and check on how Carter was getting on.

We had traveled slightly more than 110 miles and the very important first two weeks were over. I felt that what was happening was good. Each day as we started out, I was the one I had to answer to, not counting Carter, and while the pay wasn't the best the responsibility was in the right place.

When I returned to Sally and Carter a week later, Vern Bishop had just arrived with Carter's shoes with new borium tips (calks). I struggled to hold an uncooperative Carter while Vern did the more difficult job of putting the shoes back on. A couple hours later the job was done and I paid Vern $25 for the job, which had included two sixty miles drives to pick up and deliver the shoes. I considered it a bargain when I compared it to Carter's first shoe-ing, which had cost $60. That time had included the cost of the shoes and the fitting of them, but Carter had been delivered to the farrier. The fact that it was Sally who had done the actual request-ing probably had a lot to do with the excellent service and reason-able price.

Sally rode along with us the next day and it was good to have the company. Carter's wounds had almost totally healed. We trav-eled about twelve miles together and ended up in the side yard of some friends of hers. The same people seemed to think we mer-ited additional attention and called the press the next morning. Until this time my hands had been full just dealing with the job at hand but I had begun to wonder how I would ever involve the media to better spread the cooperative message.

While I was getting ready for a hot day on the road and apply-ing double doses of fly repellant to a now glistening Carter, a car drove up. A young, attractive woman got out of the car and my mind no longer focused clearly on the job at hand. I imagined that this person was lost and asking directions. Instead, Carrie Freel was a college student who worked as the editor for the Cheboygan Daily Tribune weekly supplement and she had come to interview me.

There had been ample opportunity for me to rehearse what I had to say and to explain what I was trying to do in the one hundred miles of travel, so I continued to get ready to go, explain-ing as I went. It wasn't long until we were ready to go and I asked Carrie if she'd like to ride along with us. She said that she would but first she asked what our route would be and said that she would catch up to us later.

An hour later Carter and I were slowly making progress through the forest along the narrow Old Mackinaw Trail, a surviving cor-duroy road comprised of dirt and gravel over saplings. Three cars passed us all day, one of which passed going both directions and I counted it twice. The tree lined road was pleasant and much cooler than the highway. The only sounds were Carter's steel feet and the rubber tires on the gravel, and the cries of bluejays flitting through the woods. I dreamed of a trip through rural America that took place on roads like this—without traffic and highways and people in too much of a hurry—but the dream belonged to another time and place.

The first car along stopped and Carrie jumped out. She had parked her car a couple miles up ahead and hitched a ride with the first car along. This way she could ride with us until we reached her car.

I was new to the interview game and ignorant of the rules, so I enjoyed a wide ranging conversation that included the whys and wherefores of the trip and the REA, but also the topics of religion, family, music and why I had put so much fly stuff on Carter. We laughed at how welcome it was for Carter to have a bowel movement, just to camouflage the poison of the fly goop. Too soon we arrived at Carrie's car and said goodbye.

Two hours later Carter and I emerged from the forest and stood at the top of a hill, overlooking the straits and the Mackinac Bridge. It was a magnificent obstacle to cross. When I was a boy our family made a trip "up north" to see the recently completed Mackinac Bridge connecting the upper and lower peninsulas. The sight before me on that day in July with Carter was essentially the same as the one I had seen nearly 30 years earlier.

There were differences, however. No longer did people view a trip to the UP as a hardship or necessarily as an adventure. At worst it amounted to a long drive. No longer did passage across the often treacherous straits depend on the availability of a ferry boat and the weather. Many people who had not known what it was like to have to depend on the ferry boat had no idea of what it used to mean to make the passage across the four mile body of water between two of the Great Lakes. Things change.

8

A Network of Friends
—Upper Michigan

After an uncouth beginning I had the best of luck to the end. But we are all travellers in what John Bunyan calls the wilderness of this world—all, too, travellers with a donkey; and the best that we find in our travels is an honest friend. He is a fortunate voyager who finds many. We travel, indeed, to find them. They are the end and the reward of life. They keep us worthy of ourselves . . .

—Robert Lewis Stevenson,
from "Travels with a Donkey"

Carter and I drove within two miles of the bridge. I found an abandoned building between two motels and pulled behind it. After unhitching Carter and tethering him to a tree, I waited until he disappeared into the oats bucket, then walked next door to a pay phone and made two phone calls.

The main stables of the Mackinac Island tour companies were in the UP, and horses and carriages were routinely shuttled between the Island and the UP stables. The first call was to Mackinac Island. I told them that I had just arrived in Mackinaw City at the northern tip of the lower peninsula, and asked if anyone was available to pick me up. I had called just in time. The person on the other end of the phone told me that Duane Bawks had left the Island after making a hay run twenty minutes earlier, and could come "below" to pick me up as soon as he arrived on shore.

The second call was to Jack and Punky Belonga, more friends of Sally. When I called, they had already talked to Sally and they told me how to get to their place.

An hour later Duane arrived with a large fifteen horse trailer, and in a matter of minutes we had the buggy and Carter all loaded, and were headed off across the water. Some people had said that we would never make it to the bridge. It was a sweet moment. Duane hauled us two miles outside of St. Ignace to the Belonga's home, and we unloaded Carter and buggy. I had been dealing with Duane's boss up til now.

"How much did he tell you?" Duane asked me.

I told Duane, "He said, 'no charge if we happen to be making a hay run when you need to get across, otherwise $50 to $100, depending on how far we have to drive and all that,' but you tell me."

After going through this a few times, Duane came up with, "OK, tails twenty dollars, heads forty, how about that?"

"Great." I got out my lucky coin and showed it to Duane. I felt lucky as it flipped. Tails.

"Is a check okay?"

Jack and Punky welcomed me like one of the family and I began to think of life as being part of a network of friends. Carter stayed behind the house with Punky's horse while I was treated to Jack's specialty, homemade pizza. Later Jack showed me some shortcuts through downtown St. Ignace so we could avoid some of the worst parts of the town's four lane highway. We were up till late, and when it came time to sleep, I was offered the best bed in the house.

We encountered four lane city traffic for the first time. The shortcuts helped avoid some of the blind curves and despite obnoxious whirl-li-gigs used for advertising, Carter maintained well. He simply walked and didn't wander, didn't get tired, hot or bothered. There was traffic but Carter had come to work.

We were heading for Mike and Joni Grogan's home, friends of the Belonga's. After traveling twelve miles through the countryside, I thought I recognized the Grogan's driveway, which Punky had described. As we got closer I could see Mike and Joni with some friends in their sideyard, waving to us.

We pulled up and they greeted us warmly. Mike pointed toward the back of their property to two large corrals and said that if it was alright with me, Carter could stay in the big corral on the right.

"If it's alright?! Oh no man, this is perfect!" I said.

I drove between the two corrals and unhitched. Then I led Carter to his home for the night and offered him water but he was more excited than thirsty. He saw Joni's two mares in the other corral, just 40 yards away.

Mike and Joni had just finished building this corral and Carter was the first horse to inhabit it. Carter enjoyed it, trotting back and forth along the corral's railing, checking out the two sweeties across from him, and then dipping that big head of his and running full. His golden mane was flying as he went kicking in powerful glory, happy to be free to run and play.

It was especially pleasant here. There was a sense of industry and friendship. The house had been a hunting shack but had received lots of TLC and was now a cozy house. The small barn in the back was also a product of Mike and Joni and their many friends. The current project was the installation of an automatic fly spraying system in the barn.

These two were about 25 years old. Joni was working at a restaurant and was taking riding lessons. Her next lesson was coming up soon and would be about learning how to drive using the long reins. She loved what she was doing and sincerely practiced, riding five out of seven days.

Mike operated a bulldozer. He used to work as an ironworker but a tragic fall paralyzed his legs and ended that career. When he wasn't working the dozer, he had a four wheeler Suzuki with custom footrests to help him get around their property, along with at least three wheelchairs, and lots of friends. The work around the Grogan's home was mainly a result of Mike and Joni's efforts. They were busy living life.

We gathered in the sideyard of the house a hundred yards from the corral and grilled burgers and drank fresh squeezed lemonade.

Mike needed a permanent aide and Ed Salisbury filled the bill and one of the bedrooms.

"You guys want to ride along with us tomorrow? Maybe the Belonga's would be interested too. We could have a real wagon train," I said.

Joni picked it right up. "Hey, great idea! I'll call work and see if I can switch shifts and call Punky and see if she can go!"

While she went off to the phone, I told Mike that he could drive. He replied that he might be interested, but he'd have to see how he felt.

Joni zoomed back and it was a go! She had the whole day off from work and Jack and Punky would bring Punky's horse over at 9 a.m. It would be another first.

Once the sun went down we talked and watched TV, and had some more lemonade. Joni's anticipation remained great. They insisted I sleep on the couch and I was aware that my ability to say "yes" was growing.

Day dawned and Joni had the house percolating with coffee, breakfast, and her vivid energy. Mike said that he wanted to come along.

Joni attended to her eleven year old mare while I fed Carter and began offloading whatever weight I could. Since Jack would be acting as our support crew, I planned to load the excess weight into his truck.

The Belonga's arrived on time with their newly purchased horse trailer and Punky's horse. Jack said he had some work to do in the morning but hoped to join us later and ride along. We loaded about 350 pounds of stuff into the trailer as Punky got her mare ready and Joni enjoyed riding her mare around the yard. She rode up to Carter and let the two horses touch noses. We were ready.

At first Punky and Joni followed, but it wasn't long before they passed and led the way. Our speed increased as Carter worked to keep up with the other horses, not by any urgings on Mike's or my part, but as Mike pointed out, Carter was enjoying following the good looking fillies.

The day was getting hotter fast and Carter had soon worked up a real sweat. I pulled him to a stop under some shade trees but after about 30 seconds he started off again. His sweeties were getting too far away!

Mike and I enjoyed a peaceful ride. Mike's attitude was such that I felt that I wasn't good enough to pity the man. Not only would he not want it, but if I paused to pity, I might never catch up.

We talked about plenty during our fifteen miles together on that July day. He was pragmatic. He recognized his blessings and commented that he wouldn't know what he would do if he didn't have his arms. He drove Carter for about two miles and gave an example by saying, "What would I do if I dropped the reins now?"

I had to agree but was reluctant to do so because I was secretly hoping that a horse and buggy might be a way that Joni and Mike could share a love. They both had such a strong "can do" attitude that I felt that Mike would somehow make such a situation work, but maybe I was hoping too hard.

This was the first outing of the year for Punky's horse and after three miles of blazing trails her horse suddenly went down on its belly. Her legs simply collapsed. We took a twenty minute break and all seemed well enough, so we continued. Three miles later Punky decided that her horse had had enough and she called Jack from a friend's house. They would wait for him there, and said we should go ahead, they'd meet us later.

Driving Carter ceased to be fun for the next couple of miles, without our lead fillies. He began to zigzag and tried to look behind us for his girlfriends. Gradually he came back to his gelded reality. We traveled on for another six miles and Jack and the wives rejoined us. Jack crawled into the back seat as the girls went ahead to see if they could find a stopping place for the day.

The clouds turned ominously dark, fast. We could see rain and lightening to our left, heading our way. It was one of nature's most ferocious storms, a squall line! Heavy rain began to fall and it grew very dark. The visibility dropped almost to zero.

I turned on the solar powered flashers and they very possibly saved our lives. Lightening was everywhere and the thunder was tremendous. At one place the lighting smashed almost on top of us and Carter jumped, but maintained. Mike and Jack were probably thinking that their fates were in my hands about this time, but, in fact, I had little to do with it. It was all Carter. Cool Carter.

The rain stopped as quickly as it began. The girls returned with news of a place to stay only a mile ahead and left to wait for us at Bill and Rita Lindemuth's home. When we arrived, we unloaded my gear from the truck and I said goodbye to my road crew. Bill showed me his cattle corral and Carter happily joined the dozen or so cattle.

It was forecast to get into the 30's that night and Mike had told me that the mosquitoes were devastating, so I began to prepare right away. The buggy was a convenient and comfortable sleeper but it wasn't mosquito proof. The rear doors of the buggy were fitted with Velcro and fiberglass screening, which worked perfectly, but the front sliding doors weren't sealed at all so I set about pitching my four man tent in the backyard. Just as all was made ready, Rita invited me in for a hot meal and good conversation.

After supper we went for a ride and my hosts proudly showed off their tiny village of Rexton. We saw the campground and the gravel pit, and drove past the house of the local rich guy who either used to be or still was a state senator. Rita pointed out a restaurant which they had once operated. Then we drove west of the village and visited the Larry Faulkner family.

It was dark and Rita walked up to the door and knocked. I think she had to remind them who she was but soon they walked out to the truck where Bill and I were sitting and I explained what I was up to.

"Sure. No problem. Just come on out and camp wherever you want. Be happy to have you," they said. Just like that. Thanks to the efforts of the Lindemuths, I had a destination for the next day. And the day after that.

When we returned home, Rita got on the phone and called some people she knew ten miles past the Faulkners and so the network went. As I stood up to retire to the tent, Rita told me to just come on in in the morning and fix myself breakfast. She would lay out everything I would need.

I went in like I had been told, just as Bill was lighting his first cigarette of the day. I felt welcome and went into the kitchen to heat up the still warm water for coffee for both of us. I cooked breakfast of bacon and eggs and then enjoyed a welcome shower while Bill made us another cup of coffee. There was no hurry since we only had four hours worth of travel ahead of us and Bill had plenty of stories to tell.

Bill was sixty years old and talked of the days when he drove a team of Belgian horses for the REA in its early days, assisting with the installation of poles in especially difficult areas that trucks couldn't get to.

I happened to look out just as Carter rammed the single strand of electric barbed wire with his breast. He backed up, but kept looking at the dozen cattle on the other side of the wire, now beginning to walk away from him towards the back pasture. Five minutes later he did it again, and again he retreated, but he kept looking in the direction of his buddies. A third time he walked against the wire and this time it gave and Carter went happily down the path.

Bill and I put coats on and went outside to his tractor. Bill drove and I stood on the rear. A quarter mile into the pasture we came to the cows, but no Carter. What?! We drove on to the top of a hill and there he was, grazing with two cows. All he wanted was to be with the others. I snapped the lead rope on and we walked back to the farmyard behind Bill and the tractor.

After we mended the fence, I loaded up the buggy and Bill brought a good bale of hay for us to take. Water jugs filled and everything ready, I went to the refrigerator and fetched two pasties. Rita worked at the pastie factory and had left a note with my eggs:

> Scott—Don't forget to take two pasties before you leave this morning. Have a nice day and we will see you this evening. Those pasties are made by Arlene Brown of Ozark, Mi. Hope you like them. Rita

Pasties were popular in the UP; meat, potatoes and other goodies wrapped in crust. So called depression food—good, cheap and filling.

We were solidly into bear country and I was apprehensive as we approached this stage of the journey. There was nothing that could be done except hope that we didn't run across one. If a bear did happen near, Carter would smell him and spook and no halter would hold him.

We arrived at the home of the Faulkner family without incident. On their living room floor was a bear rug, which had been a 3-year-old 300 pound black bear roaming the woods just a couple of years earlier.

That night the cinch of Carter's short picket line rope gave out and as I looked out through the fiberglass screening, I could barely make Carter out in the darkness, and he was walking away! Fortunately, he was smelling no bear and headed towards nowhere except for some fresh grass out of reach from his picket line. I hurried out of the buggy and retrieved him but bears were not uncommon in Michigan's UP and I was holding my breath.

When the trip began, my hands were full just learning what to do and what to expect. If the nature of the trip was too often solitary, my determination to break away from a routine that didn't satisfy, overruled the consequent loneliness. Boredom wasn't much of a question because of the ever present possibility of Carter going bonkers and my own anxiety level.

The scenery of the backroads was not breath taking—trees, flatland, lowland, scrub, a few critters, and very few farms. When we eventually traveled far enough west to join US–2, the scenery had changed very little, but had expanded to include a hot highway loaded with Winnebagoes and station wagons. It was Vacationtime in America and the tranquility of travel via horse and buggy was drowned out. The sound of Carter's steady clip-clops were replaced by the earth shaking and frightening sounds of many heavy logging trucks.

By the time we were halfway across Michigan's UP, the stretches of highway between souls was considerable, often lasting for hours. I had grasped enough of the task at hand so that the combination of loneliness and boredom forced me to seek entertainment wherever it might be found. My mind sought company and my company was Carter.

Carter's ears were the real show on the road. By looking at his ears I could know where his mind was at and what it saw. His eyes followed his ears. They were amazing and accurate, working much like radar. If I was quick, I could predict what was going to happen before Carter was even aware that something was going on.

While we moved down the road Carter's two early warning devices were silently at work, scanning the landscape in all directions. Plenty of miles passed as I engaged Carter in conversation down some lonely stretch of asphalt. As the conversation began, Carter's ears turned back toward me, listening to what I might be saying.

I might be saying, "Hey Carter, what's goin' on? What's new up there?"

As the words came to his ears and then stopped coming, he would return his ears to face forward, like they were automatic. Fast.

"Think we'll ever make it to Tennessee by November?" Back. Then front.

"I'll bet you wish we had a filly along with us, huh?" Flick. Flick.

Most of our conversations were one sided. Sometimes we both took part. If we were going up a long steep hill on a hot day, I might say, "Good boy, Carter, come on babe, (kiss sound)," encouraging him on.

Then he had to work especially hard and though he might get tired, he wouldn't suggest a stop, except to comment, "(exhaling wind through floppy big lips-sound)", which was his way of saying, "Hey, leave me alone, I'm busy."

Sometimes I would joke with him and say "No one said it would be easy, come on, (kiss), get up."

If the grade was exceptionally difficult, I'd be serious and say something more like, "Come on Babe, (Kiss), come on now, (Kiss)." The conversations were great, but slightly repetitious.

Most of the time was between conversations. His radar silently continued to work. His bridle included blinders as an aid in keeping Carter's eyes on the road ahead and at times his radar could be foiled. If something like a bicycle came up from behind, its tires were almost silent. The bike would suddenly shoot into his range of vision and he would spook away from the unknown danger.

I learned that flight was a horse's number one defense and if surprise could be avoided, there would be little cause for flight. Sometimes I could compensate by talking to him and getting his attention before the surprise came. The fact that my familiar voice was present would serve to reassure him. However, in the case of a bicycle, for example, if I was also unaware that it was coming, the outcome was up for grabs.

The watering ritual was as fun as any. Since it was so important that Carter get enough water I would usually bring him to a stop at least once an hour for a five or ten minute break—in the shade if possible. I'd jump out of the buggy, hook the reins over the rear view mirror, and walk up to him to say hi and rub his face.

Then I'd walk back to the buggy and take out one of the two six gallon jugs of water. When I began to pour the water into the black four gallon bucket, Carter would crane his head and watch with anticipation, as eager as a puppie in an Alpo commercial.

If he was thirsty, he would suck down the four gallons in no time and look for more. If he just wanted to enjoy the recess, he would stick his big snout into the water and make gurgling drinking noises, splashing around to make it look good, and then when I wasn't watching, he'd stop the pretenses and just stand there and take it easy. When time came to go I would start to pick up the bucket and he would resume his act of "drinking" in order to gain a longer break. I loved the game and it was this sort of thing that reminded me that life with animals was special and often playful.

Another sort of joy occurred whenever Carter talked to those along the road. Generally he ignored people and other vehicles but when we passed another horse, he'd say hi. I loved it. Other horses would run up as close as they could to the road and peer anxiously, almost saying, "I want to come too!"

Carter and the stranger would whinney to each other. I smiled every time I heard my fat Caruso sing. If we passed a number of horses, very often they would put on a show for us, running, kicking, tossing their proud and playful heads—a lovely and free way of saying howdy. There were times when we would pass a field of other big Belgians and they would thunder around their field, full of power. Other times we would pass a quarterhorse or Standardbred, so sleek and hyper sort of strong, and I'd think that they were about to jump their fence, they'd get so excited. But they never did.

Carter was particular about who he called friend. He never related in a positive way to pigs, sheep, geese or turkeys. He was tolerant and rather indifferent to cats, dogs and rabbits. But he was always open to the cow, and the cows always seemed just as friendly toward Carter.

We continued across the southern portion of Michigan's upper peninsula in an effort to avoid the hills to the north. The further we traveled, the more our route merged with US-2 along Lake Michigan. The idea remained to travel through REA co-op areas and to get to Tennessee by November but the tactics refined to focus on the route which was the flattest, the shortest, and included the greatest number of states, and rural electric co-ops.

My county map showed a bison farm near Engadine, 15 miles ahead, and I thought that might be a good place to try for on this particular day. We made it to the bison farm and just as Carter saw the bison, they saw us. Carter snorted and immediately picked up to a trot and the entire bison heard rumbled toward us. For half a mile the bison shadowed us right next to the road until we reached the end of their pasture. So much for planned destinations.

We left the bison behind just as the wind began to pick up. The sky was turning from a pretty blue, cirrus infested sky to one with increasing haze and lowering clouds. A storm front was approaching.

Our back road ended and we came out on US-2 again. The shoulder was great but the traffic was non-stop. We came to a crossroads and turned left, feeling a need to find shelter from a storm that looked sure to happen.

Already we'd traveled 21 miles. After going down a narrow dirt road for a couple more miles, the best part of an hour, we came to a house where horses were corralled in front and pulled into the circle drive. I stayed with the buggy in front of the home of people I didn't know, dirty and unannounced, hoping that someone was home and would come out. Fortunately, Ron Clark and his wife saw us and came out to see what was going on. I told the story of coming from Traverse City, trying to get to Tennessee. Was there someplace where we could weather the storm?

It didn't take long for Ron to say we could spend the night in their storage barn. He pointed to a rutted and narrow road leading to a large pole building at the top of a nearby hill and told us to meet him there. Ron came up to rearrange the equipment and I drove the rig inside just as the rain began to fall. I put up a picket line inside the barn and tied Carter to it, ten feet away from the buggy.

That night I slept in the buggy while it rained like mad. It blew like crazy. Everything outside got soaked. Carter got loose twice. Once early, when he simply pulled his lead rope apart and a second time when he woke me up by walking past the buggy the next morning, heading for outdoors and the hayfield next to us. What a way to wake up!—to look through the screening of your buggy with sleep still in your eyes, in time to see your horse non-chalantly leaving.

We spent two nights in that building. It rained the second night too. On a welcome day off, I tried to adjust the brakes. It may have helped a little. I wrote an article for the Electric Burro Travel Series, always an accomplishment. In between working on the buggy, brushing Carter, sharing meals with the Clarks, and writing, I watched a couple of young skunks playing in the tall grass next to the building.

Carter rested from seven days of travel. I wondered if a horse needed a day or rest once a week, or if it was a human practice transferred to the life of a horse. Carter was doing well. He was beginning to get into shape, hard and full of wind. He was sleek with a beautiful coat and everyone said that he looked none the worse for wear after a month on the road and 200 miles.

The following morning dawned clear and dry. Ron brought up a couple of bales of hay and told me to stop at the house before we left because his wife had a bag of groceries she wanted me to take with us. An hour later Ron and his daughter rode by on horses on their way to round up some stray cattle for branding. Carter and I moved down the hill, rested and ready for the road.

We escaped from overpopulated US–2 and disappeared down Schoolcraft County Road P433, just after we crossed Little Bear Creek. It was a good chance to daydream and return to a pace more fitting our mode of travel. I was in the middle of a thought about how I could extend my journey to include the new international economy in the cooperative scheme of things after we reached November and Tennessee, when I was jarred back to reality by a car pulling off the road ahead of us.

Sue Ellen Kingsley and her 3-year-old daughter, Karla, had stopped to say hi and invite us to camp at their place, just a mile or so away. The day was still young and I was embued with a sense of elapsed miles, so as much as I wanted to stop and spend some time, I declined.

Miles and hours later we found a place to stay and Sue Ellen showed up to reinvite. I took care of Carter and the buggy and accepted a ride to her home, a cabin without electricity or running water. It was interesting to return to a way of life that was the only way of life for most of human history, and which remained a way of life for many people in the world.

Sue Ellen's place was quiet and clean and was situated to offer a beautiful view of the woods and fields and rolling hills. Little Karla seemed as normal as any 3-year-old, unaffected by not living with juice. We had supper and I was introduced to Garrison Keillor's weekly radio program, "Prairie Home Companion," by way of her battery powered radio. Night fell and Sue Ellen and Karla gave me a ride to my buggy where we put up the tent in darkness.

We continued on country roads for most of the next day, traversing the city of Manistique (population 3962). Only two days of quiet, peaceful roads and I was restless; no buildings, no people, and no traffic to speak of. After fourteen miles we came to a farmhouse and I went to the door to ask for a place to stay.

Gail Hoholik came to the door and didn't seem at all surprised to hear my request. She told me she was a veterinarian and often had people leaving large animals with her, though she said that the buggy was a bit unusual. She pointed to a large pasture near the house and said that we could stay there. I drove over to the pasture and parked my travel home and let Carter run free. Soon he was grazing down by a large pond—next to the cattle, of course.

I checked my electric system but couldn't get the crock pot to work so I walked up to the house and met Mike, Gail's husband and a dairy farmer. Mike had an engineering degree but preferred

the life of a dairy farmer, admitting that his wife's practice subsi-
dized the farm. While we investigated the electric system, he
showed me the clinic that was attached to the house and said that
it would be unlocked in case I wanted to use its bathroom.

The battery was low though the panels checked out to be charging at an acceptable rate. We hooked the battery up to his "old
fashioned" but effective plug-in battery charger and let it charge
that night.

The next morning I retrieved the fully charged battery and
Mike came down to the buggy to help me hitch up. We talked
some more and solved most of the world's problems but then, as I
had Carter between the fills and eating his oats, one of Hoholik's
large Belgian sheepdogs sneaked under the buggy and nipped
Carter's hoof. He jumped ahead and out of the fills. It took a
couple of weeks before he would again allow himself to be positioned for hitching without being jumpy.

We left Mike and his farm by 9:30, heading for a dairy farmer
friend of his 17 miles away, near the town of Isabella. Seven hours
later a car drove up to us and a man leaned out the window and
said, "You lookin' for me?"

I assumed it was Mike's friend and kind of laughed.

"Ha! I'll bet Mike called you and told you I was heading your
way, huh?"

"Mike who? I'm Carmine Falbo," he replied.

Carmine Falbo? I thought. Do I know a Carmine Falbo?
"You're not Mike Hoholik's dairy farmer friend?" I guessed.

"Carmine Falbo. Mel Falbo. I'm on Alger Delta's board and
you wrote me a letter saying you'd be coming through here. Aren't
you Hudson?" he replied.

So that was it! I had mailed a brief letter to all of the directors
of the UP's co-ops outlining my basic trip and had asked for their
support; now I recognized Mel Falbo's name. He threw me with
Carmine.

"Yeah, that's me. So you're Mel Falbo?" I managed to say, feeling caught off guard.

"Yeah, that's what I said. Carmine Falbo. Well come on, follow
me. I live a mile down the road and Mary's cooking dinner for us
now."

Carter spent the night in a neighbor's corral half a mile from the Falbo home and I parked the buggy in Mel's driveway. Mary had prepared a real spread for supper and I learned more about these people around the table.

The Falbos had lived in Detroit and Mel had worked for Chrysler most of his life. His greatest enthusiasm seemed to be the close relationship that his family had had with many of the athletes who played for the Detroit professional sports teams. Trophies of signed baseballs and photographs were brought out and stories of the true personalities behind the images were told. The autographed baseball mitt of Hall of Famer and my boyhood hero, Al Kaline, was brought out and as I put it on my hand, Mel told me how Al had given it to him when he visited the locker rooms.

Then retirement happened and the Falbos moved north, away from the Motor City that seemed to have lost the part of its vitality they had loved. When they arrived in distant Isabella, he had never heard of a consumer owned utility but when he learned how he could participate and make a difference, he ran for a seat on the board and won. Now, 13 years later and 72-years-old, the monthly meetings had become an integral part of his life.

That night I slept on the fold out bed in Falbo's living room. In the morning, after a big breakfast, we walked out to his fully equipped workshop and began work to true up the buggy's wheels. When I had ordered it I had been told that the average life of the hard rubber tire was 7 years but the left rear tire was already wearing badly. Mel's Motor City expertise was still intact, as was his enthusiasm. For several hours I helped him as he measured and welded and painted. In addition to straightening up the wheel, he added an emergency brake arm and several supports for the brakes. Once again the buggy was ready for the road.

When we fetched Carter from down the road, he walked stiffly. After 50 yards he loosened up and seemed OK. But then I felt his breast and under his front legs and discovered a rash. When I touched the area he would tenderly lift his leg. Back at Mel's, I called Gail Hoholik and described the problem. She said it didn't sound serious and that I should wash it with soap and water and keep it rubbed down with ointment. If it got worse, let her know, but otherwise it shouldn't hurt to travel.

With that advice we hit the road as the Falbos and friends snapped pictures and waved goodbye. We kicked along US–2, skirting Lake Michigan's northern shore. Things went well with Carter in spite of the considerable traffic and his rash.

Coming into St. Jacques, there was nothing except a small cross-roads and a country store. There was no air of sophistication, St. Jacques was pronounced "Saint Jakes."

Chuck and Sue Hansen had the only store around, a small convenience store with their home attached to the rear, and gas pumps in front. I pulled up to unleaded and it didn't take long before Chuck came out. We had only covered eight miles and I felt tentative about Carter and talked to Chuck about it. Chuck led us to a wooded area behind their place and Carter was soon on a picket line, watered, fed, and content. I had dinner with the Hansens and spent the night in their hunting trailer.

The next morning I was getting things ready to go and applying ointment to Carter's rash, when a girl of about 8 years came around and noticed Carter's old rope burn. She suggested I stop at Arnie Proehl's place a couple of miles down the road and ask him about it. Arnie was the local horse expert and I accepted the sound advice.

When we came to Arnie's, paddocks and horses were everywhere. The driveway was narrow and long and I didn't want to get into a position where we wouldn't be able to turn around so we sat and waited. Only a few minutes passed before a blonde man about 25 years old came running out to us. It was Arnie and he was a soul on fire.

His enthusiasm was great and his love for horses obvious. He loved the concept of my trip and then he looked Carter over and pronounced him fit. He invited me to spend the day with him, but having just begun that day's travel, we couldn't. Arnie asked my intended route and then told me a short cut we could take. We were off.

Not for long! As Carter walked on down the shortcut road, I glanced in the rearview mirror and saw a man pedaling furiously after us on a bicycle. It was Arnie. He asked if he could ride along, so I had him hold Carter while I put the bike into the back seat. On we went.

We traveled together only about three miles, but in that space of time I grew to respect this man who seemed so alive. He continued to say how much he liked Carter and the buggy and the trip. He talked of his love of horses and spoke of the beautiful day. Everything about him seemed upbeat.

Then he told me how he had woke up one morning about a year earlier, blind. Gradually vision had returned but then he lost control of his legs, they were paralyzed. Again things returned to normal. He was diagnosed as having Multiple Sclerosis. MS has no cure. Last winter he had almost frozen to death in his home when he suddenly lost the use of his limbs and couldn't move to put wood in the stove. He was saved by a friend who happened by.

I thought of how he had been pedaling the bike so intently, working to catch up to us and I thought that the great thing was not my trip but his spirit. We talked of life and death and MS and Jesus. Arnie wanted to move to Florida or Arizona, somewhere warm. He had resigned himself to give his many fine horses away since he felt that he wouldn't be able to care for them much longer. I handed the reins to Arnie.

As he drove Carter, there wasn't the slightest hint that he was depressed or negative in any way. Amazing. I couldn't help but think how easy it was to spend hours in front of a tranquilizing television screen, whiling away the hours. If it wasn't TV, then some other inane thing. What difference was there between contracting MS and being born since both had the same ending, with equal certitude? Arnie was in touch with his life and he was living it with a glow.

We reached the outskirts of the small town of Rapid River and Arnie said he had better turn back before he got too far away—his strength wasn't dependable. He handed me the reins and retrieved his bicycle and pedaled back the way we had come. I continued into Rapid River. Church was open.

Rapid River, Michigan was a small town but a real hubbub of activity, complete with several restaurants, bars, stores, gas stations, an ice cream shop, and a lighted baseball diamond. Clip-clopping through town, it felt good to be away from the outback.

Daylight waned and Rapid River was looking relatively subur-ban. I pulled up to the home of John Skellenger. He was a man about my age and was working in his yard with several kids run-ning around. When I asked about where he might suggest I look for a place to camp, he suggested a farm down the road where I had just come from.

I thanked John and started off towards where he had suggested, but before we could travel far he ran after us and apologized, saying that we could stay in his yard. He said that he wasn't thinking and that he had suggested the farm because years earlier there had been a wagon train come through the area and they had camped at the farm, but that he had plenty of room if we were alone. So we turned around again and soon Carter was munching hay on his picket line and the boys were helping me haul water.

The Skellenger family was John and his wife, Ruth, and three sons, Billy, Peter and Danny, the oldest of which was about ten. They owned an ice making company and were very industrious and conscientious. That night, Mom and Dad were going for a getaway of sorts—a movie and dinner—while the kids were left with babysitter Nathan Boris, about 14.

As John and Ruth began to clean up, I mentioned that I was going to walk the couple of miles into town for exercise and a meal. They said that since they would be gone before I could return, for me to just come on in when I got back and make myself at home. Billy volunteered to give up his bed and sleep in the basement. It was great and amazing. I was a perfect stranger and was being given one of the highest honors of trust.

I couldn't help but wonder at the trust and openness of these people in rural Michigan. How could they be so quick to trust, when some inner city schools were using metal detectors on stu-dents as they entered the building?

I walked into town and had a meal at one of the restaurants, appreciating the opportunity to walk. My biggest gripe about the trip was the lack of exercise. It seemed like I sat almost all the time, and my rear end ached from too much sitting!

When I got back to the Skellenger's, it was dark. I gave Carter some water and went inside. The kids were downstairs playing

"Jeopardy" and I was invited to join in. I enjoyed the opportunity to play with these fun loving kids and to relax in the comfort of a home and family.

Nathan wanted to be an Air Force pilot and thought it was important to make good investments. He said that it was important to plan for retirement before he got too old and I found myself hoping that this 14-year-old babysitter was exhibiting such cautious maturity because of the responsibility of babysitting for three kids and a pretend cowboy. I wondered what traits would be possessed by those growing up in the 1980's.

The next morning Ruth insisted on washing my dirty clothes and while we had breakfast and waited for them to dry, Billy showed me a few tricks on my computer. Another 80's kid. Little Peter asked if he could help me get Carter ready, so Pete and I went outside and got things in order.

Clean clothes on board, Carter and I left the loving home of the Skellenger's with the 3 boys riding along for about a mile before being reclaimed by Mom. It was a perfect summer day and as we started on our way things felt good. I was rejuvenated by the warmth of family and children, and shower. Other things seemed brighter, too. We were leaving country that was less than exciting and entering a more populated land. Smiles seemed more frequent.

It wasn't long before we had city traffic, stop signs and traffic lights and we entered Gladstone, Michigan, population 4,500. The REA 50th anniversary logos were on the sides of the buggy and as we drove up to the headquarters building of Alger-Delta Cooperative, assistant manager Dan Roberts came out to greet us.

After a howdy-do and some water for Carter, he called the local media and the Gladstone police for an escort through town and for the next five or six hours he drove behind us with his emergency flashers on and a caution flag out the window. He made me feel like a member of the co-op family. My inclination to work with cooperatives increased because of such attitudes held by people like Dan. He didn't bend over backwards like he did because he had to, but because he wanted to.

A reporter from the Escanaba paper came out and rode along with Carter and me for a couple of miles. The police helped us get across busy four lane US–2 heading into Escanaba. Dan continued to follow and called ahead using his car's radio to obtain a police escort through gigantic Escanaba, population 15,000. It was tough.

Carter was tougher. That day we traveled 18 miles, 10 of which were nothing but busy and noisy. There were overpasses, underpasses, railroad tracks, trains, lumber trucks, bicycles—the works! We came to THE busiest intersection of town at rush hour— Carter didn't miss a beat! He was great. My nerves were whipped but with all the help from so many people, we made it past that bad intersection and I knew I was in love with my big pony.

The police turned around and Dan certainly was late for supper as Carter and I left the traffic of US-2 in favor of Lake Michigan shoreline hugging M-35. The sun was getting low and the place we found to stay for the next two nights was behind a billboard advertising McDonalds, right next to busy M-35.

We had traveled 14 of the last 16 days and covered 189 miles. That night I walked the three miles into town, both for the exercise and the opportunity to see the lights of the city. I ended up catching a Clint Eastwood movie, "Pale Rider" and then walked back to Carter and the buggy by the light of a full moon.

Ever since I had bought Carter I had only seen him lie down one time. I knew that a horse could lock their knees and sleep standing, but I had a hard time accepting that a horse would not lie down at least once in a while, especially if they were working— but Carter was always standing. Tonight as I slipped behind the McDonalds sign, all was quiet. Carter was lying down. It made me feel good just to see him rest like it seemed he should. But even better than that, when I went up to him, he stayed down and as I gently rubbed his great nose and talked to him, he kissed my hand with several sleepy horse kisses. Different strokes for different folks—but I loved it.

The next morning I fed Carter the last of the hay and a neighbor volunteered to drive me five miles to a dairy farmer. I got two bales and paid the man $3. The farmer then proudly showed me his half dozen Belgian horses, all of which were much bigger than Carter. As we talked, I learned that the man was in debt nearly half a million dollars. It was sad.

The man was obviously a hard working person and had accomplished a lot. The people around the farm were full of industry, too, yet he seemed resigned to losing all that he had. There was a sense of the impossible around this place, a "why me Lord?" kind of feeling. The $3 I left would do nothing to save the farm.

As I was leaving I felt a little gloom of my own as he told me about the drought to the south, adding, "I hear they're getting $6 for a bale of hay in southern Wisconsin." Yikes!

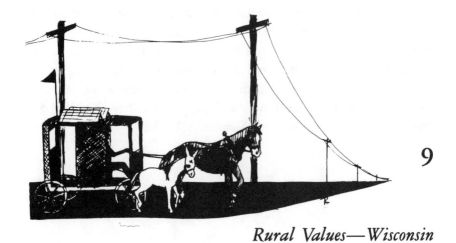

9

Rural Values—Wisconsin

If you really want to learn how to play the game, bet for more than you can afford to lose.

—Winston Churchill

On the third day out of Escanaba it began to look like the day to cross into Wisconsin. About three hours before getting to Wisconsin, it started to rain. It kept raining harder and harder. I put down the windshield to keep slightly dry but I could barely see so I was constantly putting the windshield up or down. One big drawback to having it down was that Carter couldn't hear me like I wanted him to. The reins surely gave him directions and information, but it was my voice that provided the main messages.

The roads we traveled on were wonderful. No more nasty roads full to overflowing with too many noisy cars and trucks. These were sweet things, paved and slightly used. We were back in the country and this was the kind of traveling I had been waiting for, not counting the rain.

But the battery was low again and I used the emergency flashers only when I saw traffic approaching. It rained so hard that there were times when I couldn't see them coming and was lucky that they saw us. We came to a bridge over the Menominee River and the rain became a heavy thunderstorm. Thunder and lightening were everywhere and I prayed that Carter would be steady and that no traffic would come. Two cars did come, but Carter kept on truckin'. We entered Wisconsin.

It rained for another hour. The reins were slimey and my hands were prunes. When it finally stopped raining we kept going for another three hours, making our second 23 mile day. All in all we went eight hours.

The next day the sun was hot when it rose at 6 o'clock. Since the harness was soaked I lay it out to dry and took things nice and slow. Cleaned out the buggy. Shaved and shampooed with Ivory soap.

I walked down to a mama-papa store only $1/8$ mile away with my Thermos and got some small wrapped donuts. When I asked for coffee the woman told me she was sorry, they didn't have any coffee to sell. I mentioned that I was camped down the road and that I was traveling by horse and buggy to Tennessee. She perked up. Told me that the family kitycorner to her place was Amish but that they drove cars. Real successful farmers.

I told her that I would like to travel amidst the Amish, to get to know them better. She agreed that most of the Amish she knew were real nice people.

Then she said, "If you're not in a real hurry, I'll go make you a pot. Just take a minute," and disappeared into the living quarters. People can be so nice.

It was a nice, hot day and Carter walked well, talking with some horses and cows along the way. When we had traveled about 15 miles a truck came alongside and Jerry Damitz leaned over to say, "Hi, where you going?"

One thing led to another and Jerry told me that he worked at a cabinet shop in Marinette, Wisconsin and was on his way home about three miles down the road. He and his wife, Donna, had 30 head of beef cattle and raised registered paint horses to boot. He said that if I wanted, we could stay at his place. Lovely!

When we got to Jerry's, he was quickly working his stallion in the paddock, so I undid Carter and gave him some oats and waited for a vacancy. Jerry finished and led the stallion to his stable, and I led Carter into the paddock. Then things got interesting.

It had been a hot day and Carter was acting like he was feeling it. I put him inside the paddock but he stayed around the shade tree and seemed to avoid the far side where the water trough was located.

Since the water trough was an old white cast iron bathtub I thought he might be afraid of it, so I went in and led him over to the tub in the corner of the paddock, assuring him that everything was OK. We got to the tub and he snorted his suspicion, but then drank deep and long. I thought that was that.

As he finished, I went one way and he went the other. He dipped his head and instantly I recognized that he was about to run and show that he was feeling good, and I felt good that he felt so good after a hard day. Suddenly he kicked back and his steel shoe connected solidly with my left elbow and hip.

I was stunned. It didn't knock me over, only back. I knew I was hurt but didn't want to look at my arm as it hung limply down. I held the helpless left arm with my right hand and ventured a look at the good right hand—sure enough, blood. I had watched it happen, thinking that I was out of range but unaware that the ligaments in a horse's leg allow the ball to leave the socket, and to extend further than just the length of the leg.

Carter kept running around, acting healthy, as I walked over to the gate and fumbled with the difficult latch—first to get out and then to relatch it.

Donna Damitz came outside with a visiting friend and asked if I was hurt.

"Yes."

They offered to take me to the hospital, so I went to the buggy and gathered my check book, some clothes, and an outdated medical insurance card. I didn't know if I could get into an Emergency Room without one. Since I had left the FAA I had gone bare, without medical insurance, hoping that I'd never be in such a predicament.

We drove into Marinette (Wisconsin) General Hospital where I was almost immediately taken into a room and examined. Three X-rays showed nothing broken and since I had walked in on my own the doctor determined that my hip was OK. No stitches. No pain pills. One tetanus shot. An hour and fifteen minutes later we were on our way back to Damitz's. My arm and my hip throbbed but I considered myself lucky.

People who live in the areas where the electric companies are cooperatives could get together and organize a progressive and competitive cooperative health insurance for all members. Or a health maintenance organization. Today. It's a question of will and cooperation. Fifty years ago when the same areas didn't have electricity, they got it together.

The same methods could apply many needs. One of the basic principles of a cooperative organization is cooperation with other cooperatives. Financing of such a medical co-op/insurance could come from local credit unions where liquidity is a problem—they have money to loan, and not enough good places to invest it. Or from the National Cooperative Bank. Or local banks. The point to be made—where there's a will. . . .

The next morning was predictable. A bump the size of a golf ball on my elbow, black and blue hip and arm, and real sore. I never got mad at Carter because it wasn't like he kicked me on purpose. More like I got in the way of a fit of feeling good. In spite of soreness, it was a good day. Not just the weather and the fact that the arm was still in one piece, but everyone seemed to be in a good mood. Harnessing and hitching with one arm was a bit difficult, but not impossible.

Even though I didn't feel malace towards my Joe Palooka, I was stern with him that day. I had lightened up too much when I had been kicked and I insisted on Carter doing exactly what I wanted as we traveled along. The old saying sort of applied, "Fool me once, shame on you; Fool me twice, shame on me."

The Wisconsin countryside was impressive. Very green, very colorful, very agricultural, with plenty of pretty flowers and birds. At one point a man, about 30, called out from a farmhouse and ran down to greet us.

He said that his grandparents were in the house and they were thrilled because my carriage looked a lot like an old milkwagon his grandfather used to drive. Would it be okay if he met us down the road so that they could see our rig? Sure. A mile or so later the young man brought his grandparents and for twenty minutes we talked of my trip and the old days. This kind of thing happened all the time.

As we approached Coleman, population 865, I noticed a suburban sort of home to our left. The house had four windows on its front side, five counting the glass front door. In every window there were at least one or two kids checking us out. By the time we got to town, kids seemed to be everywhere and we had our own parade. Unannounced and unexpected. No pretensions. The best of parades. Everyone was friendly.

One man asked us to pull over and said that he had seen us 300 miles ago as we started out in the UP. Could it really be the same buggy? Another man about to enter the post office diverted his walk and came over to us and said, "I really like your solars."

West of town a man in his seventies who had stopped and talked with us east of Coleman, stopped again and apologized for not having asked earlier, but he hadn't thought of it. "Do you need any oats?"

We were low on oats and the oats we had were loaded with dust, so I said that we did. He got back in his pickup and said he'd see us later.

Deloris VanLaarhoven stopped us later and wished us luck. She gave me $5 and told me to have a good meal. As we were stopped, the same man returned with a 100 pound plus bag full of top quality oats. Before I had a chance to help him, he had grabbed the bag and thrown it into the back seat of the buggy.

Eighteen people packed miles later, we found a place to camp at the end of a dead end road, next to a corn field. Three miles away was Kelly Lake, a small and pretty lake populated by vacationing Chicagoans. Once Carter was munching on his oats and a few pinched ears of corn, I headed for a welcome walk to and a bath in the lake, and the meal that Deloris had told me to have on her.

While feasting at the Holiday Inn of Kelly Lake I began asking around for possible places to keep Carter and the buggy. It was August and time for another board meeting and another column. Someone mentioned Dodie Kinziger because she had a dog kennel, and owned a few horses on the east side of the lake.

I called her and managed a meeting with her the next day. When I met Dodie she said yes almost right away. When I asked her how much she would charge, she replied, "I charge $5 a day for keeping dogs, but I board dogs, not horses," which meant, no charge.

I drove Carter and the buggy over to Dodie's and Carter happily joined her horses while I parked the buggy out of the way. Then I kicked around the lake, looking for a ride for me to Manitowoc, Wisconsin, about 80 miles away, to catch the ferry across Lake Michigan. Amazingly I found a ride that day and was picked up by my neighbor the next morning on the Michigan side.

One of the good things about taking care of business while making this trip was that I was able to check on things at home, to see friends and family, and to deal with cooperative business. On this trip home I was away from Carter almost ten days.

When I returned and harnessed up to get back on the road, Carter acted green. He let everything along the way get his attention. He didn't want to stand and he wanted to look at everything. It took a couple of hours before he finally lightened up and began doing his thing like he was supposed to.

We traveled fourteen miles on that first day out. Approaching Gillett, Wisconsin, a woman came out from the house with a Polaroid and asked if she could take our picture. Carter was so ready to stop, fresh back to work from his vacation and all, that he stopped without my doing a thing. He knew that when people came up to us it usually meant that we would stop and this time he took the initiative.

Adelaine Rank took three pictures of us, and each time she managed to cut Carter's head off. She asked where we were going and I replied that we were looking for a place to camp.

"Here," she said. Off the road we pulled.

The Ranks were dairy farmers. Carl and Adelaine had six children, two of them boys. Carl's father had farmed but none of their six kids had entered farming. Ten years ago the barn had burned down and insurance had paid $200,000 to rebuild it. At the time they had considered getting out of farming, but it was too much of their life. Carl felt that too many farmers got too big, too fast. Banks encouraged it. Bigger tractors led to bigger equipment, which led to more land, which led to bigger tractors. Bigger tractors with stereo cassette players, air conditioning, and 1985 prices. A potential death spiral.

I did and didn't have a hard time putting my finger on just what ideals came with the territory of the farmer and rural American. A large part certainly related to the way neighbors helped each other. I was a stranger made friend by the hospitality of strangers, now friends. Trust was offered and a bed was given to me, not because I deserved it but because people are good. We're family. People need each other and need to share their love. The same ideals also live in the city—good people are everywhere. But trust seemed to come easier in the country and the dollar not foremost in consideration.

The hills around Oconto Falls were numerous and some of them demanded that Carter really dig in. Carter almost always came first when it came to hills, and within reason we had an equal right to the road. If the shoulder of the road was paved, we'd stick to the shoulder, but if the shoulder was soft or non-existent, I would keep Carter on the road itself. This meant that any traffic that came along would have to follow behind until we got to the top, at which time we would pull over. It was rare that I would get off the road for the faster traffic, even if I did feel bad about making cars go slow.

One of the best improvements to the trip came as a total surprise. As we were going up a particularly steep hill, I thought that if I were to jump out of the buggy, there would be 175 pounds less that Carter would have to haul up the hill. So I jumped out and drove Carter from outside the buggy, walking beside the buggy and feeling good that I was helping him get up the hill. Once we made it to the top, I jumped back in. But then it hit me—exercise! Not only did this new style help my horse, it freed me from too little exercise.

I thought about the pros of cons of walking and driving as I rode along. The arguments that went through my mind against this new thing came down to how others might think. My solar powered buggy, no doubt, had many wondering what kind of weirdness was going on anyhow, so why worry about someone else's problem? That settled it! I jumped out as we traveled along a flat piece of land.

The trip improved 100 percent—bingo—just like that! Now instead of being bored or sore from sitting too much, I could walk. As I walked, my mind walked and I could play games with the trip. I could kick a pebble as we went along, or I could get into how close Carter might come to squishing a wooly-worm or aim at a grasshopper with the wheels. I felt better, I thought better, and while Carter was probably only marginally affected, if at all, it seemed to be a sensible thing to do.

This new method of traveling had been happening for less than 10 minutes when Don Van Deest came driving from the way we were heading pulled off the road to await us. Never before had I heard of Don, but what he brought was a growing conviction of mine. The cooperative was reaching out to lend a hand to one of its own.

Don was manager of Central Wisconsin Electric Cooperative, and he had driven out looking for me to offer me a place to stay, a steak dinner, and a Jacuzzi whirlpool to relax in. Don's home was another 15 miles down the road and there was no way we'd be able to make it that day. Don wished us luck and said that he would return towards the end of the day to see how far we had gotten and that he would help as much as he could.

"One thing though," Don mentioned as he turned to leave, "there's a man on our lines who died this morning of a heart attack. Don't stop there looking for a place to stay." He described the farm of the family of the deceased and drove back towards the town of Iola.

We continued along some nice hilly countryside and I couldn't believe how much I was enjoying the day. This style of walking and driving at the same time was close to my original concept of travel and my leg muscles were making my brain synapses happy. On we went, making a sweeping right hand turn up a shallow hill, with the radio playing some catchy tunes from the rear of the buggy.

From a farmhouse on our left three girls, all juniors in high school, came running after us. One had only socks on her feet. They had seen a TV news piece about us the day before and asked lots of questions. I invited them to ride along and they immediately jumped into the front seat. I brought Carter back to a walk, and drove while walking.

We talked. The girls were playful and added more sunshine to my already improving day. The popular song, "Money for Nothing and the Chicks for Free" came on the radio and they applied me to their imaginations and asked if that was the way it was with me.

In the middle of the laugh one of the girls mentioned that her father had died that morning, but assured me that she was alright. This was the grieving family that Don and told me about. There is courage everywhere.

The girls rode with us for about 30 minutes but decided they had better turn back because if they went much further, the one girl's socks would wear out completely.

We never made it into Iola that day but Don found a private park to keep the buggy and Carter at, and then picked me up for the promised home grown steak dinner. We enjoyed a long soak in the Jacuzzi after dinner and talked until late.

The following day I met the entire board of Central Wisconsin Electric Cooperative and many of the employees came out to greet and encourage us on the road. Before leaving the friendly town we stopped at the grade school and visited with the first and fourth grades on the playground. I tried to explain the very foreign concept of life without electricity. I think the contrast of the horse and buggy with the solar cells helped, but it was still a difficult task. Our audience was appreciative and as we hit the back roads out of town, I enjoyed a hot lunch from the school cafeteria of chicken and mashed potatoes.

August neared an end and as we approached the Wisconsin River in central Wisconsin, darkness arrived near 8 p.m. The skies to the West betrayed an approaching storm and I tried to gauge just how far we could go before it hit. Usually I would begin looking for a place to stay between 6:30 and 7:30. It was almost 7 o'clock when we came to the first house in a long time. Three dogs came out to stand their ground and began a non-stop barrage of barking. Under the circumstances I had little choice but to bring

Carter to a stop and hope that someone would notice us so I could ask the big Q.

Finally a cautious man about 65 emerged from the dairy barn in back and came out to the road. He offered us the use of his cornfield but he recommended that I check with his neighbor first since he had horses. Just then lightening struck and the man turned without a further word and hurried back to the shelter of the barn.

Heavy rain began to fall and I trotted Carter the quarter mile to his cornfield but there was no way to get off the road and into the field. No choice and no neighbor in sight, we slowed to a walk and kept on in the rain. It turned cool and windy. Two miles later, the sun gone and the dark clouds making things even darker than normal, I pulled into the driveway of the first home to come along, that of Doug and Sue Hambach. There were many signs of horses. I went up to the door and knocked.

Doug answered the door. Dirty, wet, and unannounced, I asked for a place to camp for the night. Without hesitation Doug turned to grab a hat and called to his wife to say he'd be right back.

"You can stay in the arena. Come on, follow me." Within 30 minutes Carter was enjoying the green grass of a manicured arena, the buggy was set up for the night, and I was inside drinking almond coffee with Sue and Doug.

Doug was about 50 years old. As a younger man he had worked as a teacher before going back to school and becoming a dentist. He had then practiced dentistry for 20 years locally and knew everyone. A few years back he had given up his practice to work full time with cattle. This arena of Wisconsin was the best cattle country in the world, he claimed, if it was worked right. They had a thousand head. We talked of many things, including electricity in the country. Doug was in favor of nuclear energy and considered himself to be pragmatic. He also didn't like pointy headed intellectual types of people.

Doug was knowledgeable about horses and told many stories. He talked about how horses have such terrible immune systems and how their digestive systems barely worked. About how stupid they could be—but despite it all, their saving grace was that they were incredibly strong.

Sue was about 35 and a horse trainer by trade. Originally from upper New York state, she was interested in the details of my trip. I mentioned that Carter's left front shoe had lost it borium calk and she immediately got on the phone to her farrier, Warren Beamish, and asked if he could stop out in the morning to have a look. Yes, he could rearrange his schedule and would be out first thing. It was midnight when I headed out to my home on wheels and sleep.

The next morning Doug and Sue were off early for a meeting in Madison. Not long after they left Bob Luce from Adams-Marquette Electric Cooperative drove up and introduced himself. He had heard that our REA Speedwagon was coming and he wanted to do whatever he could to help out.

A few minutes later Warren Beamish drove up and he soon had the bad shoe off. He didn't have any borium but he did have another hard carbide material called Drill-tex. Drill-tex was commonly used on drill bits, and while it was as hard as borium, it was granular and gripped even better.

He applied it to the tip of the shoe, and put the shoe back on. As he finished and hurried to keep up with his original schedule I asked him how much I should make the check for.

"No charge," he replied. He had always wanted to make a cross country horse trip but never had, so this was how he might contribute to his dream for now. By 9 o'clock we were on the road.

Once during a particularly lazy stretch of road when I was almost dozing at the reins, I was brought to life as Carter jumped quickly to the right and off the road. I looked up to see a 10 point buck standing in the middle of the road in front of us. He, too, had been surprised and had brought his bounding leaps to a sudden halt. I was lucky because when the deer stopped, Carter stopped, just shy of a big ditch.

That night was spent in Friendship, Wisconsin at Adams-Marquette co-op's fenced in backyard amongst poles, transformers, and miles of electric wire. For the second night in a row Carter shared the same corral with me and nosed around the buggy for oats and company, roaming the yard at leisure. I wondered what choice comments the line crew at the co-op would have the next day when they returned to a storage area that contained 7 or 8 big bombs lying everywhere. Bob told me not to worry about it. I hadn't brought a pitchfork.

Bob Luce not only provided us with a place to stay but had brought 100 pounds of oats and a couple bales of hay. Further, he had gone ahead and talked with people at the Woodside Dude Ranch in Mauston about us staying there. We arrived at the resort after 22 miles. I had never been to a dude ranch before and wasn't sure what to expect. I had visions of Perrier water for Carter. It was interesting because except for the periodic interruptions, I was coming from a "pure" horse life to one where city people escaped to a life that included horses—compatible but exclusive, two different life styles.

One of the original owners, Lucille Nichols, came out to greet us as we drove into the ranch. She had talked with Bob and we were welcome to stay there. Already I had another meeting, this time in Philadelphia, and needed to leave Carter and the buggy. I asked her how much it would cost to leave Carter and the buggy at the ranch for five days.

"Nothing, but you deal with Roy as far as the horse is concerned," was her reply.

As Lucille mentioned him, he walked up. Roy was working as the head cowboy at the dude ranch but in better times he had been a farmer. About 50 years old, he thought and talked without pretenses, arriving to work by 6 a.m. everyday. He told me to bring Carter and follow him to the stables.

I began to do so when an electronic bug zapper overhead suddenly zapped—not once but three times—and each time Carter checked in for the races, almost running me over. Things had changed. I was laughing and having fun.

Roy took us to Carter's new home and we talked horse details. Carter's shoes needed attention. He said he would try to get him shod while I was gone. I mentioned that for about a week there had been an occasional darkness in Carter's urine and asked Roy what he thought might cause something like that.

He calmly asked if Carter was getting enough salt. I immediately realized my mistake! How stupid! When we had entered Wisconsin in the heavy thunderstorm, our four pound block of salt had melted. Ever since then Carter had not had any salt. I had meant to get some but had been negligent in replacing it. Roy offered Carter a salt block and he immediately began to lick it.

The dude ranch was celebrating its 60th anniversary that night and Lucille encouraged me to stay and take part in the festivities, but I had a ride to the airport in Madison that night and had to decline the invitation. I wanted to stay because the party would be fun and it fit right in with the 50 years of REA.

Lucille was a lively, interested, and interesting woman in her 70's, who carried an air of authority about her. She thought what I was doing was wonderful and remembered the days when the ranch had its own Delco system to provide electricity. At their home down the road, they had only had lanterns for lighting. She told me of the never ending daily chore of cleaning the blackened chimneys of the kerosene lamps. How she hated it! She remembered her distaste complete with the disgusting facial expressions which went with the job.

"No matter how much you turned the wick up, there was never enough light," she said.

I left the dude ranch that night, heading first for Madison and then onto Philadelphia where the national electric cooperative group was having its regional meeting. It was a three day affair and included many speeches and seminars. At 50 years of age the electric cooperatives found themselves in the throes of middle age and were struggling to become more relevant and better understood.

As I sat through some of the meetings I couldn't help but think about Lucille Nichols in Wisconsin. People like Lucille, older than us Baby Boomers, remembered with relevancy just what the REA had done for them, or more precisely, what the REA had allowed them to do for themselves. My generation was in the middle. Most of us had grown up with electricity and thought of it as something that was supposed to be, if we thought of it at all.

The greatest part of the story of rural electric cooperatives was the role of cooperatives and cooperation. In instances where the profit motive didn't exist to provide the incentive to supply needed services, a cooperative could do the job and prosper.

Quiet lights below

Baby Pete—ten weeks old

Edwin Martin and Don Buschert rolling the virgin buggy out of the shop

The new carriage, loaded onto the truck and about to leave Elmira, Ontario, Canada for Michigan—a storm approaching

A buggy and a burro at the barn—but now what?

May 11, 1985 at the state capitol in Lansing, Michigan on the 50th anniversary of the REA

This sandy two-track shortcut deteriorated from here but eventually led to Gaylord, Michigan

Carter watches Joni Grogan work her mare in Moran, Michigan . . .

. . . and reacts!

Joni and her horse say good morning to Carter

Big Bill Lindemuth, Trout Lake, Michigan

Adjusting the photovoltaics (PV's) in bear country, Naubinway, Michigan

Cooling heels in Lake Michigan, Fox, Michigan

Kids in the windows for a one-horse parade—Coleman, Wisconsin

Clip-clopping through downtown Gillett, Wisconsin, population 1,356

Carter happily munching hay on a picket line near Hancock, Wisconsin

Two old-timers travel back through time, without leaving Lil's Bar, Friendship, Wisconsin

Roy, foreman at Woodside Dude Ranch, Mauston, Wisconsin

Animal magnetism

Tom Pardee driving in Wisconsin, sipping morning coffee

Tom driving from the side

A can-do attitude on the part of people and government allowed for the rebuilding of perennially-flooded Soldiers Grove above the floodplains and incorporating designs stressing solar and conservation.

Jack Brown of Boscobel, Wisconsin

Snooping for oats

On the road in Wisconsin

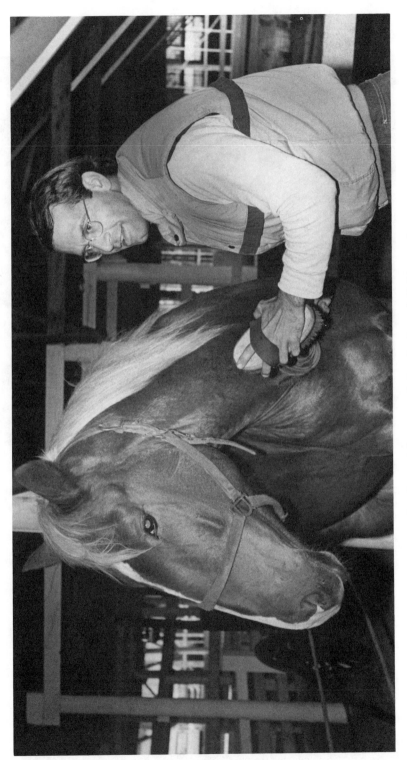

Carter and friend, out of the rain at the Dewitt, Iowa 4-H fairgrounds

Leaving the Dewitt, Iowa fairgrounds

Hard rubber tire wired and clamped to the steel and hickory wheel

Climbing the bluff southbound from the Mississippi River, Andalusia, Illinois

Lore Booker and Carter, New Canton, Illinois

Bridge across Mississippi River, from Pike, Illinois to Louisiana, Missouri

A Bowling Green, Missouri hitchhiker

Eugene Parks with "So Impressive," St. Clair, Missouri

Melissa Corbin, veteran teamster

George Radin and his mules out for a Sunday ride, Festus, Missouri.

Paul Cready and Ray Cox at Fruitland Livestock Auction Company; buggy in background.

Cape Girardeau, Missouri KFVS-TV came out into the rain along Highway 61 for an interview

Bud Campbell shows how a cotton picking machine works, and how the accident happened

The approach to Tennessee from the Leek's home in Caruthersville. The levee is on the left and beyond is the Mississippi.

On the bridge leading into Tennessee, with Tennessee in sight and a barge steaming up the Mississippi below

Stopped short! The goal of Tennessee is at the top of the bridge and fills the scenery!

100 feet above the Mississippi, the goal was in sight—then came the jackhammer

Carmon Epley—proprietor, Bogota, Tennessee

Dominoes at Carmon's, an everyday thing

Prentiss Johnson, director at Forked Deer Electric Co-op and Carmon show off a 50-year-old "REA/FDR fan"

Cooperation on Iwo Jima, 1945

Cooperation in Bogota, 1985

Carter nudging a goodbye with his large head while Weldon Schramp looks on

The first modern cooperative, Rochdale, England

Pheasants for sale in a Loughborough street market

*People come from all over the world to attend the Cooperative College in Loughborough,
England—pictured here are students from Nepal, India, and Africa*

Carter, at home in Michigan

I listened to people talk about doing more. Of expanding services. Why not expand the successful and democratic concept of cooperatives and start new co-ops to serve the needs of today? The established and respected rural electric cooperatives could be the cornerstones of such enterprise.

There was another aspect of cooperatives that was vitally important and too easily overlooked. They are locally owned and operated. Because of this the local economy receives a large degree of protection from companies moving out-of-town or out-of-state, even out-of-country. Built-in economic development.

Meetings have never been my favorite way to spend my time and in spite of the interesting ideas being bantered around, I was anxious to get back to the reality of traveling with Carter. When I finally got back to the Woodside Dude Ranch it was a real scorcher, close to 100 degrees. Roy had managed to get Carter shod and I made noises about leaving that day.

Lucille came out to the garage where I was working on the brakes and told me that a livestock alert had been issued and I should plan on spending the night. It was September 7 and I felt that I needed to hurry or we would never make it to Tennessee, but when I visited Carter in his stable and decided to wait another day. He was soaked, just standing in the shade.

All night there were tremendous thunderstorms. When I got up at 5 a.m. the rain still fell and I despaired that we might suffer another delay. By ten o'clock the rain stopped and I put the harness on Carter. It felt good to be on the road and away from the distractions of travel.

The clouds slowly cleared and the roadside gradually dried. Back in the travel mode, I set about figuring just what speed we traveled at. I knew that we traveled roughly 3 m.p.h. on a daily basis but now I counted Carter's steps per minute.

I learned that Carter took 48 steps per minute, counting only one of the four feet, while I made 52 steps counting one foot. He was Mr. Consistent. For the entire trip his standard was 12 steps per quarter minute, either on level ground or up long, steep hills. It became so deeply embedded that I knew if we were slow or fast just by the sound.

About the only time he would slow down was going downhill. Then the brakes would be inadequate and the harness would push against his muscular rear legs. His downhill speed was 11 steps per 15 seconds.

Each step was a consistent 73″ apart. At 48 steps per minute that worked out to 292 feet per minute or 17,520 feet per hour. And so, according to my Casio and Lufkin, we were traveling at 3.31 m.p.h., not counting stops.

We spent the night in the city park of Elroy, population 1504. It made for an easy night since it was located right on the highway and equipped with animal stalls. It was also the location for the temporary dog pound and it caused Carter to get loose once again.

I roped off an area between stables and Carter was grazing while I walked 200 yards to a pay telephone to call my friend, Tom Pardee. Just as I made the long distance connection, I could barely see Carter trotting toward the only open gate to the park, leading onto the highway! I hung up on Tom and ran to block his way but by the time I got to him he had calmed down and slowed to a walk. What happened was that he was grazing with his head slightly under the single strand of rope and was startled by one of the dogs chained to the other side of the stables. As he lifted his head, he found himself out of his little pasture and off he went!

Captured, I roped him into a stall and returned to the phone. Tom planned to begin his vacation from his job as a respiratory therapist the next day and would be taking the ferry across the lake, driving about 400 miles to find us somewhere on Wisconsin 82.

I had known Tom since high school in Pontiac, Michigan in the late 60's. He was the kind of kid who went to the parties, loved his friends and wasn't afraid to show it. He was the guy who was at the center of action and partying the hardest—but his was a natural high. He didn't need booze or drugs, and at 6′4″ he attracted that much more attention.

Tom and his wife had helped and encouraged me with my travel project from the beginning. He had helped me string the fencing for the baby burro's corral and had been with me on the very first day. It was their home where I rested after the first week of travel and I looked forward to having him join me.

Tom appeared around one of the many curves near sunset. After saying hi and welcome, Tom went ahead to see if he could find us a place to spend the night. It wasn't long before Tom came back and said he had found a place about a mile away. That night we camped in the buggy at Rita and Jim Scala's place. The buggy proved too small for two of us to be comfortable.

The next morning held the most rude incident of the entire trip. We had met Mike Nelson from Vernon Electric Co-op by 7:15 a.m. and the people at the co-op had graciously agreed to help us shuttle Toms' car as we moved through the area. After coffee, around 9:30, as we were getting things packed to go, a green and rather noisy V-8 pickup drove up. A husky, gruff sounding, full bearded man rolled down the window of the truck and introduced himself by saying "What are you doin'?"

I figured he was kidding, he couldn't be so rude, so I jokingly replied, "Oh, we're planning an invasion of Canada and we're guerillas," and as I spoke I continued to carry some hay over to Carter.

"I say again, what are you doin'?" His tone was harder.

I've never liked the phrase "Say again." It's radio talk and should be restricted to the radio. No need to militarize everyday life with something so cold and impersonal. I knew I was prejudiced and was glad that Tom jumped into the scene because I was only about to get smarter.

Tom calmly told the man that he had talked to Jim and Rita and they had given us permission to camp there for the night. He added that we were just about to leave.

With that the man settled down a tad and explained that Jim and Rita were renting the place from him and they had no business giving us such permission.

Tom repeated that we were about to leave. Finally the guy left and we got on the road. Considering that this was the worst incident of the entire trip, life was good.

I drove for awhile, enjoying Tom's company and explaining some of what I had learned about driving a horse and buggy as we went along. Tom was green at the buggy game but with little traffic, he soon took his turn at driving. He did well. We took turns driving from the front seat and then I introduced Tom to the walking/driving method. Sometimes one of us would ride while the other drove alongside. Often we would both walk.

Even though Tom was inexperienced with a spooked horse, I needed to take some pictures for the Electric Burro Travel Series column. Alone, there had been little opportunity to get a shot of a moving Carter, so I threw caution to the wind and as Tom walked and drove, I ran and shot pictures.

Tom made history as thousands of years of tradition were thoroughly ignored by this lanky lad from Michigan. Bo Diddeley and Little Richard would have both been surprised and proud. Saying "giddy-up" or making a kiss sound wasn't good enough for Tom. Instead Tom made his solo driving debut by singing to the heavens, "Ro-o-o-ck Me-e-ee!", slapping Carter's rump with the reins at the same time and updating the history of humankind and the horse with current jargon. It will likely be a while before it catches on with the Amish, but the first, not-so-tentative step was taken that day by Tom.

Since the winter before our trip, Soldiers Grove, Wisconsin was one of the places I had hoped to see. While dreaming dreams, before any carriage was ordered, I had been painting the remodeled walls of my barn home and was listening to a program on television. It was about a village of 664 in southwest Wisconsin that had been rebuilt using the sun to provide at least 50% of the heating needs. While I had been interested in solar energy for years, I had only seen single projects—never an entire town. They called it "America's First Solar Village.

As Tom, Carter and I hurried along at 52 steps per minute, it slowly became clear that all routes leading into Minnesota included hills with uncontrollable Bad. Shoot! Along with Wisconsin some of history's greatest cooperative beginnings took place in Minnesota. Reluctantly I decided not to attempt the crossing into Minnesota and we began a more southerly route. Soldiers Grove became our official destination and our second day of travel brought us to the Kickapoo River and the village that helped itself.

Since the turn of the century there had been six major floods in Soldiers Grove and each time the village was destroyed. The village people had initiated plans in 1976 to relocate the downtown area by buying a relocation site uphill from the Kickapoo. In 1978 the Kickapoo flooded worse than ever. Local, state and federal agencies then gathered to discuss what to do. It was decided to rebuild the commercial area with energy needs in mind and the agreements included strict inclusion of solar power for heating purposes. Four years after construction began the village was completed.

As we approached Soldiers Grove, tobacco was being harvested. The world's first solar village wasn't very big but the concept was. These Wisconsin people were helping themselves in much the same fashion as the farmers had fifty years earlier when REA was started. There was an IGA grocery store, post office, a 16 unit senior citizen's apartment complex and many other solar buildings, including a gas station. While the world's first solar powered buggy cruised through the world's first solar village, John Feyen came up to us and invited us to spend the night with his family.

Again, trusting hospitality. That night we had dinner with the six member Feyen family and slept inside their old farm house. They were remodeling it to include solar heat. Tom and I waited our turn the next morning for the single bathroom. While we shared breakfast, phone calls were made to find a place to stay that night. Jack Brown and his farm became our destination, since his farm was along our route and because he was an old time horseman.

The next day the people from Crawford Electric Cooperative came out to help us shuttle Tom's car and as Tom left with them, I continued alone with Carter. Tom had been gone no more than 15 minutes when three men emerged from a commercial sort of pole building and came out to the road to talk. I told them a little about the trip and that I was looking for Jack Brown. This was Jack Brown! We talked some more and Jack told me that he lived only a few miles further down the road and that he'd meet us just before we got to his place.

When we had driven up to where the three men had met us, several horses had followed along in a pasture on the other side of the road. With me walking next to the buggy, we started out for Jack's house. Suddenly the horses ran up from behind and Carter took off at a dead gallop! There we were, booking down the highway at full speed with me eyeing the buggy to see how and if I could jump in. I knew things were precarious but just when things looked like I'd have to make a jump for it, Carter began to listen to me talking to him and he began to slow down to a trot. I began to smile and then laugh as I enjoyed the non-stop good that life was bringing me.

The co-op folks brought Tom back to the rig and then, a mile before we got to Brown's farm, Jack drove up behind us. Jack took a place in the buggy and Tom played musical chairs, climbing into Jack's pickup. I handed the reins to Jack and he proved his hand at handling horses. We drove on to his place where there were several Percheron horses in the corral. Jack led Carter into the barn and handled him with authority, putting him into a large stall and feeding him some hay. Harness was hanging neatly everywhere.

It was time to go home for the monthly meeting and I resented having to leave the trip. I explained things to Jack and he offered to keep Carter while I was gone. The collar had come apart the day before and the new shoes that Carter had received at the dude ranch were already loose. Salt of the Earth Brown said that he'd try to get the harness repaired and Carter reshod.

Jack, Tom and I went into the house by way of the storm cellar where Jack took off his coveralls and hung them up with half a dozen others and we washed up. Jack's hands were made of leather. He hadn't missed a day of work around his Boscobel farm in 20 years.

We went upstairs to where Mae Brown was fixing lunch. Not lunch really—dinner. A real spread. We sat and ate and talked. When we finished eating and talking, we ate some more and continued talking. The Browns remembered REA beginnings well. The large cooperative that supplied power to the local co-ops, Dairyland, had just replaced the poles on Brown's land using the latest equipment. Jack recalled when the first poles went in and how he had worked a team of horses for the REA co-op in the most difficult areas.

When the electric cooperatives were getting started, transportation was nothing that could be taken for granted. People who worked on the original lines would board at places along the way since it took too long to get to the work sites everyday. Many people have never known or have forgotten that it has been a relatively recent phenomenon for people to commute long distances to work on a daily basis. The reality of installing electric lines has changed a lot. In the "old days" there were a lot of wasted efforts due to rough terrain and the nature of horses.

We discussed which way to go when I returned in a few days and any direction included hills or difficult bridges. The Boscobel bridge itself was long and narrow with a steel grid deck. Not only would Carter's steel shoes make a loud and spooky noise, but the Wisconsin River would be visible below. It was scary. The alternative was to head towards Minnesota, but the hills leading into Minnesota sounded even worse.

For the time being it was a problem for the future. For now things were perfect since I could ride home with Tom. We left in his car and returned home via the Lake Michigan ferry. When my meeting was completed and my monthly column mailed out, almost a week later, I returned to Boscobel.

Jack was in the middle of getting in his silage and busier than ever. He had gotten Carter reshod and the harness repaired, like he had said, and now he offered to help me get across the bridge. That morning I watched as Jack harnessed up and I learned how to "throw" the harness onto Carter. I estimated how long it would take us to get to the narrow bridge and Jack told me he'd meet me before the bridge and would drive Carter across. As we headed out that morning, Mae told me she was very surprised that Jack had offered to do it because he steadfastly refused to go anywhere near water.

Two hours later we came to a caution sign that read "NARROW BRIDGE—STEEL GRID DECK—1500 FEET."

I pulled under a nice shade tree and waited. Jack drove up fifteen minutes later and we changed vehicles. I drove across the bridge in Jack's truck and waited on the southern end, hoping for light traffic.

Jack brought Carter to a walk. I watched as they came up to where the solid road turned into steel grid. Just when Carter began to twist his head for a better look at the spooky looking deck in front of him and just before he was about to decide to balk at the whole idea, Jack reached forward with the whip and cracked him on the rear. Carter broke into a trot. The bridge was about $1/8$ of a mile long and steel shoes on steel deck echoed with noise but the team of Carter and Jack performed flawlessly, trotting the entire length. Jack was a busy man and after thanks and goodbyes we re-exchanged rigs and parted. Carter was rested and ready for the road.

One thing he wasn't quite ready for caused him to spook a couple of days later as we passed through Fennimore, Wisconsin. There was a cheese shop with a 10 foot mouse in front named Igor, towering over a hunk of cheese. I looked at Igor as a sign, but Carter saw it for what it was—a ten foot tall mouse! He shyed away from Igor and broke into a trot. A funny spook!

A generally forgotten factor in 1985 was the relative slowness of horse and buggy travel. People would come up with statements like "only ten miles," or "only ten minutes" and I would have to remind them that ten miles was half a day's travel. Once, while talking with some people who had ridden bicycles across the U.S.A., they had told me of a "no backtracking rule" that they had adhered to out of necessity. I decided to do the same, otherwise we'd never get to Tennessee by November.

As September neared its end, it rained every day. It seemed like we would never dry out or warm up and it stayed windy and about 50 degrees. One day as we drove along in the rain, two cars pulled over and a man, his wife and their teenage son got out of the first car. The second car held one man and two women in their twenties. The girls were introduced as two visiting friends from Texas and they were having a pig roast at their farm a couple miles off the road, behind us. Would I like to come? I did, but it was 4:30 and I felt that if I was to make my goal I needed to travel as far as

I could. I thanked them but said no thanks. I had a long way to go and had a new "no backtracking" rule.

As I was about to drive on the wife said, "I sure wish there was some way to make you stay. We could put your horse and buggy in the barn."

Discipline has its place but this was one rule I should have broken. But I would have had to backtrack to get to their farm. Woulda, coulda, shoulda. I was nuts.

As we neared the Mississippi River and Iowa, I spent the night at Ronnie and Charlene Esser's, sleeping in their travel trailer. The next morning I woke to Carter trotting down the road and hurried to pull my boots on and give chase. Nothing bad happened and I caught up to him and led him back.

The Essers had called the local TV station and a reporter joined us for a mile or two as we got underway. I had never been interviewed in my life before this trip and didn't particularly relish the delays incurred, but felt it was good and necessary if people were to be reminded of the roots of the electric cooperative movement.

The Essers followed along and exchanged their 13 year old Rhonda and 9 year old Dane for the reporter. The day before getting to Esser's home, I had heard my rear wheel making more than its usual noise. I ignored it, thinking the ground harder or more gravelly than usual. Fifty yards later I looked back and saw that the hard rubber tire had come off the right rear wheel. The wheel had an exposed steel rim and the tire looked like a snake on the shoulder of the road.

When we started out with the TV reporter that morning, I had strapped the rubber onto the wheel rim with soft electric fence wire. With Rhonda and Dane riding along, I noticed that many of the wire straps were snapping in two after only a couple of miles, so I stopped at a house along the road and went up to the door to ask if they might have something I could secure the tire with. The man came up with eight stainless steel hose clamps in his garage, refused any money, and on we went.

Dane and Rhonda had a good time, seeing and being seen by their friends. After about seven miles their parents picked them up and Carter and I continued. I knew we were getting close to the

Mississippi but when we topped a hill and rounded a bend I wasn't ready for a sign saying "Dubuque 2". I could see the city and in front of the city was the mighty Mississippi. The bridge was wide and solid and lightly traveled. Carter crossed without incident.

10

Cooperative Innovation—Iowa

The country needs and, unless I mistake its temper, the country demands bold, persistent experimentation. It is common sense to take a method and try it. If it fails, admit it frankly and try another. But above all, try something.

—President Franklin D. Roosevelt

Now in Iowa, we had to wait for a one year old dog racing track's parking lot to empty but then went down to a park next to the river. It was wet, cool and windy and if I wasn't so pleased at having reached the Mississippi, I'd have been miserable.

I fired up a new gas burner which I had purchased in an effort to use "appropriate technology" and to avoid using the 500 watt electric coffeemaker that seemed to be defeating the best efforts of the PV's. With endless clouds, the battery never had an opportunity to recharge. Nevertheless, as I savored the hot coffee, a car drove up. Since we were some ways off of the park road I thought that I was in for some "touristy" sorts. What I found instead were Bill and Mary Foley and their uncle Ralph.

Bill's father was a captain on the steamboats, the Mississippi Queen and the Delta Queen, and the Foley's had spent the last week on their annual vacation with their father and mother, traveling on the Mississippi Queen. They were visiting their Dubuque uncle while waiting to continue later that day to their home near Moline, Illinois. They were curious and had come over to say hi.

I asked if they happened to have any 2¹/₂ inch stainless steel clamps with them. The clamps from the previous day had only lasted about ten miles before they wore through. Not surprisingly, they didn't, but they offered to give me a ride into Dubuque to see if we could find some.

Years before when I had canoed down the Mississippi, someone had stolen my knife from the canoe when I had stopped in Dubuque to buy a loaf of bread. Hmm-m-m? I asked if it would be safe to leave my things unprotected in the buggy, not to mention Carter. They said, "This is Dubuque, it'll be O.K." I wasn't sure that I agreed with their logic, but decided to throw caution to the wind. Besides, what choice did I have?

We stopped several places before finding a lumber yard that stocked the clamps. After finding out that each clamp sold for $1.24, I ventured an explanation of my situation and boldly asked for a discount. I ended up paying 55¢ each for the three dozen clamps in stock. Was I lucky or making my luck? I thought about it but decided I didn't care, I had the clamps.

Back at the undisturbed buggy an hour later, I began to put the clamps on the wheel. The Foleys left only to return with Bill's dad and mom and after going through my story again, Bill said that if I made it to their place in Andalusia, Illinois 90 miles away, they would give me a ride to Kolona, Iowa where there was an Amish community. Perhaps we could get the wheel repaired there. I said thanks and we said goodbye.

Carter and I left the following morning, driving in cold rain, enjoying neither the weather nor the impatient traffic of the city. We reached the southern edge of Dubuque where the road out of town was steep, blind and fast. I procrastinated and stopped to replace some of the deteriorating clamps. A woman named Peggy walked up and said, "Do you give rides?"

Without looking up, very concerned about the dangerous road ahead of us, I said, "Nope."

Then I looked up and felt bad. Peggy stood there with her 3-year-old son. I explained my concern about the busy roads and some of the drivers' impatience.

"Follow me. I can show you how to avoid the bad roads," she said.

By 4:30 we were out of the city and Iowa began to look like Iowa should. I could tell I was in Io-way, as the locals say, because there were isolated cornstalks literally growing on the shoulder of the road.

By 5 o'clock the wind began to blow hard and cold, and when it reached 6:20 the sun was very low in a black and overcast sky. I stopped at a farm—no one at home. I drove on to the next one, up a big hill, down the other side and saw some kids in the yard. I stopped to ask the kids about a place to camp.

One of the boys ran inside to ask his dad. He returned and said, "Dad said sure, pull into the barn."

I put Carter at one end and positioned the buggy in the other. It felt good to be out of the lousy wind. I was cold in spite of having on a down vest, T-shirt, hooded sweatshirt, hat, Insulite boots and overalls.

The kids got Carter some hay, his first since I had run out the night before. I went inside to meet the family and have a burger, fries, coffee and wine. My photo and story had appeared in the day's Telegraph Herald so the Larry Sawvel family knew about me already. The family consisted of Larry, his wife, 9th grade Cory, 6th grade Kevin, and 4th grade Jeff. Larry's 86-year-old mother also lived with them in their rented farm house.

Larry was about my age and a disabled Vietnam veteran. He spent most of his life, not farming, but returning to VA hospitals. While he was in Vietnam he had been exposed to Agent Orange and it sounded like he was slowly, painfully and courageously dying. Too often it seemed that justice didn't prevail when the expense got "too big." It happened everyday to the people exposed to Agent Orange in Vietnam or in Washington state or in Kansas. Larry's medical treatment was being provided, but his life was ruined.

The next morning Kevin and Jeff came into the barn where I was sleeping in the buggy to invite me in for breakfast. Snowflakes had been seen the night before in Des Moines and the air was cold as I went in to a warm family breakfast.

After breakfast, Larry's wife brought over some drawings by

Kevin. They dripped with talent. Kevin reacted by saying that he hated to draw. I grew self righteous and told him, "You have a wonderful talent. Love it." If Kevin listened, then perhaps I would have served my purpose in life.

More courage surfaced with Jeff who had written about his experience of being severely burned as a 5-year-old. As a 6-year-old child he had written an article about the experience with unusual insight and an unbelievably stiff upper lip. He remained scarred, but cheerful and fun loving.

The school bus came and the kids left, but not before getting two bales of hay for us to take along. Larry and I walked back to the barn and he told me that he had received a Dear John letter from his first wife while in Vietnam. He said that he hid his emotions from his boys. It seemed clear that he thought it only a matter of time and that he was thankful that his boys would have a guaranteed education.

By 9:30 a.m. we were gone. Even though it was cool and windy, getting only as warm as 57 degrees, it was a good day because it was drying out. The rain had quit. Not for long.

It rained everyday we were in Iowa. Rain clouds hid the sun and the weakness of the photovotaics was apparent. No sun meant limited radio and no crock pot use. What juice remained in the battery had to be saved for the flashing lights.

The wind was cold and gusting to 40 knots as we approached Dewitt, Iowa. In addition to five layers of clothes, I had a wool blanket draped over my legs and a plastic raincoat over that. Puddles of water gathered on the raincoat as the rain came through the opening in front. Without a windshield wiper the windshield had to be left in the open position just to see. It was a bummer.

It was a day in the trenches of horse and buggy travel. Highway 61 was infested with semi's and as they passed the buggy would shake. I seriously wondered just how much harder the wind would have to blow before the buggy blew over. I was chilled to the bone and stopped Carter under an overpass to fire up the propane cooker. When it rains it pours and I discovered that the gas canister was as low as the battery. It took 50 minutes to perk some coffee, and about ten before it cooled enough to drink. All the while Carter stood still in the cold rain.

The coffee break helped to warm the bones but I remained cramped inside the buggy. Hours later a man in a $100,000 John Deere tractor drove out to the road to say hi. We talked for a bit and then he invited me to camp at his place. By this time it was after 6 o'clock and getting dark fast. We were still two miles from Dewitt and my hope was to stay near the town so I could insure myself a restaurant or some commercial place to warm myself. I declined the invitation and pushed on.

It was dark by the time I found the 4-H fairgrounds near downtown Dewitt and received permission to spend the night. I drove Carter and buggy into one of the livestock buildings, narrowly missing the roof with the PV's top. In fact, with Carter already under the roof I had to reach up with one hand and unhook the two bales of hay and throw them off while holding Carter still with the reins in the other hand. There were no walls, but there were stalls and a roof, and I felt relieved just to be off the road and out of the weather.

Once Carter was fed and watered and with our home for the evening covered in darkness, I grabbed a book and walked the mile or so into downtown Dewitt. When I reached Main Street, only a block from a warm, lighted and dry restaurant, a car drove up with three well dressed men inside. The passenger in the front seat was Joe Hatch, and Joe rolled down his window and said, "Hey, we'd like to talk to you. You're interesting. Can we talk with you for a bit?"

They parked their car and we got a booth in the restaurant. They were returning from some sort of civic meeting and told me to order whatever I wanted. I ordered a bowl of hot chili, hot french fries and hot coffee. As we had driven into Dewitt, Joe was one of the people I had asked directions from.

After going through my oft-repeated story, I learned that Pete was a local realtor, Arj was an old man, knowledgeable about co-ops, and Joe was the manager of the senior citizen's center. We had talked for about an hour when Gary Beck walked in. Gary was about 37 years old, dressed in a Boy Scout uniform and fresh from a Boy Scout meeting. He was also the branch manager of Eastern Iowa Light and Power Co-op, with headquarters on Main Street. Gary sat down and joined our discussion.

Dewitt impressed me as an All-American sort of place with a lot of civic pride and a population of 4,512. These men liked their town. They were proud of it and what they had done for themselves. After a second bowl of chili, everyone went their separate ways. Joe offered to show me their senior citizen's housing project. I readily accepted.

As Joe showed me through Dewitt's senior center and I saw how the people had cooperated and innovated, I felt bad that the cooperatives hadn't already started to expand their relevancy. But I felt good that the idea was realizable. Joe Hatch and friends had done it without an organized or funded organization. The co-ops could do it too, if the will existed.

Maybe the electric cooperatives will be phased out, not so much by any administration in Washington, but by the co-ops themselves. Cooperatives are formed to serve needs. Needs change with time. Like any business if cooperatives fail to address the changing needs of its membership, they will die.

Before leaving Dewitt the next morning I made phone calls to the Davenport police and State Police about crossing the Mississippi River from Iowa into Illinois. The answers I received weren't encouraging. Both said no to providing an escort across the bridge. Both said I could cross either of the bridges, providing I maintained 40 m.p.h. They were serious!

The rear tire remained held on by clamps which wore out every ten miles. Carter had a loose shoe, the bridges were busy due to one bridge being closed for repairs, and here it was, almost October and our goal of Tennessee by November was more than 500 miles away. As we left Dewitt I wondered how we were ever going to get across the river.

Thirteen miles later I met a retired farmer, Lawrence Schult. He called a few neighbors and arranged to borrow a horse trailer for the next day. He would take me across. That night we pushed the buggy into Lawrence's truck and I slept in the buggy.

The next morning, before loading Carter into the trailer, Lawrence called Al Schnekloth, another neighbor. Al came over and brought a few shoeing nails with him and tightened Carter's loose shoe. Then he told me to hop into his truck and he'd show me a couple of horses. We drove a few miles to his family's ranch. Here the Schnekloth's had some of the finest Belgian horses in the world. Finest also meant biggest. There were young ones and old ones, big ones and—no small ones. Carter was a large horse at 1475 pounds, with his head well above my own 6'1" when he stood up tall. Schnekloth's horses towered over me. Most of them weighed well over a full ton!

When I returned from the Schnekloth tour I led Carter into the trailer. In less than an hour we drove across the river to the Foley's place in Andalusia, Illinois and unloaded. No one was home. I put Carter on a picket line and went down to the river to watch it flow.

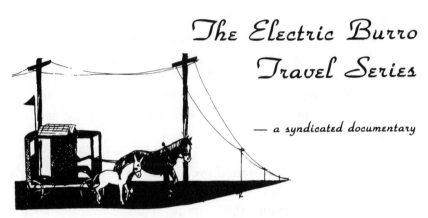

The Electric Burro
Travel Series

— a syndicated documentary

"WAGONS RO-O-OLL - WAGONS WHOA"

Twelve weeks on the road through the great American Mid-west, our trip has taken us 662 miles. We have gone through 14 RE co-op's areas and two states and have eight weeks remaining before we expect to reach Tennessee. As colder weather approaches, Carter is in supurb condition and our daily average is up to about 18 miles per day, our record is 23 miles. The style of travel has evolved for the good, now allowing for exercise as I walk for about half the day, driving alongside the buggy. This helps Carter, especially while going up or down hill, and helps me by giving me exercise. Depending on road, weather, and horse conditions we usually travel 6 - 9 hours. Besides allowing for plenty of horse talk, the hours on the road at 3 m.p.h. give opportunity for thought.

One thought that came along was the 1960's TV western, "Wagon Train". Remember the program with Ward Bond as wagonmaster, which started with the old man shouting, "Wagons Ro-o-oll"? At the end of one of our hourly breaks from walking I thought I'd play wagonmaster and called out, "Wagons Ro-o-oll", expecting Carter to take off like the wagons did in the program. I had included the drawl like Ward Bond used to do and it sounded like "Wagons Whoa" and Carter just stood there! I had meant to go, but my 1500 pound pony heard otherwise. A breakdown in communication had occured.

As this trip clip clops along I often reflect on just what it is that I am doing. It is meant to be a commemoration of the 50 years of the REA program. Surely any effort at acknowledging the past should also address the future and so I find myself looking down the road, say for the next 50 years. Lets look at a few facts and see if we might glean some direction.

*** Most Americans alive in 1985 were not alive when FDR said REA.

*** Technology and knowledge are changing faster than ever before and the rate of change is only going to increase. If you have seen the world come from a horse and buggy era to one of the space shuttle and computers and think that that is incredible, stick around for the second act!

*** The rural area now served by RECs now has twice as many retired people as it has farmers. Not the case in 1935.

*** The majority of Americans expect electric service; it has become a necessity.

One thing that surfaces again and again as we travel the co-op countryside is the unique spirit that existed as REA first got off the ground. People were doing for themselves, hand in hand with the government. There are many people in the REC program that know this better than anyone because they lived it. The only way to have such a special cooperative spirit is for the members to be aware that co-ops are serving their needs.

One way to revitalize our rural electric cooperatives would be to reach out and address our existing needs. Our imaginations are our only limits. Why not turn our energies towards the seniors among us? Our population is getting older. Federal and state funds for senior housing are being cutback when they are most needed. By becoming involved in CFC's Associate Member program most any REC could build their own senior citizen's complex, let's say 100 units. Look at the benefits! The co-op would be directly involved in economic development. The co-op would be helping to ease the almost universal multi-year waiting list that exists at most such housing projects. By insisting on state-of-the-art building methods and materials we could demonstrate to members "how-to" build efficiently. Load management procedures could be built in, before the fact. We would be addressing the needs not only of the seniors but their children, who are us.

As IOU"s agitate for an expanded market and prowl the countryside in takeover bids, it seems to be important for us to revalidate our existence, to work to breathe renewed life and cooperative spirit into our neighborhoods. Our strength certainly lies in our democratic base, in our doing for ourselves. Cooperative education has its place and is important, but if we are to be sure that our "Wagons Roll" cry is heard as it is meant to be and that our neighbors are not hearing "Wagons Whoa", then we need to grow. The REA program spoke for itself in the 30's and 40's, no educational program was needed. People believed in their own program and through continued efforts to help ourselves that spirit will speak for itself.

Once upon a time people scoffed at farmers running an electric company. It was said that they didn't have the ability. Likewise we don't have the ability to build a large senior citizen's housing project. Reminds me of something that Charles Lindbergh said before he flew across the Atlantic, "How can I do, why should I dare, what others, more experienced and influential, have either failed to do or not attempted"?

Copyright — 1985
The Electric Burro Travel Series — Column #5
Scott Hudson

(NOTE: As of September 15, 1985 Carter and the buggy are 6 miles north of Boscobel, Wisconsin and the Wisconsin River. Goals are Cape Giroudeau, Missouri by Oct. 12 and Memphis, TN by Nov. 11.)

Sample column from the Electric Burro Travel Series

11

Good Samaritans—Illinois

"And who is my neighbor?"

Jesus replied and said, "A certain man was going down from Jerusalem to Jericho; and he fell among robbers, and they stripped him and beat him, and went off leaving him half dead.

And by chance a certain priest was going down on that road, and when he saw him, he passed by on the other side.

And likewise a Levite also, when he came to the place and saw him, passed by on the other side.

But a certain Samaritan, who was on a journey, came upon him; and when he saw him, he felt compassion, and came to him, and bandaged up his wounds, pouring oil and wine on them; and he put him on his own beast, and brought him to an inn, and took care of him.

And on the next day he took out two denarii and gave them to the innkeeper and said, 'Take care of him; and whatever more you spend, when I return, I will repay you.'

Which of these three do you think proved to be a neighbor to the man who fell into the robbers' hands?"

And he said, "The one who showed mercy toward him."

And Jesus said to him, "Go and do the same."

It was Friday afternoon and when Bill and Mary returned home they asked if I wanted to try and get the wheel repaired that day. I did, so we went inside and Mary made phone calls to many people, asking if they knew of any Amish carriage maker in Kolona, Iowa. She managed to find one person who gave vague directions to someone who might know who to ask when we got closer. Kolona was 50 miles away. Soon we had the bad wheel off the buggy and in the back of Bill's truck and were on our way.

When we reached Kolona we turned off the main road onto a dirt road per our directions. We passed barefoot Amish school children on their way home from school. There were crews of men dressed in black and white working in the fields with a steel wheeled tractor. We pulled alongside an Amishman in his buggy trotting a very sweaty horse. He stopped and I asked if he could help us find the carriage maker. He filled in the missing blanks in our directions and by 5 o'clock we pulled into Tobe Yoder's drive.

There was a man parking a large tractor with rubber tires. As we pulled up, he jumped off the tractor and said hello. It was Tobe. I told him my problem and he sort of nodded and said that yes, he could fix my tire. Tobe had an Amish sort of hat on, like a Swiss yodeler's hat. He had a beard, trimmed on the cheeks, and no mustache. About 40, his eyes were clear and full of sparkle. It was the sparkle in the eyes that spoke loudest to me about the Amish, the same sort of sparkle that I usually associate with innocent children. It wasn't just Tobe either, but most of the Amish I met.

Tobe led the three of us into his shop and it was obvious that he worked on buggy and tractor wheels. The hub and spokes of my wheel were made of hickory. The rim was steel. The hard rubber tire was solid, with a length of steel wire running through the middle. What puzzled me was that the rubber was a full 6″ longer than the circumference of the wheel. When it had come off I had tried to clamp the rubber back onto the rim, but had to cut 6″ off so that it wouldn't overlap.

Tobe took the rubber and wheel to a special machine that compressed the rubber and allowed the metal in the middle to be brazed together. By tapping the wire Tobe knew when it was tight enough—not sophisticated at all, yet coupled with experience, as sophisticated as the space shuttle. It took ten minutes.

Bill asked if Tobe would mind if he took his picture. Tobe said that he did.

I asked what he attributed the plight of the American farmer to. No sooner had I asked the question than I realized it was a poor question since Amish were also farmers and Americans, and they prospered. Tobe was thoughtful and polite. He said it was a combination of high interest rates and expensive machinery—that a $100,000 machine was worn out before it could be paid for.

Tobe and his wife were interested in my trip and asked many questions as we prepared to leave. One thing they did not seem interested in was the PV electric setup. I looked for wisdom in their non-electric approach to life as I prepared to continue my trip commemorating rural electrification. Tobe's wife commented that the Foley's were good Samaritans. Wisdom.

It so happened that it was the first day of the annual Kolona Historical Days, a weekend of baked goods, homemade ice cream, and equipment displays set up in downtown Kolona. Basically the Amish and Mennonites used the occasion to mix with Englishmen and to do business.

I appreciated the library which was staffed and open for the occasion. I learned that the Amish and the Mennonites had common roots and that there were several orders throughout the world, with most in the United States. Photographs were scorned by some orders based on the Bible's dictates of no idol worship. Mustaches weren't allowed due to their historical relationship with the military. Some orders believed that rubber on wheels was a temptation to use vehicles for pleasure.

About the time Martin Luther was leading his revolt against the Roman Church, the Anabaptists were born in Switzerland in 1525. From the Anabaptists came the Mennonites and the Amish. There was a story dating back to 1569 when the Anabaptists were widely persecuted. A man named Dirk Willems was being chased by the sheriff who wanted to arrest him because of his faith. Dirk crossed the ice over a river and as the sheriff followed, the ice broke and the sheriff fell in. Dirk turned around and pulled the sheriff to safety. The sheriff then arrested Dirk, the man who had just saved his life. Dirk was burned at the stake.

The Amish paid taxes, but were exempt from paying into the Social Security fund, not because they didn't want to pay into it but because they didn't want to receive from it. The origin of these people's teachings was the Bible and when it says in Galatians 6:2, "Bear one another's burdens," they meant to live their faith. When they appeared before Congress for special consideration from the Social Security Act, what they sought was the right to look after their own elderly, not to have the government do it for them.

Returning that night to the Foley's, we called around for a farrier and managed to find one who could make it out the next day. I spent the night in a king size bed in Foley's basement, complete with my own shower.

The next day at 10 a.m. Ladd Moering came out with his wife to take off Carter's shoes, apply new borium, and to put them back on. Ladd was about 21, tall and thin, and had worked as a farrier's apprentice for two years rather than go to jail for some problem. He was still seeking a regular horseshoeing job but until he could find one he was working full time at a Dunkin' Donuts.

Carter wasn't cooperative and Ladd was plenty flustered. After a trip into town to pick up some Bondo for Carter's poorly trimmed hooves (thanks to Ladd), and with me holding onto a reluctant Carter, the job was finished by 3 p.m. Five hours to complete the job—the road was postponed another day.

While Ladd and I were attending to Carter, Bill and a friend replaced the wheel on the buggy, discovering that the reason why the rubber was wearing so poorly on the left rear was because the round bearing had been mashed onto the square axle without any consideration for doing a proper job. I thought back to when I had picked up the buggy in Canada and recalled the extra set of bearings I had been given. Now, more than 800 miles later, I knew why.

The following day dawned beautiful. After breakfast with Bill and Mary, it was time to travel for the first time in my mother's home state. Bill and Mary were so easy to be with, I felt that I was leaving family.

For the next ten days as we traversed Illinois, we traveled a record average of 19 miles per day. That was the good news. The bad news was that I wasn't to have another shower until Missouri.

There began to be frost warnings at night and when I rinsed the soap from my head after shampooing, it would go numb.

That evening we pulled into the first place to appear in a long while. It happened to be a hog farm. It began to rain. Doris and Merle Hyett were just about to sit down to eat when I drove up and knocked on their door. By now I had extended my faith to the extent that even in the driveway of a pig farm I would wrap the reins around the rear view mirror on the right side of the buggy and hope that Carter would stand.

Merle was 67 and he came outside. After a few questions he helped me get Carter settled in one end of a tractor garage. Then I readied the buggy for sleep and closed it up for the rain. Just as I was recording the day's events, Doris came out and invited me in for supper.

Over supper and apple pie purchased in Kolona the same day I had been there, I learned that Merle had been an M.P. in World War II, guarding B-29's in India and later on Tinnian, the A-bomb island. He was on Tinnian during preparation for that first terrible bomb. As for my trip, Merle volunteered his belief that it was my mode of transportation that opened so many doors for me.

Doris worked for the Argus newspaper and she promised to get a reporter out the next day. As the trip progressed interviews became an almost daily occurrence, sometimes more. As much as the intent of the trip was to spread the word about REA and the good job done by cooperatives, I felt that it wasn't natural to have such a one way meeting. Not only were the interviews too self centered for my liking, but I was bored by telling the same story so many times.

It was raining hard when I went out to my buggy that night. 38 degrees. The next morning I got up by 7, fed Carter half a bale of hay and was invited in for coffee. Coffee became eggs, toast, coffee, and an interview with the Argus reporter, and a chance to meet the kids and grandkids. I met their son, Al and learned that his first wife had been murdered while teaching at school. He had remarried but I thought of Merle's statement the previous night, that it was my mode of transportation that opened doors for me. I saw some truth in what he said, but thought that there was more to it than that. When I had knocked on their door, I had been a total stranger. Carter might open hearts, but people opened doors.

After pictures, goodbyes, and thank yous, the wheels were rolling. It was cool but the rain had stopped. The first six miles were on a gravel road with some real sharp stones. I wished I knew more about horses' feet. Even with shoes and Borium calks, did these sharp stones hurt Carter? He didn't seem to be bothered, but I couldn't understand why they wouldn't cut the frog of his foot.

We came to the little town of Seaton. With a 20 m.p.h. wind and temperatures around 40, I was ready for something hot. It was noon when I pulled in front of THE restaurant in town and hoped for attention. It only took a minute before a waitress came out and took my order for "something hot." She suggested hot chocolate. I said, "How about a burger and fries?" She went inside while Carter and I waited on Main Street. Soon she returned with a large hot chocolate to tide me over while waiting. As we waited seven men came over and we talked. They knew of a bridge out ahead and said that I'd be better off if I changed my direction from east to west, away from busy roads under repair, toward the more lightly traveled roads closer to the river. Before long the girl brought out my burger with a triple order of hot fries, plus a hot cherry cobler—all for about $2. We turned around.

Harvest was in full swing and there was activity everywhere. People were in the fields, driving trucks and tractors, and operating grain elevators. There was a good feeling in the air.

We were stopped for the first time by police on US–34 west of Gladstone, leading to the bridge across the Mississippi into Burlington, Iowa. It was rush hour and the road had no shoulder. I felt bad about slowing traffic but had little choice. We were proceeding along when an Illinois Highway Patrol car turned on its flashers behind me. I wasn't too concerned about being illegal but I was concerned that he chose such a bad place to stop anyone. The cop was simply curious, that's all. It turned out to be good actually. I wasn't sure where the turnoff was to the Great River Road and the patrolman gave me directions, "Turn left at the next road."

We arrived at the Great River Road and it was lightly traveled, but also old and slick from accumulated rubber. Once, as I was driving and walking, Carter slipped and went down on his front knees. My feet automatically adjusted, skipping to catch my balance, as if it might help Carter. I felt bad for Carter, but he was alright. I could not separate Carter's fortune from my own.

One day we found ourselves near sunset and in the middle of nowhere, that is, in the middle of a bunch of cornfields. Having just climbed a long hill I pulled over and waited for a large tractor to get to our end of a row so I could ask where we might stay.

The man on the tractor was 26 years old and his name was Mike. Something seemed strange, something didn't fit. Most farmers I ran into spoke with the authority that comes from the land, from making their own decisions and being their own boss. This time, however, Mike said he didn't care. He didn't say if I could camp, nor did he say where I should camp, he just said he didn't care. I pointed to a hill off the road, under a large tree and asked if it would be okay to park my buggy there. "Yeah, that's O.K." was his reply.

So I did what I had suggested to him. I tied Carter to a picket line and went about the chores of getting things settled for the night—bringing the oats and water out from the rear seat, putting up the mosquito netting on the rear doors, putting the back to the front seat down to form the bed, unrolling the sleeping bags and putting the warm Insulite bag inside the cheap nylon bag. The usual.

I prepared a gourmet meal of peanut butter and jelly on rye as Mike finished up one field and drove over to where I was parked. He asked if I wanted to ride along with him. I asked how long he would be working and if I could ride a little later, after I finished some notes. He said that he'd be working till he finished all of the fields, till about midnight. Whenever I wanted to join him would be fine.

About an hour later, the headlights were on and I climbed up into the sound proofed cab of the $35,000 John Deere to share the large seat. Mike's job was to plow the cornstalks under with the $14,000 plow. As we rode along, Mike adjusted the stereo and offered me a beer. Then he reached back and slid open the rear window and tossed out an empty beer can. We watched as it was plowed under with the stalks. Mike got a big charge out of plowing under his beer cans. That night I drank three beers with Mike. He had started with a twelve pack and by the time we were done, all twelve were planted.

Mike claimed to be a farmer, though most of the time he worked as a drywaller. He had done contract farming since 1979 and he liked the job of being a "farmer" because he could put up drywall in the daytime, and then come out to the farm and drive the tractor during the night. He especially liked it because no one hassled him and he could just do his job and catch a good buzz while making extra money. Mike lived in town and wasn't from a farm or a farm family. His favorite pastime was cocaine. If he hadn't told me, I would have guessed that his favorite pastime was plowing beer cans under.

By 11 p.m. Mike was finished with the fields he had been assigned and we drove over to the farm house where Scott and Jim were playing Gin Rummy and drinking beer. They were also so-called "contract farmers." As we came in Jim got up to cook some eggs and sausage. We played cards for an hour and then the "farmers" said that they needed to get some sleep. Their supervisor was visiting from Davenport the next morning and they needed to get things ready for him.

I wondered at these "farmers" and the changes they represented. I knew that the percentage of farmers in rural areas had been declining for years and that the population was an increasingly mixed bag. I thought of the efforts in Washington to privatize the economy and as I looked around me I felt that the strengths of rural America and decentralization were being sacrificed and ignored for wrong reasons.

If public power projects like the Tennessee Valley Authority and the Hoover Dam were sold off to the highest private bidders, as was proposed, then the cost of living in rural areas would go up. What kind of argument could possibly stand that would allow private concerns to make short term profit at the long term expense of the entire country? The first to be hit would be the countryside. Should quality of life be defined by the bottom line, or was there something more important to be gained by allowing the population to spread out?

Mike's state of Illinois had lost 19% of the number of farm operations it had only six years earlier. While it might be Mike's state, by no means did he represent the farmer or values of old. Mike was an employee of one of the big conglomerates that were replacing the small family farmer. If the expense of doing business in rural America was allowed to go up and up, were we doomed to having the farmers of America replaced by "contract farmers" putting in their time like the person on the assembly line, getting high to get by?

Mike gave me a ride back to the buggy in his 1975 Pontiac. The window was broken in the down position. It was 44 degrees. When we got to the buggy we sat in Mike's car and talked for another hour. Mike wanted to know why I had musical eighth notes on the rear of my buggy next to the "serious sign." The serious sign was the REA 50th anniversary logo. In more then 900 miles, Mike was the first person to ask what the music notes were all about.

I explained that it had to do with an attempt at balance. The music notes represented lightheartedness. I tried to explain about the electric cooperatives and why I believed that they had been so good for so many people. In the same breath I tried to say that while soapboxes had their place, life was very short, and it was important to have fun.

Mike invited me to spend the night at his place. He said that we could "get wasted," plus I could stay warm and have a shower in the morning. The thought of a shower was compelling but I wasn't interested in partying. Mike was friendly but I thanked him and said goodnight.

The next day was brisk and as we pulled into Lima, population 166, we were greeted by Maggie Thomas of TV10 from Quincy, Illinois. I talked with her for about an hour and felt sorry for her as she stood outside of the buggy in a very cool breeze. Her lips were shivering. I invited her inside the buggy to get out of the cool breeze but she preferred to interview while standing outside.

I felt two good things about the TV interview. One, it would serve to spread the word about REA and cooperatives. Two, Mag-

gie Thomas, well known local TV personality, was very pleasant
and fun to talk with. She was nothing more and nothing less than
a normal sort of person and it was nice to meet someone who
handled her achievement and recognition as no big deal.

I questioned the very powerful media drug of television. Instant
recognition. Associated credibility. But like a relationship, fame
was so much easier to achieve than to shed. How many people
reached for the brass ring of renown without ever thinking just
what it might mean?

The TV10 interview helped us out right away. As we entered
Quincy, population 42,000, it was apparent that we were in a big
city. In fact, we were trapped in the city with the sun sinking fast.
Asking around I was told to check at the fire station. There was a
park behind the fire station—maybe we could stay there.

We pulled up to the station and asked permission from a couple
of hard waiting firemen. As they called for the park ranger on the
police band radio, Carter and I waited for permission, which I
expected to receive based on the theory of trusting in luck. We
watched a dozen kids having a birthday celebration in the park,
but when the kids discovered us I began to think that a night in
the city park might be less than relaxing.

Thirty minutes went by and the sun went down. What was
taking so long? Just then, Kerry Maxwell drove up. He had heard
the firemen calling for the park ranger on a police band and then
had seen us on TV. He drove over to the park to offer us a place to
stay behind Maxwell's Roofing. With car headlights on and no
more sun, I couldn't wait any longer and for thirty minutes we
traveled back through the city. All pavement, no shoulders and no
lights. Ugh! As we moved through the city streets, a mile now from
the park, the park ranger drove up to say we couldn't use the
park. He was sorry but rules were rules. Thanks pal.

Kerry's kindness overshadowed any ugh. He opened his two
story business building as I tied Carter out to graze in a field
behind the building.

The next day was Sunday and warm and sunny. Kerry had told
me not to be in any hurry, so we relaxed there for half a day. I
walked to a grocery store to buy film and a pound of salt for
Carter. While I stood in the checkout line I couldn't help but
notice the guy in front of me. After several glances my way, the

man asked me if I was the guy he had just seen on TV. So that was it! I told him I hadn't seen it but that I was the one. He wished me luck. Said he remembered REA coming to his house as a kid.

It was noon before we got under way that Sunday, and the idea was to get out of town before busy Monday. I was surprised at the friendliness of literally almost every other car. It seemed everyone was waving and wishing us luck. Whew—the power of TV!

I wondered just what had been said by Maggie Thomas in her interview because I couldn't believe how extra friendly people seemed to be. I was pleased that people seemed to be picking up on some of the details about the "why" of the trip. One man offered, "You're going overseas next, right?" and a 13-year-old boy said, "Something about electricity and you're 52 years old." Their facts weren't entirely straight but they obviously learned something about our "why."

While traveling close to the Mississippi River, I sought the flood plains, the area along the river where the land is flatter. That area shifted with the bends of the river, one mile being on the Missouri side, the next twenty miles being on the Illinois side. With seemingly endless hills I couldn't wait to get to flat land. The decision seemed to be either stay in Illinois and deal with shallow hills and no shoulder, or cross into Missouri and get good shoulders but heavy duty hills.

These decisions and daily details of horse and buggy travel were increasingly mixed with thoughts of international travel. If we ever made it to November, the idea was to travel outside of the USA and to deal with the relevancy of international cooperation. So as I steered Carter and the buggy to miss a wooly caterpillar on the pavement, or jumped into the moving buggy to change from a walking to a riding mode, I found myself thinking more and more about how to actually accomplish travel abroad. I was excited by the prospects, but also distanced from the thought by the total attention that everyday travel required.

I camped without permission for the first time on the trip when we were south of friendly Quincy and our local notoriety was at its highest. People were busy harvesting and were everywhere. However, as darkness approached we found ourselves amidst corn and beans and the only house within shooting distance was empty. There was no more hay, very little water, and an equal amount of oats. Exasperated by our situation and sincerely trying not to be staying anywhere without permission, I pulled off of Illinois 57 and between a corn and bean field. Once I got Carter tied and the buggy ready I walked back to the vacant farmhouse only to find it still empty. Back at the buggy I tried to read, but the 33 watt florescent light dimmed from an inadequately charged battery.

I heard a gun. It sounded like a machine gun, firing 20 rounds or so at one burst and the sound was coming from a wooded area in the rear of the same field. Oh boy, I could see it now! Some Neo-Nazi group was in the area and while I slept that night they would find me in their field without permission, and I would become a victim of their justice.

When the sun rose the next day, I was still alive. I wanted to get on the road fairly early because I expected farmers to be pulling into this field at any time since it was one of few not yet harvested. The day was a wonderful autumn day, sunny and sixty degrees. Shortly after starting we stopped at a farmhouse to get our water supply replenished. Then we traveled.

When we drove into quiet New Canton, population 400, I stopped and asked a lady about the location of a park I had been told about. A truck stopped with two women in it, then another. It was fantastic. People were bending over backwards to help me, yet the entire area was reeling from the devastated farm economy. Before I knew it Marvin and Candy Booker invited me to spend the night at their place just ahead.

It was good to get to Booker's place. It was better than staying in a public park and there was a pond and plenty of room for Carter to graze. Marv brought out a large bale of hay for the star of the show and another man who had seen us on the road dropped off two more.

That night I was inside with the Booker family and a couple of their friends. Candy and Marvin had been married for 18 years and had given up hope of ever having children, when they were surprised by the birth of their only child, Lore. Lore was a cute redhead and the apple of their eyes. Carter was the apple of Lore's eyes. Such a world!

It rained. Of the three bales of hay that we now had, only two had been covered from the rain, so one was soaked and heavy. Shortly after resuming travel, I pulled the heavy bale off at the bottom of an incline and left it on the side of the road. Anything to help Carter.

An hour later a truck pulled off the road ahead of us and the driver got out and pulled that same bale of hay out of his truck to return to us. He had seen it and assumed that it had fallen off the buggy. When I explained to him why I had left it, he asked if he could help us. I told him that we were out of oats. He said that he had some oats but that they were two years old and he used them for pig feed. He added that they weren't dusty and he could bring us some. Good deal!

Then he told me about a shortcut past Dutch Creek. He drove off and the rain began to fall again. We came to Dutch Creek and turned right towards the river. The road was gravel and we were nearing the "bottoms" which was another way of saying flood plains or flat.

The shortcut was a good one. Almost no traffic, and the gravel improved to good pavement. About five miles from where the man had tried to give us back our bale of hay, he showed up again. This time he brought with him about 50 pounds of usable oats. He also brought a styrofoam container with dinner of hot turkey, dressing and gravy, mashed potatoes, cole slaw, corn and hot coffee. The lunch made my day as the rain continued to fall.

An hour after having my day made by the hot meal it was made again when we suddenly came to Pike, Illinois and the bridge over the Mississippi leading into Louisiana, Missouri. Without stopping to worry about it, and skipping our hourly break, we kept going.

It was a narrow two lane bridge with lots of overhead bridgework that could bother Carter. As we were going across and before we got to the superstructure there was only a 3 foot high railing between the road and the Mississippi. I concentrated on Carter, watching him closely, keeping the reins tight. I started playing "what if. . . ?" and thought of what might happen if Carter did panic and jump over the railing. Could I grab the knife and cut him free of the harness. Would I have time to grab the camera or computer? Would anything even matter? I remembered hearing on the local radio that morning about a 22-year-old man that had killed himself by jumping off the Hannibal bridge to the north just last night. I paid even stricter attention. Just then a semi-tractor trailer came onto the bridge behind us.

The bridge shook. If he tried to pass us, would there be enough room? As I tightened my grip on the reins, he began to pass. If that wasn't enough, just as he got to us he blared his horn. Nice guy. Even nicer, but for real, was the angel in front of me. Carter never missed a beat and we entered our 5th state, the Show-Me state of Missouri.

12

An All White Sparrow
—North Missouri

The nomadic instinct is a human instinct; it was born with Adam and transmitted through the patriarchs, and after thirty centuries of steady effort, civilization has not educated it entirely out of us yet. It has a charm which, once tasted, a man will yearn to taste again.

—Mark Twain, 1869

Missouri felt especially good. As it was, we were only ten miles shy of 1,000 miles but until now it didn't sound like much more than a day outing. WJR radio in Detroit had been following our progress on a monthly basis and they had asked us to call them October 9, which was tomorrow. If I had had to call from Illinois it would have sounded pretty weak. But Missouri—this was a different story. Missouri was the home of St. Louis and it was here where western exploration had historically had so many of its beginnings. To people in Michigan, Missouri sounded considerably more distant than did Wisconsin or Illinois. Iowa sounded respectable, but Missouri was better.

The first two miles west of Louisiana, Missouri were largely uphill but Carter didn't complain. When we got near the top of the large hill I saw a man stretching his legs, a Harley parked on the side of the road. He saw us and walked over, snapping our picture as he approached. The guy was dressed in full leathers. He had been on the road for the last four months and had left Denver yesterday. Wow, what a comparison. We had both been on the road for comparable times but he had traveled pretty much as far as our total in one day. He asked how much further until he got to the river and I told him only a couple of miles.

The biker biked and we walked. With only an hour or so until sunset US-54 was like an interstate with no homes anywhere. About that time who should pull in front of us but Marv, Candy and Lore. They brought us apples, a spare tube of grease, and their phone number. If we needed any help, call, and when I was ready to travel overseas and needed a place to leave Carter, they would be happy to pick him up and take care of him for me. Meanwhile, "What can we do to help you out now?" Marv asked.

Since I didn't have any idea where to look to spend the night, they drove ahead to check things out. Ten minutes later they returned saying there was a Baptist church a mile and two-fourths ahead. For the next three miles I tried to figure out what "two-fourths" meant. Had he meant 1.2 miles or $1^1/2$? And where was the church?

Finally we did come to Emmanuel Baptist Church and preacher James Bachman offered the yard behind their parsonage for us to camp in. That night I walked to an all night gas station about half a mile away to satisfy a chocolate jones. Both that night and the next morning when I returned to call the radio station, two different attendants asked if I had hitchhiked or walked—and they were serious! You could practically look across the field and see the buggy yet these people were amazed that I had walked so far.

Why would people think like that? There I was trying to gear up for travel to places that traveled at the speed of the human foot as a matter of everyday living, and two people in a row were surprised that someone would exert themselves in such a small way. As I walked back that night a few cars sped by. Was the best definition of life in the U.S.A.—55 m.p.h.? The speed of life said a lot about how things had changed in the last 50 or 100 or 5000 years.

When we left the church the next morning Carter walked tentatively. His shoes were worn and the shoulder was patched with tar in many places. Each step was a slippery chore and I had to constantly watch the road, steering away from the shiny spots.

On the outskirts of Bowling Green we came to a used car lot, with a sign saying that the dealer's name was Bill Betts. As a kid I had a friend named Billy Betts, but I had lost touch with him. Could this be him? We pulled over and as I learned that Bill was not Billy, several others gathered around. One was a reporter from the Bowling Green newspaper and by talking with her I was able to answer many questions that the small gathering would have asked. I was also able to ask if anyone knew of an Amish farrier for Carter. Since I had heard that there were Amish communities around Bowling Green, I didn't want to miss the opportunity to learn more about them.

One of the people saying hello was Sally Crofoot, the first to have stopped. Billy and Sally discussed Amish farriers and then Sally said that she would drive ahead to Country Classics, a place that repaired, constructed and sold carriages. They would know who could help. She told me how to get there and said that she would meet me there.

Carter and I arrived and I got a kick out of tying Carter to the hitching post in front of Country Classics. How long had the hitching post been gone from most corners of society? Another first. . . .

Ken Sisson and Ethel Worthington were expecting us. Ethel sold antiques in the front of the building while Ken made "new antiques" like wagons, stage coaches, chuck wagons, sleighs and buggies in the back. When I arrived I got a quick tour of the place and saw a large chuck wagon under construction in back. It was beautiful, sturdy and certainly built with lots of attention to detail. In another storage building Ken had more than a dozen vehicles waiting for refurbishment.

Sally offered to give me a ride to wherever we might have to go. Ken told Sally where Levi Schwartz lived and off we went in Sally's shockless van, with her 8 year old son, John, and their cockapoo, Suzie. Sally was about 40 and knew more than most about the Amish community. She used to be a "driver," giving rides to Amish people on a regular basis, and had helped to deliver at least one of their children. A job with no money for pay.

We drove along paved roads rutted by years of iron rimmed wheels. Sally told me that this was the worst of Amish country, in fact, the place where some were sent by church elders as punishment. The area did look poor. She pointed out an Amish store which looked like any Amish house might look. The school looked the same. The old pavement turned to rough dirt roads and we bumped across a creek several times as it snaked back and forth across the road. John had a wonderful sense of humor and helped to make a great trip even greater. It was clear that he had been with his mother for many of her trips into Amishland. He interrupted a shared laugh and pointed, "Look, a good sign!", and Sally and I turned to see an all white sparrow next to the creek. We smiled and agreed.

When we got to Levi's there were two men standing next to a red pickup, talking. We got out and I walked over to the couple and asked for Levi. The one man was obviously Amish, the other looked English. The Amish looking man pointed to "Red," an Englishman. Didn't sound right to me as I asked Red, "You're Levi?"

Red pointed to Levi. "Ha, Ha, Ha."

I waited until Levi recovered from his little joke and then told him that I was coming from Michigan and trying to get to Memphis in another month. My horse needed new shoes. He had no difficulty with the shoes but he couldn't quite believe the part about 1001 miles already traveled. He told me that Drill-Tex was better than Borium—that it wore better and didn't slip. Red had just had eight shoes Drill-texed. I told Levi that I had had one calk of one shoe built up with Drill-tex in Wisconsin but that it hadn't seemed to wear too good. Levi replied that the Drill-tex he had was a new type of Drill-tex. He had a little bit left.

Levi went inside and brought out Missouri and Kentucky/Tennessee maps. He was more interested in my trip than doing the shoes for my absent horse. St. Louis was the place to avoid. There would be hills, even big ones, but The City was the problem. Levi thought aloud, "Some of our people have taken long trips, up north of Hannibal." I didn't say a thing. Hannibal was about 40 miles away.

An older man appeared with a team of six horses abreast. Four of them were Belgians, two were half Belgians. Levi asked if I'd like to see them and I said yes. We walked over to them. The other man seemed to defer to Levi. Levi told him which wheat field to work. As they stood there Levi asked me if my horse was as big. I said probably not. These guys were BIG. As they drove off he said, "Lot of horsepower there, lot of horsepower there."

We walked back to the others and somehow age was brought up. Red was 70. "How old do you think I am?" Levi asked.

Levi had plenty of grey and looked 60 or more so I said, "Oh, you might be pushing 54." Levi said 37! Was he pulling my leg? Sally thought not.

Sally needed to return home, so two hours after arriving at Levi's, we began to talk about whether or not Levi could help me. Levi said that he would put new shoes with Drill-tex on if I brought my horse back the next day.

"We'll be here," I said, happy to have been with the Schwartz family.

"Look—John is in his glory," Sally pointed over to the house where young John was talking with a woman.

As we were driving back into town, I asked him what he thought of the Amish. He said that he liked them because no one was getting killed on three wheelers or with cars, and that there was lots to do living on the farm.

Back at Country Classics, Carter was standing quietly at the hitching post. Ken and I went looking for permission to spend the night at the VFW rodeo grounds a third of a mile away. As we drove Ken told me that he could build a copy of my buggy for $1200. I said I doubted that if I actually ordered one from him that the price would remain so low. He insisted he could do it for that.

That night was enjoyable as I spent the night at the fairgrounds. Sally and her boyfriend and two kids visited and then Ken dropped by with a huge bowl of chili and sandwiches. Darkness fell but floodlights came on next to us and the local trap shooting club appeared for about three hours of shooting. I was surprised that Carter didn't spook. Instead he rolled in the arena's dirt, a happy pony.

Sally was a waitress in downtown Bowling Green and she invited me for breakfast the next morning. Ken told me to meet him at Country Classics with Carter at 10 a.m. and he would see that there was a trailer to take us back to Levi's. I would have preferred to drive out with the buggy but time and distance dictated otherwise.

For the umpteenth time I left my unlocked computer and camera laden buggy and walked the two miles into downtown Bowling Green for breakfast at Sally's restaurant. The bank didn't open until 9 o'clock so I enjoyed a leisurely breakfast. Then I walked across the street to the bank to get some cash.

I rushed back to the fairgrounds to harness and hitch Carter and then hurriedly drove over to Country Classics. It was 10:20. I loaded Carter into the waiting trailer and Ken had his helper, Jim, drive us out to Levi's.

When we arrived the man who had driven the team the day before was standing next to a large, copper kettle outside of Levi's shop. The older man was Levi's father. The women were helping him make apple butter, heating a concoction of apples, seventy pounds of sugar (Domino), water, and cinnamon, heated by a wood fire. The old boy joked that of all the ingredients in apple butter, there was no butter. He also got a big kick by saying that he cooked with water instead of kerosene. What he was talking about was his method of keeping the brewing apple butter at just the right temperature by throwing water on the fire, thus keeping it at a temperature that wasn't too hot.

While I was learning about apple butter, Levi came walking from the direction of the barn. One of their cow's was bloated and Levi had been working with it. He looked at Carter inside the large trailer and said to bring him up next to the shop.

Jim and I got Carter out of the trailer and as Levi began to take Carter's shoes off, I could hear the people around the kettle talking in their German dialect. I heard "Michigan" and "Tennessee" and I realized that I was the subject.

About a dozen kids were around on this day, going to and fro, and they joked and laughed at my red hat that had a pig on the front with the caption "Durocs—They Grow on You." The Duroc is a type of pig and it was fun to hear the kids get such a big kick out of my baseball hat.

Once Levi had two of Carter's shoes off, he had me take Carter to the barn. His father let two Belgian colts out of the stall and I led Carter inside. He asked if Carter would want some oats or corn. I chose oats and Carter pigged out.

We went back and I watched Levi put the Drill-tex II, or whatever, on the shoes. Levi had several piles of Drill-texed horseshoes stockpiled high on the side and as he used his torch to "melt" the Drill-tex, we talked. He was a lot of fun, stating that his shoe job would last till Memphis.

The extended family was around and it seemed obvious that they were genuinely interested in my trip. Levi said, "It's something, it's really something!" I told how I drove from the side, walking for the exercise. One of the women asked, "How?" I couldn't believe that I was in any position to answer any question relating to horses and driving from these people. They wanted to know if I drove in the rain.

Levi finished making the shoes and I fetched the Fat Boy. After feeding him oats it was predictable that he wouldn't stand very still, but Levi knew many disciplinary tricks. He had a very authoritative "Whoa," and wielded his rasp with similar strength, whacking Carter on his rear when he failed to be still. If his rasp wasn't handy, he'd use the side of his hammer, and lacking that, he would use the top part of his foot to kick Carter flat on the belly. Carter became obedient.

It was 47 degrees and a light mist began to fall. I reached inside the truck cab and got my down vest to add to my hooded sweatshirt. Levi was sweating hard in only shirtsleeves and when he noticed me working at keeping warm, he said that ordinarily he would be working inside his shop but since this was apple butter time there wasn't enough room because of the apples and plastic jugs stored inside.

An Englishman drove up to Levi's shop and jumped into the middle of all conversations. He wanted to set up a time for Levi to shoe his mule and as he talked, he talked loudly. I thought he was sort of obnoxious. As he pestered the apple butter squad, Levi told me that the man was the state milk inspector and that he was always allowed to come around "our people."

Levi finished filing Carter's hooves and then brought out a couple of homemade tricks like a disappearing dollar bill. Another good one was a puzzle made out of horseshoes. It seemed so obvious, so easy, yet I could never figure out how to do it. Levi told me that the best bet of all was to bet someone that they could not find a 13″ long ear of corn. They could find 12″ ones, even 12¹/₂″, but never could anyone produce a 13 incher.

Before loading Carter back into the trailer, three hours after Jim and I had arrived, I asked Levi if he would sell me four bales of timothy hay. Levi told me to ask his father. I walked outside to his father and he told me to ask Levi. I went back to Levi and he sent me back to his father, who then asked Daniel. Daniel was about 25 years old and said that he didn't know how much hay sold for. Levi's father said, "How does 50¢ a bale sound?" Not only was 50¢ a bale a good price, but I was happy to resolve such a major purchase.

I paid Levi with a check for $40 for the four shoes. He invited me back the next day and said that he would give me some apple butter and bread. I wanted to do just that, but my time table—that lousy time table—said I needed to travel.

As I said goodbye to these warm people, Levi's father said, "Take care."

I replied instinctively, "I am watched," and I opened my hands to the sky. Levi's father smiled and nodded. I didn't want to leave.

That evening in Bowling Green I got a room at a motel across from Country Classics so I could have my first shower since Andalusia, Illinois. After the shower Ken and Ethel took me out to eat and then loaned me their truck so I could take my clothes to the laundromat and not get wet from the rain.

The next morning I harnessed up and off we went, saying goodbye to a good place with good people. It was cool and very foggy, and when it wasn't raining, it was misting. No sooner had we gotten out of town than US–61 lost its shoulder and gained too many blind curves. It was infested with large and fast moving trucks. I was sore from sitting, and my neck tired of constant craning to the rear, looking for traffic. It was a dangerous stretch for horse and buggy and when we came up to local road HH, we took it. It led slightly away from our direction of travel, but it beat the alternative.

HH was great. It was barely used and until near the end of the day's journey the hills remained tolerable. That night we met Merton Carlson who was trying to snap a picture of a Red Tailed Hawk. He invited us to camp at a place he owned down the road a few miles. We arrived at sunset and situated ourselves in a small clearing next to Mert's rented house.

The next morning, a couple of hours after sunrise, Carter was finishing his hay, when up drives Melissa Corbin and her family. Melissa had met us the night before with a couple of her girlfriends, and had stopped to bring a huge sack of lunch and to see us off. Once everything was packed, I asked 11-year-old Melissa if she would like to ride along. Did she ever!

The road remained basically empty and for the first two miles I had Melissa drive. She did a good job. Carter broke into a sweat early in the morning and I was pleased to hear on the radio that the relative humidity was 88%, because otherwise the 67 degree temperature and the bright sun weren't enough to make him sweat so much.

After a few miles, Melissa's mom picked her up and left a thermos of coffee. A short while later they returned and Peggy needed to do some shopping—would it be okay if Melissa rode along a little further?

As we drove I took the opportunity to get to know Melissa better. Her favorite musicians were Cindi Lauper and Madonna. Her favorite TV programs were "Punky Brewster," "Three's Company," and "Little House on the Prairie." I enjoyed the fresh little blonde riding along with us, not uptight, not too talkative, but good company and good conversation. When Peggy stopped to pick her up about three miles later, I picked Melissa a bouquet of wild flowers from the side of the road. Peggy snapped our picture just as Carter reached in for a bite.

Levi had warned me of St. Louis and everyday brought us closer to the city and the suburbs. Lindbergh and the Spirit of St. Louis had first captured my imagination and later, when I saw the Arch for the first time, I became a real fan of the city. I approached the area of St. Louis with good feelings.

About 40 miles northwest of the city we drove into Troy, Missouri, home of Cuivre River Electric Co-op. Arriving an hour after dark we spent another night without permission, this time in front of the 4-H grounds. The following morning I called the home of Billy Ramsey, manager of the co-op. He came right out and gave me the dickens for not calling him the night before. He asked which route I would be taking and he told me to call him when we finished traveling that day. He would come and pick me up.

That Sunday we drove through rain and a changing countryside. Farms were interspersed with subdivisions, bulldozers were parked next to corn fields. The "feel" of the country was different, charged with impatience. We were off the main roads, yet the cars seemed faster than usual.

One mile north of the "Great Divide," otherwise known as Interstate 70, we pulled into Shorty and Hazel Slatten's drive and asked if I could leave Carter and the buggy for the night.

"It'd be our pleasure," but Shorty felt bad that he didn't have a pasture for Carter. Just that day he had taken down fencing that completed his pasture and the only reason why he had done so was because for the first time in three years they didn't have any horses. Another subtle sign of Pac-Man Suburbia eating up the countryside.

Hazel hadn't lost any country hospitality though. She offered ribs, catfish, beer and more. I settled for a cherry RC Cola and a phone call to Billie. While we waited for Billie to drive the 20 miles from Troy, Shorty hooked up my battery to a charger and I tied Carter to our 23' rope and let him graze. Billie arrived and as I climbed into his car, I promised to see the Slatten's in the morning.

Part of the trip was an effort to learn about the doings of America's electric cooperatives. I was especially happy to be in the Cuivre River co-op area because it seemed to exemplify much of the good that can be found in cooperatives. Of 22,000 members, 5,000 attended the annual meeting. A fantastic turnout!

Participation, not apathy. Less than a week later I passed

through a neighboring REA area, one of the few borrowers of low interest government money that wasn't a cooperative. The difference between the types of REA borrowers was apparent but sad, because the non-cooperative REA borrowers were happy that only five members showed up for the annual meeting! Such a pity. An opportunity for neighbors to grow amongst themselves, ignored and allowed to wither.

That night at the Ramsey home we watched the St. Louis Cardinals defeat the Los Angeles Dodgers in the playoffs. St. Louis was on fire for her team and pennant fever was rampant. Everywhere around St. Louis people could have something in common with almost anyone—the awareness that this team was hot in the hunt for the World Series. A devout Detroit Tigers fan, I faked it and joined in the fun by wearing a red shirt.

While the Cardinals played their game to perfection, Billie's wife, Laura, and I talked about the times they had spent overseas with the national cooperative organization (NRECA—National Rural Electric Cooperative Association) in the international programs division. Two years in Egypt, and another two in Columbia had brought them many memories and as many really nice artifacts. Since I was theoretically within a month of leaving for overseas destinations, including Egypt, I was considerably more interested in just how the international programs worked than whether or not the pitch was a strike or a ball.

NRECA got involved in electric cooperative formation outside of the U.S. in 1961. The United States Agency for International Development (USAID) needed a medium by which to administer foreign aid programs, the general thought being that for a country to become self sufficient, it must first develop an efficient agricultural system. The REA and cooperative program in the United States had successfully addressed the same question and NRECA was looked on as a capable organization to carry out the wishes of Congress.

NRECA's international program developed to help create some 200 rural electric systems, serving 15 million people. Some of the systems were organized as cooperatives, while others were not. The international division expanded to address projects funded by the World Bank and other international banks and was designed to function, not so much as the developer of the system, but as a representative to help assure that various projects were being administered properly. Some projects existed to satisfy World Bank overseer loan requirements and as such were occasionally failures. Many others made genuine contributions to improving living conditions.

The next morning Billie and I were off to a local restaurant and I plied this capable man with questions. I considered Billie a good person to ask tough questions of because something very positive seemed to be going on with his co-op.

I asked him why more of the cooperatives didn't join together for more efficient operation. He replied that in many cases they should but for a variety of reasons they didn't. In some cases, different cooperative headquarters buildings were only ten miles away from the neighboring co-op! They didn't look at mergers, even if the members would realize benefits, because the number of people serving on the board would be cut in half, or the manager might lose his or her job. In the face of administration accusations that REA was no longer needed and that cooperative electrical systems should be done away with, it seemed a shame that the people who represented the cooperative system would refuse to streamline themselves, yet they rarely considered consolidation.

After pancakes and coffee, Billie drove me back to Shorty's, and then turned around for another 20 miles to Troy and work. A cooperative spirit.

I readied the buggy for travel and Shorty reconnected the newly charged battery. Hazel called me inside to talk with KWRE radio for a live, on-the-air interview. One of the things mentioned in the interview was my apprehension of a steep hill about ten miles ahead, called Hopewell Hill. I had been hearing about the hill for days and my fear grew with each story.

Visibility was less than a mile in fog, and traffic was fast and heavy, so close to I–70. I bade the Slatten's farewell and found comfort in having a fully charged battery. There was no other comfort to be had. I was uptight about the killer hill, and the road was an endless stream of big dump trucks, no shoulder and drizzle. The drivers seemed impatient and I yearned for quiet rural roads.

Carter undoubtedly picked up on my mood because he wasn't being being his usual plodding self. After three hours of crud, THE hill was just ahead. A man and two women came out from a side driveway with camera in hand. I was impatient and only wanted to deal with the problem of the blind, steep, dump truck infested hill. I had had this big obstacle in front of me for so long, all I wanted was to get it behind me. As I approached the trio, the youngest woman asked if I would like for them to follow us down the hill with their flashers on. Whoa Carter. Now that was a good idea!

Stopped, the man suggested that I tie off the rear wheels because the hill was, in fact, steep. I had considered this on many occasions but always chose not to do so because I kept hearing about spokes being snapped and I preferred to deal with the possibility of a hill, too steep, than to have to repair or find another wheel. It was a gamble. My new friends snapped some pictures and we continued.

The "apparent" hill turned out to be another 1$^1/_2$ miles down the road and when the descent began, I wondered if my volunteer help would show. Come hell or high water, I intended to do this hill without added hesitation. While I wasn't counting on help, I was hoping for it. The descent began, and I looked in the rear view mirror with trepidation. I was surprised with the beautiful sight of a van with emergency flashers flashing!

The brakes were almost non-existent, even though I pushed the brake pedal as hard as I could with both legs. Most of the 1600 pounds transferred to Carter's rear legs via the 2″ wide britchin strap. He didn't like downhills and tried to steer left or right, but I was intent and insisted on a path that put the skinny right wheels onto a shoulder only inches wide for added braking. I talked to him constantly as the trucks continued to rumble down the hill and others downshifted to climb up. Three years later we arrived at the bottom of the nasty hill, my shirt soaked, but the tension released.

Our safety assured for the present, the van passed and went ahead to wait for us. In the van were Tiny Kenoyer, her mother and daughter, and three kids. Tiny's daughter was about 18 and she said that if she had been as forward as her mother had just been, her mother would have killed her. We laughed. Tiny claimed that it was the horse that had made her want to help when she had heard the interview on KWRE radio that morning. She said that if I had been hitchhiking, it would probably have been different. Moral: Take a horse with you when you hitchhike.

We talked about my planned route and I mentioned that it was about time for me to return home for a final time. Tiny suggested I give Eugene Parks a call. He was a horseman and Tiny thought I should ask him.

Back on the road we made excellent time. Hopewell Hill faded in the background and Carter and I walked along with few breaks. Carter must have been as charged as I was because it wasn't until several hours later that I realized we were going non-stop, up and down some good sized hills. The land was gradually leveling out as we approached the Missouri River and everything was judged relative to the hill behind us.

We spent the night within shooting distance of the Missouri River, at the pig farm of Kenneth Engemann of Marthasville. I felt free and easy. The weather was cool and clear. The sun was below the horizon when I saw 9th grader LaVon Engemann and asked her if she knew who I could ask about a place to stay.

She replied, "Why don't you stay here?" as though it was the only thing to do. I asked if she thought I should ask her parents or anything and she said "okay," and walked up the hill to where her father's girlfriend was preparing charcoals for dinner. Same answer.

I gave Carter his end-of-the-workday oats, and barefoot LaVon took it upon herself to fetch Carter six gallons of water. Without hesitation she lugged the 50 pounds of water from the hydrant next to the pig sties 100 yards away. Her freshness fit in neatly with having survived THE hill.

The Engemann's lived next to Wanda's Green Gables and that night I walked next door to celebrate by ordering a dinner of clams and a beer. Wanda told me that Marthasville had been named for Daniel Boone's wife and that Daniel was buried a couple of miles down the road.

As I ate, the liar's table filled up with farmers. Harvest was still happening and they had a lot to talk about. I jumped in, playing Devil's Advocate, and for an hour we discussed and cussed. The tone was friendly but serious. Just next door at the Engemann's, the same questions were being asked and survival was a big and very real question.

I asked Wanda if there was a pay phone anywhere close and she handed her phone across the bar. I called Gene Parks like Tiny Kenoyer had suggested and he had already talked with her. Gene said that he hadn't seen Tiny in two years but told me to come on—he had room for my horse and I could leave him there while I headed home. As I set out that morning, with the Hopewell Hill behind me and the Missouri River ahead, I felt like I was on vacation.

The sun and pavement were hot and I couldn't help myself when some funky music hit the radio. Since the trip was dedicated to a 50-year-old REA and the cooperative philosophy I tried to maintain a certain level of decorum, shaving kinda regularly and keeping relatively clean clothes on my back. However, I wasn't holding back on this somehow special day and was bopping down Missouri 94 to music like the Hooters', "And We Danced." Walking next to the buggy, holding the reins in one hand and doing some steps a la Michael Jackson, must have made a few people look twice, but I didn't care. I was enjoying the day.

I looked for some shade for my pony but there was none to be had. We rounded a bend and suddenly, without warning, we were at the bridge leading across the Missouri River, into fast growing Washington, population 10,000. The superstructure was impressive. I didn't know anything about the quality of the bridge but since we were already there, we kept on. It was noontime and the bridge was long, the traffic heavy in both directions. There wasn't much opportunity for anyone to pass us. By the time we reached the southern end of the bridge there was a long line of cars and trucks behind us. Oh well, what can you do?

Carter proved smarter than me, again, as he suddenly came to a stop. I was concerned about traffic and had forgotten to look for some shade, but he hadn't. He found a real nice shade tree next to the hospital and we enjoyed a nice break from the hot sun, watching people scurry for lunch.

We were getting into the Ozark mountain range. Hopewell Hill had been exceptional, but good sized hills were essentially non-stop. I was hoping to make it to St. Clair and Gene Park's ranch that day and we were making good time. After traveling about 20 miles rush hour hit us. We topped a bridge, and I saw construction ahead. Missouri 47 merged with Missouri 50 and after a stoplight we needed to turn left. Cars were lined up.

We got in line, advancing with each light change. When it was our turn to go, we were first in line and and I broke Carter into a trot. I loved to watch his mane and tail fly and it was fun to travel faster than a walk yet I did not like trotting him for any distance because of those heavy legs. As soon as we started out, sirens began to blow and an ambulance and police cars came rushing from the opposite direction. There was barely a road, let alone a shoulder, and the people behind us didn't appreciate going slow. There was little alternative and we kept on until we finally came to a place where we could get off the road and Carter could take his blow. We had hurried for only a quarter of a mile but my mood had changed to serious.

We tied our record of 23 miles that day, traveling along newly rebuilt Missouri 47. The road itself was very nice but the heavy traffic didn't let up and the shoulder was narrow, falling abruptly away. Darkness caught us and we stopped in front of a house that had a horse trailer in its drive, a field across the street, and someone looking out the window.

It was the home of Ben and Mary Wieda. Ben came outside and told me that his wife had passed us twice. He had asked her if I was Amish and she said that I was wearing shorts, so he knew I wasn't Amish. He offered us a spot next to his house and I climbed two trees and tied up a picket line, got Carter fed and brushed, and went inside. Ben told me that if he hadn't offered me a place, his father would have turned over in his grave because he had always told Ben, "You never know when a stranger might be the Lord in disguise."

Ben and Mary had a couple of friends over and it was forecast to get down to about 45 degrees that night. One of the friends asked if the PV's on top were for solar heat for the buggy. They weren't the first to ask. My only heat was body heat inside the sleeping bag. Many people had very little idea what solar energy was all about.

Ben was a farrier and Mary was a hard charging realtor, probably Type A personality. They told me that I was still five miles from Gene's and offered to show me how to find his ranch that night. I was enjoying the fact that we were about to take our monthly break, having driven 18 days in a row, and 26 of the last 28. I thought the work was largely done. Half a mile from our destination, we came to two of the steepest hills of the trip! They weren't long but the shoulder we needed for braking wasn't there, and they were very steep.

Back at Wieda's, I called Gene to tell him where we were and that we could be to his place before noon tomorrow. He told me to meet him in St. Clair at his son's car lot and that we could go to his ranch from there.

It was October 16 and the leaves were turning gold and yellow and red. As we drove into town the next morning, Carter walked slower than usual. Maybe he was tired.

Traveling through town, I noticed a frail, white haired old lady watching us approach as she stood on the sidewalk. She smiled, and as we drew closer she began to nod approvingly. When we came to where she was standing she stepped up to the curb, leaned forward and said quietly, "Nice." That's all she said.

I returned her smile and thought of what memories must have been evoked from the recesses of her mind. St. Clair wasn't growing quite as fast as Washington, Missouri but it still possessed the hustle and bustle that cities do and our clip clopping certainly represented something less fast, less noisy, and more personal to this woman. Memories can be kind.

I found the car lot and Gene Parks and his son, Larry, came out to greet us. A reporter from the paper arrived, but before I gave a rundown on the solar powered buggy, Carter needed water. I asked

Gene to hold Carter while Larry showed me the hydrant.

When I returned, Gene told me how Carter had started to follow me when I had walked away, and that he had listened for my voice. I thought that was neat, and strangely remembered a long forgotten boyhood desire to be a veterinarian. It was a warm and nostalgia filled memory.

An old man joined our small crowd and asked how old Carter was. "How old do you think?" I asked.

He took hold of Carter's mouth and said with certitude, "He's no colt. He's 12 year old."

I asked the professional in our midst what he thought. Gene corrected the old boy and told him, "Closer to six."

I wondered. Supposedly he was four, but if he had a half sister named Reagan, that would probably make him 1980 presidential election vintage, and so, closer to Gene's estimate.

I intended to fly home that day but didn't know how I was going to get to Lambert Field, so we shoved off for the remaining two miles and two hills. The downhills taxed Carter to his limit.

Gene met me at his road and led me up another hill to his ranch. We unhitched Carter together and as I put the harness into the buggy, Gene led Carter into a stall with clean sawdust. Carter commenced to eating some leftover oats and seemed happy to be done with the hills and ready for a break.

Gene showed me around his 20 horse ranch and introduced me to his horse, So Impressive. Gene had been offered $250,000 for the stallion on two occasions and had turned them down. He almost took $500,000 on a more recent occasion, and had gone so far as having an accountant come out to tell him how he could avoid paying too much to the government, but then he turned down that offer too. Standing at stud So Impressive brought $1,000 per session and was as beautiful a horse as any I had ever seen.

Gene was a professional. He had learned the horse trade from a man he had worked for as a kid and at 54 years of age figured that he had been riding for 50 years. He mentioned a popular demonstration that the Amish put on every year, showing their crafts and working six horse teams. He compared himself to the Amish, telling how he acted as his own vet most of the time, doing his own breeding, training and shoeing. He had saved mares from being sold to the "killer market" (Jello, dog food, glue, some restaurants, et cetera) by being able to artificially inseminate them by hand. By doing much of the work himself, he was, in essence, paying himself. Gene was proud to be old fashioned and sounded like Amishman Tobe Yoder talking about the $100,000 tractors wearing out when he complained that 1985 cars were worn out before they were paid for.

He told me that I was bound to learn much from this trip, not the least being patience. He told how he had had to learn patience when he had broken a leg years earlier with six kids to feed.

Time was getting on and I asked if there was any bus into St. Louis or to the airport. Gene didn't know but offered a ride to a gas station that sometimes had buses pulling in. He left me with, "Don't worry, I'll take care of your horse."

This would be the last time I would be returning home for my monthly meeting. I planned to drive my pickup truck back to Gene's, shuttling it along as Carter and I continued to Tennessee.

I stood on the entrance of I–44 in the 87 degree sun, waiting to hitchhike to the airport sixty miles away. For 20 minutes no cars appeared and things looked bleak. But then, just as things had been going the entire trip, "Squeaky" Marquart entered the ramp in his old Vienna Potato Chips & Snacks step van and stopped before I had a chance to stick out my thumb. Squeaky had seen me at Larry Park's car lot and though it was against company policy, he told me to hop in.

I told him that I hoped to get to Lambert Field. He said he would do his route backward so that he could drop me off at the only bus stop between St. Clair and the airport. He didn't know but maybe there would be a bus through there yet today.

Squeaky dropped me off at a restaurant/motel/truck stop and I went in and asked about buses. Yes, there was one bus today and it would be arriving in 20 minutes, leaving for the airport. The plane I needed to catch left at 5 p.m. What time would the bus get me there? 4 p.m. Incredible. Then again, maybe it was to be expected.

The Greyhound that arrived was the Los Angeles to New York City bus, and it was not non-stop. Speaking of incredible, the people were the sorts you might expect to find on such a transcontinental bus. Many of the people on board had been there for $1^1/_2$ days and had $1^1/_2$ days to go! They were bus sore and tired of the many stops at every little town. These people were living at the speed of the big city and were impatient. I felt slow and good.

I thought of Carter and how he breathed. I remembered putting my ear next to his nostrils as he caught his breath after a big hill and exhaled deeply and slowly. The recent memory was calming. I felt I was leaving an innocent in Carter and felt sorry for these city people because they were in such a hurry. Interstate 44 into St. Louis was crowded and everyone seemed rushed.

In the seat behind me sat a pretty girl from California. She had pink hair. From the ghetto blaster on the seat next to her I heard the words of a song, something about not trying to live life in one day, of not speeding time away. Was anyone listening?

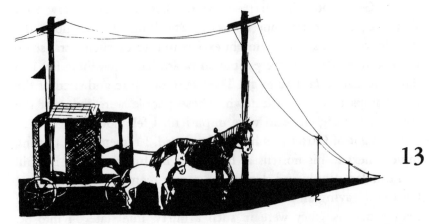

13

Into the Bottoms and Over
the Levee—South Missouri

*For me the world is weird because it is stupendous, awesome, mysterious, unfathomable;
my interest has been to convince you that you must assume responsibility for being here, in
this marvelous time. I wanted to convince you that you must learn to make every act
count, since you are going to be here for only a short while; in fact, too short for witnessing
all the marvels of it.*

—Don Juan

A friend died unexpectedly of Marfan's Syndrome the day after
I returned home. No one was ready. The mysterious cycle of life
and death seemed numbly short, but meetings happened anyway
and the EBTS column was mailed out.

We buried the father of two with our own hands. The burial
acted as a cleansing catharsis on both personal and societal levels,
serving to remind dust to dust. I left Michigan for Missouri directly from the cemetery.

Driving along, I thought of how far Carter and I had traveled,
and of how little time remained. Of life and death and God. Of
travel overseas. I was happy to be so full of feelings and thoughts
and life.

My truck's shifting column had almost disintegrated. Reverse
usually wasn't available and the other three gears were always

questionable. Turn signals were messed up. But the engine and brakes were sound and she made it to St. Clair.

Gene said for me to park my truck at his ranch and to pick it up when I could. Then he loaded us up with hay and oats. "You know, for the rest of your life you'll remember this trip as the big thing in your life," he said. I recognized the truth in what he said though I hoped for continued big things.

We were south of the east-west Missouri River and I–44 and sufficiently far from St. Louis so that our path of travel turned eastward. Now to stick with the Mississippi and hope for flatland instead of continuing south into the thick of the Ozarks.

The first day back on the road found us making 16 miles after a full week of commuting, meetings and the funeral. As daylight neared an end, we chugged up a big hill. Halfway to the top we stopped for a breather. It wasn't particularly hot, but it was very humid. Carter was breathing heavy and sweating a lot. We stopped at the top for another break. Two women stopped to ask if we needed any help. I mentioned the usual and they mentioned the man down the road who had Belgians. As the three of us talked, a man and his daughter walked up. The man was Oli Ziegler, otherwise known as "the man down the road who had Belgians." Oli invited us to stop at his place.

When we arrived at Oli's, I led Carter to the barn behind the house, Oli showing the way. Carter got his own stall and then Oli showed me two of his Belgian stallions and two Belgian colts. He had just bought one good looking 1800 pound stud for $300. Horse prices were down.

Oli offered to give me a ride back to Gene's to pick up my truck. On the way I learned that Oli was 54 years old. He worked for a sandblasting company in St. Louis and planned to retire from his job as a truck driver in three years. As a teamster it was 30 and out, and with twenty head of Belgians, Oli had plenty of work he could do that was more like play.

When we arrived at Gene's, Gene was at the barn with a farrier. Missouri was famous for mules. And mule talk. These three Missourians knew mules first hand but none of them really liked them. Respect them, maybe, but as Oli said, "I've always said that mule men are born, not raised. You either are or you're not. I'm not." Having said as much, he told how he had just bred one of his Belgian mares with a jack. The horse market might be down but the mule market was up.

On the way back, Oli showed me a shortcut that would let us miss a bad hill on the shoulderless, paved road coming out of little Cedar Hill. The short cut took us back to the smaller roads like BB and A, and for the next couple of days we worked back to good old highway 61 and the Mississippi plains.

The following morning we woke up and were getting ready to go, when a team of mules pulling a wagon with George Radin of Festus, Missouri happened by. The team was beautiful and the first I had ever seen. I remembered what Oli and Gene had said a couple of nights earlier and thought back even further to when I had envisioned using the same animal to do my bidding. George was on his way to a gathering with some other wagons and mules and invited me to come along. I wanted to but was still trying to gauge if and how I was going to make it to Tennessee. Time was running short—only fourteen days remained.

For the only time during the trip we struck out two times in a row when we asked for a place to stay that night. With sunset nearing, the first strike out occurred when a family recommended St. Genevieve, 11 miles and four hours away. Then, a mile or so later, two men, a woman and two kids congregated by the road with a camera. When I asked, one of the men pointed down the road to a barn about a mile away and said, "Why not ask them? I'm sure they will help you."

Car lights were coming on and we kept going. Several times I had to hit my flashers for traffic. The sun set. As we came to another hilltop I saw a man going from his truck in the driveway to his house. The drive was asphalt and with Carter's Drill-tex shoes I couldn't drive up to the house because the shoes would eat the blacktop. I pulled Carter alongside the road to a patch of grass and walked up to the house, hoping that Carter wouldn't take off. By the time I got to the door, the man was inside. I didn't like the idea of such blatant soliciting and turned around to leave. There was still some light and I would just continue on.

Then I glanced down the darkening road and saw nothing but fields and woods. I had little choice and turned around. I knocked on the door and Mrs. Schaefer came out. We talked. She went to get Ed, about 80 years old. Both were friendly and distinguished looking.

Ed told of an older man who had stopped with a horse named Brownie years ago and asked if I was him. Then he answered himself and said, "No, of course not, but let me see your horse."

We walked down to the road and Carter was standing quietly. Ed thought that Carter looked like Brownie. He told me that he would get his truck and for me to follow him. We came to a barn and a vacant house a quarter of a mile back on darkened US-61. As I unhitched, Ed told me to help myself to the hay and water, and he'd see me in the morning.

While I settled in, the neighbors, Tom Kertz and two of his sons, Tony, 15, and Matt, 8, came down to say hi. Later Tony returned with a large plate of spaghetti and a soda. He told me that he had school the next day, but planned on doing his homework in front of the TV so he could watch the deciding game of the "I-70 World Series" between St. Louis and Kansas City.

He also said that Ed was a millionaire and owned thousands of acres. Four years before Tony and his brother had asked Mr. Schaefer if they could trap on his property. He had outlined an area they could use, and each year he had expanded the area because he trusted them more and more. I was lucky, Tony said, because Ed trusted me. I could have told him that it wasn't a question of trust. Ed had met Brownie, I mean Carter.

Ed drove over at 6:30 the next morning just as I was finishing up a shampoo and shave. It was a beautiful day, though at 50 degrees a bit cool to be wet and bare chested.

He asked me how I liked the final game of the series. I asked him who won, my radio had pooped out. Kansas City had performed a real comeback to win. Ed was a little disappointed.

He offered to buy Carter when my journey was completed. He had always liked draft horses and with 4000 acres there was plenty of room. Plus he wanted his grandchildren to know about horses and the way life used to be.

He talked about when he had driven all over the country as a young man selling banking supplies. We talked about 1929, the Mexican/US border and the Farm Bill in Congress.

Carter interrupted with his first dump of the day. I said something like, "Oh, No Carter! I'll have to clean up again," since I had just cleaned up about four of his piles from the night before.

Ed spoke up, "No, leave it there. That's the first horseshit that's been on this farm in fifty years." Changing rural values.

Ed was one of the first people to be hooked up to Citizens Electric of Ste. Genevieve. There was much about FDR that he didn't like, but REA had been a good thing. It provided local jobs and had brought electricity to be area. The Schaefers had had a Delco electric system before REA and I asked if that meant they were some of the better off people in the area.

"Yes, but even at that, when my wife would turn on the iron, the lights might go off, or if the lights were turned on, the radio might quit," he said.

We left Ed, heading into what he called "the oldest, permanent white settlement in America," Ste. Genevieve (1735–1985). We arrived in "St. Gin," as it's called, just in time to beat the noontime rush.

Since I hadn't eaten, and especially since I liked the idea, I pulled into a McDonald's drive thru. I pulled Carter up to the order microphone but nobody came on to take our order. I tried talking to the quiet machine but nothing happened. The cars were beginning to pile up behind us, so I pulled up to the window. Just as I suspected, metal activated the mike and since the buggy was mostly hickory, they never knew we were there. Being lunch time, the girl said she had wondered why no one was ordering.

I got two large orders of fries and began to look for a quiet place to eat. Before I could get to wherever, Bob Land of Citizen's Electric Corporation drove up, saying that he had been looking for me and would like to help. I mentioned that I needed a place to stay in about ten miles, and that I had a truck about forty miles north that needed to be shuttled. He said that he could help and would find us later.

Carter walked as I chewed on cold fries. It was a nice day and with most of the traffic using the paralleling I-55, old Highway 61 showed itself to be an awfully nice road. Now traveling south, the road was generally flat, with small bluffs on our right hand side. Several hours later as we approached the town of St. Marys (pop. 565), a couple of women turned their car around and came back. We talked and I asked if they could suggest a place I might look for to spend the night.

"Oh, look up Bob Bartels. He'll help you. Ask anyone in town and they'll be able to tell you how to find him. In fact, his wife works for REA," they responded.

No sooner had they left than Rob drove up to tell me he had arranged for us to stay at the home of a woman who worked for Citizens. I asked if her last name was Bartels.

"Yes, how'd you know?" Rob asked.

"Is her husband's name Bob?"

"How'd you know?"

When I told him what had happened, Rob drove off, telling me he'd meet me at Bartels' to give me a ride back to my truck. We continued into town and found Bob, who told me how to find his home. Finding it was no problem, but if the hill leading to his house had been one iota steeper, I'm not sure that Carter would have made it. I tied Carter to a picket line and Rob gave me a ride 40 miles backwards.

This shuttle ride allowed me to learn more about Citizen's Electric Corporation, not cooperative. Citizens was one of the few borrowers of REA that operated other than as a co-op. Originally C.E.C. had been a privately owned utility, but years back it had needed to borrow money from REA. Now it adhered to REA standards, but that didn't mean that it had to operate as a cooperative. Instead, its 18,000 members were stockholders, only five people attended its annual meeting, and each director voted several thousand proxies. While it did operate as a non-profit organization, it was the only REA utility in Missouri that did not fall under the regulation of the state commission.

I appreciated the ride back to my truck, but I felt that with a change to cooperative principles, there would be a better feeling of community and a greater practice of democratic principles. It seemed preferable for five thousand people to participate directly like the Cuivre River Cooperative in Troy, instead of five! Where was it written that people were incapable of deciding where their energy comes from? Certainly no one asked the people of Kiev or Chernobyl what kind of power they preferred.

When we got to my old truck, it started right up and I drove back to Bartels'. I intended to drive on south to Cape Girardeau, ahead of us for a change, and to return to St. Marys any way I could, probably hitchhiking. Bob and his wife, Henrietta, saved me from such a fate and offered to drive the fifty miles to "Cape" and give me a ride back.

I learned that Henrietta's brother had died and just been buried the day before. She had returned to work today and Bob said that he appreciated being able to help me, if for no other reason than as a way of keeping her busy.

I followed them to an Amoco station at the edge of Cape. After showing the 18-year-old attendant a picture of Carter and the solar buggy, he said I could leave my truck there—no problem. I promised to return in four or five days.

We stopped for dinner on the way back and got better acquainted. Bob was president of St. Mary's bank at 45 years of age. He was also a farmer and retailer. Bob farmed a piece of land west of the Mississippi called Kaskaskia, which was part of Illinois. The weather was changing rapidly as Hurricane Juan moved north into the midwest and threatened to soak the ground. He and his six employees were working hard at harvesting soybeans.

The business of farming was changing for everyone. In years past Bob had hired twenty to twenty-five helpers. Gradually he needed less help but still felt an obligation to the workers and tried to keep them on the payrolls as long as he could. If they weren't working for him, chances were that they wouldn't be working. There simply weren't other jobs in the area. Sometimes Bob initiated his own St. Marys economic development work crew and had the men do civic chores, like patch the road or paint a sign. Human values.

Hurricane Juan lost the wind of a hurricane but retained the wet overcast nature of a storm for days. Temperatures were in the 40s and it was raining when Carter and I headed out from St. Marys. Before we left Bob mentioned that one of the directors of Citizens Electric worked at Fruitland Livestock Auction yards. Two days later we arrived at the yards.

It was raining lightly at quitting time and the last trailer of cattle was being loaded. I expected Carter to bolt from all of the noise of cow hooves on metal ramps and cows saying "ouch!" to the electric cattle prod. Instead, a man came up to me and said that he had heard about us on his CB. He showed me pictures of a two-year-old mare that looked a lot like Carter and said that he would like to buy Carter, especially since he knew he was so well broken. Ain't it amazing.

I found the owner, Ray Cox, and asked him if I could camp on his land. He told me that I should push the buggy under the roof and out of the rain and that there was plenty of room for Carter in one of the countless stalls. There wouldn't be another auction for two days. The man who offered to buy Carter helped me push the buggy under the roof. Better than a motel.

Once that last trailer was loaded, it wasn't long until Carter and I had the place to ourselves. It was clean, with no odor. Carter had his own stall with plenty of good hay. The buggy was in the next stall. There was a bathroom and a pay phone in the lobby where the auction took place, so I went to the lobby to make a few phone calls and wash with hot water.

When I walked back to the yard, I met Paul Cready. About 50, he had just dropped off some cattle for the upcoming auction. Paul had seen the buggy and Carter and liked them both. We talked for hours about the trip, the general state of affairs and how the developing world economy impacted the American market. Beef could be raised on the hoof outside the U.S., processed and shipped to U.S. destinations cheaper than it could be done by American farmers. Same with pigs from Canada. To make a living with beef cattle in America was increasingly difficult.

Paul had worked as a pipefitter until six years ago when he had chucked it all for a life dealing cattle. He dressed the part. Cowboy hat with feather band. Chewed tobacco. Tonight Paul was driving a one-ton truck and hauling only a few head.

A year earlier he had a semi-tractor trailer and things were much better. He had been busy enough to hire a driver, cutting expenses where he thought he could so that his business could grow and he could afford to send his two kids to college. He gambled, foregoing full coverage insurance, and saving $5,000.

No sooner had he adjusted his insurance than his driver drove the truck over two dividers on the interstate, ripping out the under-bottom of the trailer. Half the cattle were killed. Insurance paid nothing.

Paul talked about the nature of the farmer. How farmers would sooner take a loss than to see someone else make a big profit. Farmers weren't able to unionize because the minute they banded together, someone would bolt to take advantage of a good price, the others be damned. Happened all the time. They'd hang onto their goods when the price was high, but then sell when the prices were low. Paul said that he could accurately predict a busy auction by prices being up or down. When prices were down, the auction block would be busy, when prices were up, things would be slow.

The next morning was Halloween and the metal roof was drumming like mad. It always rains on Halloween. After saying good morning to Carter, I walked to the restaurant next to the lobby for a breakfast of hot pancakes. This four-star living was especially welcome because I intended to travel regardless of the weather.

As I ate, three men sat at three separate tables and had a conversation over coffee. All were involved with farming to one degree or another. One was working at the mall in Cape, helping get a new store ready to open. Their talk was mixed. Of the poor prices that livestock was bringing and of the new Ramada Inn sign going up next to the interstate. About how milo was all that remained to be harvested, and how "the rain won't hurt it none."

I walked back to the buggy and looked out at the steady rain. With the auction set for the next day, the stalls were slowly being filled as people brought in truckloads of animals. Ray invited me to spend another night. I thanked him but explained that I needed to make some miles. He suggested that I move my buggy into the same stall with Carter for the time being and invited me to ride with him later when he made a trip to pick up some cattle. That sounded good. It'd give me time to write, and hopefully time for the rain to let up.

For the next hour I sat in the buggy in the same large stall with Carter. Horses might not be overly smart, but they were friendly and playful. I had fun, writing, then brushing the big lips of

Carter away from me as he repeatedly stuck his head into the buggy and nudged me.

It was about ten o'clock when Ray came and asked if I was ready to go. I rode as he drove his pickup and large stock trailer. For 45 minutes the roads got smaller and the pavement disappeared. We arrived at Willa Gerler's tidy farm home overlooking the Mississippi and Ray expertly backed the large stock trailer to the barn door. There was no room to spare. Ray loaded eight calves while Willa handled the barn door.

The two had a spoken agreement that he would charge her $3^1/2\%$ of whatever price the cows brought and send her a check for the balance. He had done business with her husband before he died and he picked up the calves from Willa as a service. The auction house usually got 12% of the going price. I felt certain that this kind of service was non-existent at the stockyards in Chicago. I took a deep breath of country.

When we got back to the auction yards, Ray again extended his invitation but I knew that hurricanes were big weather systems and usually hung on for days. I didn't have any days to burn, so as the rain continued, we shoved off.

Carter worked well for 12 Halloween miles. Traffic was impatiently citified when we went through Jackson, Missouri at rush hour. The dark skies made the approaching sunset even darker and at one point cars were passing us on both sides at the same time. Rush, rush rush. I was scared and wished to be elsewhere. It was dark when Jerry Lorberg saw us and offered us room in his barn half a mile off the road. With pleasure we accepted and once again Carter, the buggy, and I shared a barn.

Just as I began to relax, a man in his 20's drove up to our new home. Tom Fields had seen us on Cape Girardeau's local TV news and heard that we were at Jerry's. He invited me to spend the night with his wife and five-month-old daughter.

"Donna's cooking supper now. Wish you'd come. I'll show you my donkeys," he said. Again I accepted, leaving Carter with half a bale of hay to munch on.

Tom and Donna were both social workers and after supper Tom showed me the farmer side of his life. This Virginia born and bred man had two jacks, six jennies and three Belgians. My loyalties had changed from donkeys to Belgians, but to Tom, Belgians were second. Or third. Tied with his love for donkeys was his half acre plot of tobacco. A true Virginian.

I mentioned that I needed to pick up my truck so after showing me his animals we drove into the Amoco station where I had left my truck. The 18-year-old who had given me permission to leave the truck didn't work there any longer, but at least they still had my key. The truck wouldn't start. We pulled it with Tom's truck and sprayed it with ether, but it wouldn't go. Splendid. I left the truck that night, promising to return as soon as possible. The new manager in charge, a mature 19, said not to worry. I left hoping that he would work long enough to tell the next manager about my truck.

November arrived the next morning and Tom gave me a ride to my buggy on his way to work. The rain had stopped. I kept hearing that the hills disappeared soon and turned into flat cotton land. Like the Michigander who forsakes four seasons for one, leaving the northern snow for the Florida sun, I was more than ready to get away from the never ending ups and downs, ready for the monotony of flat, less scenic, country.

I gave Carter breakfast of half a bale of hay and while he stuffed his face, I tried to make some notes. There was a calico kitty who lived in the barn. As I wrote a letter he crawled around, first playing around my head and then swatting at my pen and paper.

The map was a constant companion. I looked at where we were, and how we might get to Tennessee. We were about level with Kentucky and I could see Tennessee and Arkansas on my Missouri map. We were getting close. It looked like there might be only 100 miles or so until we'd be in Tennessee. I wasn't in a hurry for a change. November 11 was my rough goal, six months since the May 11 start, and only fate could stop us from traveling the limited mileage in 11 days. I contemplated crossing into Kentucky at the Hickman ferry, traveling south to I-155 in Tennessee, recrossing the Mississippi into Caruthersville, Missouri, and on south from there into what could be our eighth state, Arkansas—all before November 11. If Lady Luck never left our sides, then perhaps we could even get into a ninth state, Mississippi.

Soon after we started out, Carter began to sweat. I began to think that as close as we were to Tennessee, we still might not make it. Carter could come down with pneumonia, or break a leg, or who knows what might happen? It wasn't a fever that was making the sweat, but the humidity. It began to rain. A cold 47 degrees. On we went. Things were flattening out.

We had been on the road about six hours when Robert Ross pulled over and invited us to stay at his place. He said he had a rig just like mine. I declined since there was still three hours of daylight remaining. Bob said that he would like to drive ahead and see if he could make some arrangements for us. An hour later he returned with the news that he had found a place for us. He'd drive ahead and wait for us.

We drove on, enjoying the flatness. One of the few hills we encountered was just before entering Oran, Missouri. A railroad overpass. Carter handled the hill with no problem, but suddenly took off at a gallop! What a hole shot! Some pigs to the right of the overpass had spooked him. Carter just never hit it off too well with the porkers. As always, he slowed down fairly soon.

We came to where Bob was waiting for us on the side of the road. He turned off of Missouri 77 and we followed. The rain had turned to a mist by now and I hopped out to drive. As I began to walk I noticed a police car. He beeped his horn and pulled up, saying "I'd like to talk to you."

"Whoa, babe."

He drove the car in front of us and got out, swaggering back to me.

"Where are you going?"

"We're going to Tennessee, coming from Michigan."

"Do you have any I.D.?"

"Yes, I do. Have I done anything wrong?"

"I'd like to see some I.D."

"Are you serious?"

"I'm very serious."

This officer was working to protect the citizens of Oran, population 1266. I reached inside the buggy to retrieve the sixth Electric Burro Travel Series column, hoping that this guy would accept something "official looking" as easily as a driver's license. It was quicker than digging my billfold out. While I was getting the column, I asked, "Did you happen to see TV 12 news two nights ago?"

"I'm working ten hours a day. How'm I gonna' watch any TV?"

"Well, if you had seen it, it would have explained things," I handed him the column.

"I'm just doin' my job," and he turned and left. He wasn't a bad guy. A little overzealous maybe, but he really was just doing his job. Later I learned that he was the new cop in town and the kids had nicknamed him "Bonehead."

Carter was a mudder and had plenty of steam to climb the last few hills after another day of wetness. I drove Carter into the driveway of the Eugene Kluesner family where Bob was standing with Eugene and his wife Evelyn, and two of their seven children.

"Surprise," I said.

I was right. Gene had just returned from the auction at Fruitland and wasn't expecting me. He told me that he had seen us on the road that morning as he drove two cows up to the auction. He had waved at us and we had waved back. I waved to a lot of people and couldn't remember for sure.

We unhitched and unharnessed Carter together. Gene led Carter into his barn and fed him some excellent hay and oats. He invited me in and treated me like a son by telling me where the bathroom was and to wash up for dinner. Evelyn was getting dinner ready while son, Pete, continued work on fixing the kitchen sink.

The Kluesner kitchen would never make it to a Better Homes & Gardens magazine, but without a doubt there was a lot of loving interaction that took place in the clean but non-fashionable kitchen. The entire farm home for that matter. If sides were ever picked, I wanted to be on the side with the leaky faucet, filled with the love of the family.

The Kluesner family was All-American. A farm family that dealt with changing realities in the manner of the small American farmer, pragmatically. All were soft spoken and friendly. All were intelligent and hard working, able and fun loving. The kids ranged from 20 to 27 and helped Gene with several hundred head of cattle.

Hands of leather were not limited to Papa Gene. The farm and family remained the center of these people's lives, yet the future did not promise to continue with the farm as part of that future. Even though the kids had an in-depth knowledge of farming, none were working full time as farmers. Several of the sons were employed at the concrete factory in town. One son was with the National Guard in Honduras. I wondered how many generations it would take before some values from the farm disappeared or changed. Two generations? One and a half?

I slept in one of the son's bedrooms that night, getting in line for the bathroom in the morning. After breakfast, Gene gave me a ride to their family built cabin, back in the back, next to a nice pond.

While we were there Gene asked what I planned to do with Carter after November 11. I told him about Marv Booker's offer and of some of the possible trailering scenarios. I added that I didn't know. He told me that they had a young filly and that they would come to Tennessee to pick Carter up and keep him until I could pick him up in the spring after my overseas trip. By doing this it would help me and give the Kluesner's a well broken horse with which to teach their filly to drive. Sounded good to me.

Before we got the rig ready for the road, Gene gave me a ride into Oran to Dirnberger's Feed Store so I could get some oats. Dirnbergers gave me fifty pounds of oats and a Nutrena hat. We returned to the farm and Gene and I harnessed Carter. Before we left, Evelyn said that they would bring me lunch the next day. Gene handed me a bag of pecans. As we traveled, the warmth of the Kluesner family traveled with me.

We headed south out of Oran and walked down the last hill. The long awaited flatland had finally arrived! Our new territory of cotton and flatness was not a wealthy land. Many houses were boarded up. Maybe some of those that weren't, should have been. There was no evidence of a population boom.

After traveling all day we entered the northern edge of Sikeston, population 17,000. A reporter met us at the outskirts. While the reporter interviewed, I cracked pecans. We both ate. During the interview one man stopped to offer us a couple bundles of fire-wood. I declined. Kids were always popping up around Carter. Several others stopped to talk, including a farrier.

The beat went on as this particular farrier added his estimate of Carter's age. He estimated 14 years old. Gene had called him "smooth mouthed," which implied that Carter was 8 to 10. Gene Parks said 6, the old timer in St. Clair declared 12 or 13. Glen Stafford, 4. Carter's first vet agreed with Glen; Levi Schwartz was diplomatic, saying 5 or better. Nothing like the democratic process to determine someone's age.

The flat land and closeness to Tennessee made me slow down. The interview continued for an hour. It would have lasted even longer but we were just entering this relatively large city and I didn't want to get stuck in the city without having a place to stay. We said goodbye and clopped on down the four lane. The reality of the city lasted way too long. The sun was already at the horizon and I thought seriously about stopping at the Holiday Inn or the Arby's and asking where we might camp, but instead, we kept walking.

We watched the sun set. By now we were out of the city proper and I pulled up to the first house out of town. A lady came to the door and said that she would like to invite us to stay but her husband had just been involved in an accident and was at the hospital. She suggested we continue 3/4 mile to Dewitt's Garden Center where she worked, and apologized that she couldn't be of any more help.

On we went. It was dark. No streetlights. No shoulder. Time after time I had to turn on the emergency flashers. It was common for slow moving vehicles to be on the road at this time of year, so as headlights approached from either direction, they could see our lights and slow down. After half an hour we still weren't to any place called Dewitt's.

The cars piled up behind us, sometimes four cars, sometimes five. A few times seven pair of headlights were behind us. I was concerned for our safety and was also hoping not to slow people too much. The situation was often aggravated because an ap-proaching car might slow down, interpreting the flashing lights as a signal "Do Not Pass," which in turn made it a longer time before the cars from the other direction could pass. Still, most people passed with smiles and waves and could be seen turning around to look.

After traveling about two miles we came to a trailer park. Nobody home. We began to pull out, not knowing what to do. A pickup truck drove up with Wayne Parker and Bud Campbell. Wayne didn't hesitate to invite us to stay at his building almost directly across the street, next to Dewitt's Garden Center! Not only that, the 19 year old husband of the woman who I had first asked help from worked for Wayne and the accident had occurred with one of Wayne's machines.

Wayne opened up his 40'x100' metal building for me and wished me well. That night I climbed the steel pegs at the front of the eight foot high trailer and stepped onto cotton piled six feet deep. The trailer was one-quarter full and I slept with a full foot of raw cotton underneath my sleeping bag. I slept fine with an indoor temperature of 40 degrees. It was also 40 degrees outdoors where Carter was tethered to an empty cotton trailer.

I dreamed while sleeping in the cotton trailer. Someone was diagnosing Carter as having had a heart attack. What a nightmare! More crazy dreams followed. By the time 6 a.m. rolled around, I was more than ready to get up and go.

I went outside with Carter and brushed the Fat Boy. I planned to cross the Mississippi by way of ferry into Hickman, Kentucky, and as I studied the map, Bud Campbell drove up with breakfast of biscuits, eggs and sausage.

Bud was about my age. He owned 11 acres where his home was at and rented another 1050 acres, farming both plots. Along with his wife and two sons, ages 18 and 14, he employed one full time hand. Bud believed that farming was unlike any other business. In most businesses, with hard work, intelligent business decisions, and a good personality, you stood a reasonable chance of being successful, but even with such qualities, in farming, you might fail anyway. Bud's father had been forced to quit farming three years earlier due to failing health and Bud wondered how long he would be able to continue to farm. He felt that government policies favored the big farming operation, not the small cotton farmer like himself, farming "only" 1061 acres.

Bud showed me the works of two of Wayne's John Deere cotton picking machines. The 19-year-old husband and father had lost two fingers when a machine like these jammed and he failed to stop the motor to unjam it. Not only did it rip off two fingers, but it broke his arm in four places.

Because of the high expense involved in owning such expensive machines, the Parker brothers made annual migrations south to work the Texan cotton harvest, just to be able to make their high investments pay. I couldn't help but think of the "typical" and generally prosperous Amish farmer on a farm of 150 acres or less.

Before blasting off Bud asked which way I planned on going. I told him of my hopes of getting into Kentucky but then realized that the road towards the ferry came up in only a few miles. How would Gene and Evelyn find us for lunch if we left 61 before noon? I didn't even know what time they would be arriving. Bud suggested that I stop at his place about two miles down the road and call the Kluesners.

In less than an hour we were at Bud's and on the phone with Gene. I told him that I wanted to take the ferry across the Mississippi and he considered the idea in his reasoned manner. Not only were horses unpredictable, he said, but with steel shoes on the steel deck of a ferry, it might be better to continue south on Highway 61. Gene closed by saying that they were just lighting the charcoal to grill the home grown steaks.

We left Bud and continued along the cotton lined highway. I stopped to pick some sprigs of cotton to take home to my young nephews and nieces. A shirt might be made out of cotton, but to someone not from cottonland, cotton came from, simply and ignorantly, "the store," or in more enlightened places, a spool of cotton.

Things had evolved since months and miles earlier when we had started. Now I walked more than half the time, and instead of being sore from sitting, I felt good. I loved Carter and the trip. Tennessee was getting close and as we went slowly along, I went slowly along.

I noticed a car pull off ahead and since it was close to noon, I thought that the Kluesners had found us. Instead it was people from the Scott-New Madrid-Mississippi electric cooperative. Just then the Kluesners drove up from behind, and surrounded by cotton fields and skinny wire strung next to a strip of asphalt, introductions were made. We talked and talked. Evelyn finally asked if I'd like to have lunch before things cooled off altogether.

Evelyn went back to the car and brought the picnic lunch to the buggy. Gene and I sat in front while she had the back seat to herself. The steak was marinated in something delicious. Cole slaw and vegetables and bread. Sweet iced tea, southern style. They even remembered to bring steak knives.

There was food left over and Evelyn wrapped it up so I could take it with me. I asked if they'd like to drive Carter, while I drove their station wagon and took some pictures. Sure.

How much variation to "giddy up" can there be? Or maybe the proper question should be, how used to one voice can a horse become, because when Gene said "get up" to Carter, snapping his rump with the reins as he spoke, Carter just stood there. Gene began driving horses when he was a boy of 9 and certainly had the required authority to his voice and technique to his snap of the reins. Yet, after repeating himself three times, Carter still hadn't budged. Finally he took the whip and cracked him on the rear. This time Carter began to walk.

They drove for a mile or so and then we switched. Gene said that he would take my truck to a relative who lived close to the Amoco where it was still parked. As they departed, he again mentioned that he would be happy to keep Carter for me while I traveled overseas.

We entered New Madrid predictably near sunset. I could practically smell Tennessee. By the time we reached this sleepy town of 3200, the Mississippi almost looped, forming a nodule to the south that appeared to be part of the land mass of Tennessee but in fact, was Kentucky. So close and so far. In 1811 and 1812 major earthquakes destroyed the town of Madrid and created Reelfoot Lake in Tennessee. The Mississippi took a new path. The town of New Madrid (pronounced MAD'rid) was built after the earthquake and like so many river towns, this sleepy little berg had a nice feel.

By the time we were through New Madrid, the sun was down and we were next to the river. We stopped at the home of a couple of ex-Michiganders, Farrell and Marge Etheridge, and I was able to park Carter and the buggy behind their house, next to some grain bins. Carter munched his oats and evening hay, and I had a huge meal with the Etheridges.

After dinner, Juanita and Timmy Colwell stopped by. Juanita was Timmy's grandmother and a cook at one of the schools. Timmy was 14 and went to the high school two miles down the road. He was alert and intelligent, and had a delightful southern twang. We talked for a couple of hours at the kitchen table. I asked Timmy if he would like to go to school in the buggy. Juanita encouraged the boy. She didn't need to. He was excited.

That night there was frost outside, getting to 34 degrees. I slept in Etheridges' spare bedroom and enjoyed a shower. Southern hospitality.

We got up early and I was eating breakfast when Timmy and his grandma arrived. After "Good Mornings," I returned to eating and Timmy dropped a brand new cowboy hat on my head. My first.

We left by 7:20 a.m., our earliest start of the trip. We drove into a stiff cold wind and Timmy learned a little about what travel used to be like for people before the automobile. For someone born after man on the moon, that's quite a contrast.

Two miles were actually three and we arrived at school twenty minutes late. I tied the reins around the foot brake (the only thing it was good for) and left Carter standing next to the school buses in front. Timmy and I went into the principal's office and I explained what was going on. I suppose the atmosphere was appropriately stern as the secretary wrote an excuse slip which read, "Reason: Rode in horse and buggy."

Carter and I stayed on old Highway 61 all that day, constantly in sight of its replacement, I-55. I wished I had a CB radio so I could listen to some of the comments that must have flowed between the drivers. Many honked and waved as we shared the same vista. I thought of the teamsters of the Civil War and how important they had been for the success of any army, as vital as the combat soldier in achieving victory. Never before had I given the job of the teamster any thought, but now I could relate. The Teamsters of 1985 were acknowledging us along I-55.

The next day was a beautiful 65 degrees and sunny. By now I hoped to travel 1400 miles and get as far as Hickman, Kentucky before November 11. We only had about 85 miles to go and another week to do it. Carter looked in super shape.

We drove on toward Caruthersville. Every step was exciting. All I could see on my left was a levee to hold back the flood waters of the Mississippi but beyond that levee, I knew, were the Mississippi waters, and beyond the water was my goal and destination. I constantly thought of what I might find and how we would be able to get over the river into Tennessee. Could we make it all the way today, or not?

The excitement of the day was equaled by the friendliness and kindness of everyone we met. Before we reached the town of 8000, Earl Bullington of the Caruthersville Production Credit Association stopped to see if they could help us out.

The PCA worked intimately with farmers and surely this man dealt with some truly heartbreaking stories. Some government employees were just that, employees doing what their job description called for and nothing more. The other sort took the approach of genuinely trying to help their neighbors and of doing the best job they could. Earl impressed me as the latter sort. A couple of miles later Earl brought us a bale of hay.

We had two newspaper interviews as we went through town, including one with the high school paper. We passed the U.S. Department of Agriculture building and took a break when several people came out to say hi. One of the people was a woman named Betty Leek.

On we went, closer and closer to the bridge into Tennessee. I caught glimpses of the superstructure on the horizon. We entered the edge of a ritzy sort of neighborhood and I joked with Carter, telling him that we would fit in better if we had some chrome lanterns on our rig but, oh well.

The shadows were getting along and a man drove up in a Chevy Blazer and asked me if I had a place to stay yet. He told me his name was Jimmy Leek and how to find his place about three miles away. The bale of hay on the rear of the buggy, from Earl, was originally from Jimmy.

Just as the sun was setting, the manager of the Pemiscot-Dunklin electric co-op in Hayti, Missouri, David Wilkerson, drove up behind us. By now the road was unpaved and a couple of miles remained before we would get to the Leek home. David had two of his grandchildren and he asked if they would like to ride along. The kids jumped in and David drove ahead to wait for us. The lights on the bridge served as beacons.

We pulled into the Leek's driveway and it was dark and getting colder. David reclaimed his grandkids and Jimmy showed me a paddock where Carter could spend the night. They had several horses which Betty and their daughter, Kim, rode in competition. With Carter cared for, Jimmy told me to get into his Blazer. I had mentioned that I didn't know how we were going to be able to get onto the interstate because there was a weigh station between the entrance ramp and the bridge. Jimmy told me not to worry, "I can show you how to do it."

He drove to a place about two miles from his house where a path departed from the road. He pulled onto the little used path and over the top of the levee. We parked on the river side of the levee and walked from there up to where the levee joined the interstate, leading to the bridge. It was well beyond the weigh station. Just like that! It could be so easy. The bridge was only about eight years old, and had never been as busy as the plans had projected. It was being repaired and one of the two eastbound lanes was closed. It should be no big deal. The shoulder was as wide as a lane.

We went back and got on the interstate the proper way and Jimmy drove me into Tennessee. I didn't feel anything special, like I had made it or anything, because "I" wouldn't make it until "We" had made it. Still, I felt good and learned that the first exit off the interstate was only another mile past the apex of the bridge. Tomorrow would be the day I had been waiting for. I hoped.

As frost warnings flew, I was clean and warm in Kim Leek's bed. Kim was off to college. I looked around the room and saw a Garfield the cat poster. Garfield was dashing for a cookie jar, but by the time he reached it, there were chains and locks on it.

Garfield moralized, "It's hard to take what you want in life when they see you coming."

On the way into Caruthersville people had asked where I was heading and I had said the bridge. One man had stopped to talk and told me that he had just heard on the radio that a horse and buggy were planning on crossing the bridge into Tennessee!

The next morning Jimmy came to my door at 5:50, ten minutes before my watch alarm was due. He had been awake since 4:30. His large debt bothered him and he wasn't sleeping well these days. The harvest promised to be a bumper crop for soybeans but he was losing money. He had farmed all his life. Tomorrow would be his 44th birthday and he expected to be driving the tractor, harvesting.

We gave Carter some hay and drove into town to have coffee and breakfast. We sat at the liars table with Jimmy's friends. People were waiting for it to dry up enough to get back into the fields to finish the harvest. On this morning in Caruthersville, people had the time for another cup of coffee.

Talk shifted to me. I said that I planned to cross the bridge into Tennessee today. That I thought cooperatives were a good way of operating an electric business. That REA had provided a real service, and still did. That it could do even more and could help provide the answers for many needs.

One of the men remembered his boyhood days when he had to work hard to pump the water for the mules. The mules would drink up the hard earned water faster than they could pump it, so he would get some wire and chase the mules away from the trough. Sooner or later the mules would drink, and sooner or later the kids would have to pump more water into the trough. The point was that there was a lot of work involved in pumping water by hand, and that it was an electric pump that had enabled people.

Jimmy told how they used to keep geese around the farm. During the day they would let them into the cotton fields and the birds would supply effective weed control by eating the grasses and weeds but ignoring the cotton plants. At night they would let them back into a coop for protection from the varmits and dogs. One of

Jimmy's chores as a boy had been to pump the geese's water trough full, but the geese would get into the water and start flapping their wings, splashing the water out. Jimmy and the other kids would throw dirt balls at them to keep them from causing more work. Today's younger people didn't hold the same appreciation for what their cooperatives had enabled. You kinda had to've been there.

On the way back to Jimmy's, we drove over the levee to the bottoms to check on how wet or dry his soybeans were. From there we drove to the secret path onto the interstate and Jimmy and I walked the attack route to learn exactly which way to go in the daylight. Premeditated? Yes, indeed. Premeditated what, I wasn't sure, but I suspected that horsedrawn buggies weren't allowed on the interstate.

14

Down in Bogota!—Tennessee

". . . Perhaps I have begun to trust my luck more than I used to in the old days"—he meant last spring before he left his own house . . .

—Bilbo Baggins
from Tolkien's, "The Hobbit"

At 9:06 a.m. Carter and I shoved off, saying thanks and good-bye to Jimmy. The road was dirt and slightly used. Only one car passed us. Stretching at right angles in front of us was the raised I–155. Visible a mile to our right was the weigh station. I felt like one of Lincoln's generals again and thought of strategy and tactics. A state highway truck passed on I–155 just before we got to the path onto the levee—both men inside were looking at us. Time to strike, all irons were hot!

As the truck disappeared toward the weigh station, I hurried Carter over the levee. Jimmy unexpectedly showed up at the right instant, hurriedly parked his blazer, and walked ahead to spot for approaching cars.

Up we went, onto the road leading across the Mississippi River and into Tennessee. This time I shouted "thanks" to Jimmy and as soon as we crossed the westbound road and got onto the shoulder of eastbound I–155 I brought Carter to a trot. This was it and I told him so. We were a mile from the bridge itself and Carter

maintained a trot for half a mile. I brought him to a walk to let
him catch his breath, looking for official sorts of cars, practically
holding my own breath. Then back to a trot until 100 yards before
the bridge and we resumed our walk. Carter was performing perfectly. This was the 14th day in a row and we had covered 242
miles. I promised him that I'd give him the day off tomorrow.

We got onto the bridge and began the walk up the incline, using
the closed left lane since there was more room. As we neared the
superstructure and the top of the bridge, we were over the Mississippi's waters. The entire panorama was the river and Tennessee. I
could see the sign reading TENNESSEE STATE LINE. Just then a
white car pulled in front of us. On top were big blue bubbles.
Agh!

A man got out of the car, and put on his hat, looking way too
official. "Where are you goin?"

I pointed to Tennessee and said, "Tennessee." I grabbed an
Electric Burro column and an info sheet and handed them to him.

"Do you have a Coggins test?" he asked, requesting the equine
health report on Carter. I told him that I did and I got it right
away. It was the only time on the trip that anyone requested any
sort of health papers.

"You're doin' good. I have to write up a report. Wait here."

Carter and I waited, watching a barge far below heading up-
stream. How close can you get, I thought, looking just yards ahead
to our goal.

After five minutes the officer walked back and had me sign the
"Livestock Enforcement Inspection Report" that he had just filled
out. He handed me a carbon copy. In the space for MAKE, he put
"buggy;" in the space for YEAR, he wrote "?" Then he asked if
anyone had said anything to me about being on the bridge. I said
no, (they hadn't). "Well, if that's the case, it's alright by me," and
left, wishing us luck.

Free to go, how wonderful! It was windy on the bridge and as
we neared the top where the construction was underway we
crossed to the shoulder next to the 30" concrete railing. As I
peered over the edge to the churning Mississippi 100 feet below,
Carter walked on. We passed underneath the metal sign declaring

Tennessee. We had made it! 10:31 a.m. But we couldn't stop there.

There was a large, noisy compressor for a jackhammer between us and the end of the bridge. Just what we needed! At least the ending wouldn't be anticlimactic! But again we were fortunate, and no one appeared to use it.

Finally we walked off the bridge and past all the construction activity. I pulled Carter to the side and let him eat some Tennessee grass. I kissed him on his big electric nose and then kissed the free soil of Tennessee. Now we had really made it!

After one mile of interstate we got off at the first exit. We had traveled as far south as we were to travel, and turned northward onto the new River Road toward Kentucky. It was November 6, sunny and sixty degrees.

Ten minutes before noon the same law enforcement car pulled in front of us again. Now what?!? He walked back to us and said that he had done some checking and that we were not allowed on the bridge or the interstate. However, since we weren't on them anymore, "everything is honky dory as far as I'm concerned."

As far as I was concerned this man was enforcing the law in the spirit it was meant to be. If I suspected that we weren't supposed to be on the bridge, however lightly traveled, this man surely knew it all along and had allowed us to cross. He could have stopped us and turned us around. Before he left we talked of wet soybeans and Jimmy Leek. He said that Kim Leek was a lovely girl and that it was too bad she was gone off to school.

After the policeman left, we walked a mile further and pulled off. Carter enjoyed a lunch of grass and I enjoyed life. I wrote in my computer, "How unlikely all of this has been. What goodness it is to be able to practice and live by faith. Do good and believe in yourself, you can't go wrong."

When we arrived at Tennessee 103, it was the first road leading to the backroads and we took it. We were in soybean and milo country and as the day dried out, the harvest was being resumed. It was a rough road for the many grain trucks, and I watched the drivers being bounced around their cabs. The same trucks and drivers passed all day long. After waving to each driver several times, we began to pass without acknowledgement, each going about his job.

The sun left us and I thought I could see the lights of a settlement ahead. I hoped so. I was more anxious than usual because I had a special place in my heart for Tennessee people. My father was from Tennessee and I was proud of my southern roots. Tonight I felt I would be back with family. We entered Bogota, population about 100.

At the corner of Tennessee 103 and Tennessee 178 was a country store and forty-five minutes after sunset I pulled next to a gas pump and tied the reins to the brake. Carter seemed happy to stand still.

I walked inside and was happy to see that there was food available. This was the only commercial building in town and it served as the restaurant, gas station and garage, pool hall, pinball hall, domino and checker center, and general meeting place. I looked on the wall and saw the menu: Hamburger—90¢, Cheeseburgers—$1.00. The words French Fries were on the menu but there was no price. They were out of fries. I asked for a couple of cheeseburgers and a Dr. Pepper.

As the excitement quietly spread, I told them where we were coming from and what I was doing. The proprietor was 73-year-old Carmon Epley and he retained a fire for REA. I inhaled my gourmet meal and began to pick candy from the large selection available. Carmon handed me a bag and told me to fill it up. Said he couldn't charge me for my burgers. Then he told me where I could spend the night on some of his property 1/3 mile away, down a dark road.

Before I left he asked me what time I planned to get going in the morning. He wanted to fix breakfast for me. I ventured, "Sunrise too early?" Carmon said it was perfect.

As I climbed into the buggy to leave, the woman who lived next door to Carmon's store walked out. Lanea Clark offered to keep Carter behind her place with her horses. I thought she meant that the buggy would be 1/3 mile away, and I would have to walk Carter to and from Lanea's house, so I declined. Carter and I drove down the dark road to our first Tennessee home.

I tethered Carter to the 23′ rope and he spent part of the night grazing. He looked in superb condition. Like the person facing death who promises God a 100% tithe if He spares their life, and then reneges as the danger fades, I decided we'd travel one more day and then take the promised day off.

It rained a little bit that night. At sunrise I walked down to Carmon's. He was there frying eggs and sausage and baking biscuits, all special. He didn't usually make breakfasts.

Carmon was an original believer in FDR, the Tennessee Valley Authority (TVA), and REA. These programs had allowed Carmon and his Tennessee kinfolk to enter the 20th century. They had meant that if you were from Tennessee, you weren't relegated to being poor, isolated or ignorant, just because of where you lived.

Carmon pointed to a dingy old fan on the floor in the corner. He said not too many people remembered but when FDR had started REA, he also said that rural electrification promised to be the thing that let everyone have an electric fan in their house. That fan had been around since REA began. It looked it.

Carmon had retired from International Harvester and received a pension of more than $1,000 per month. He really didn't need to operate this sometimes busy little general store, but his wife had died one and a half years ago and Carmon felt that companionship was what everyone needed. Marriage, kids, and sex were secondary. He ran the store for companionship. The commotion caused by the overflowing kids on the weekends was good for him.

Carmon had a dizzy spell the week before and his doctor had told him that even though he had been a drinker and smoker and coffee drinker all his life, the real cause of the dizziness was from missing his wife. He had three boys and two girls and was welcome to live with any of them. Brenda lived with him in Bogota. The others were gone, to North Carolina, Texas and Memphis.

"Besides," he pointed to a tree in the field across the road, "that's where I shot my first rabbit." If Carmon moved to Texas he would have to leave behind a large part of himself.

While I was eating breakfast people came and went. Farmers met to discuss how wet the beans were, and to have a soda or coffee. Students would wait for their rides. People on their way to work would stop to pick up a pack or two of cigarettes.

Carmon's store had a charge system that used to be common but was a rarity in 1985. People would write down their own purchases on a notebook sitting next to the Redman tobacco and just below the 3 Musketeers. These charges were usually cigarettes, chewing tobacco or soda. An occasional pair of gloves.

Two southern institutions were usually being practiced, namely the chewing of a toothpick and spitting of tobacco. The toothpick trick was to chew the same toothpick all day without blunting either end. Those that did toothpicks knew the tricks. Like the Buddhist ascetic, the boys from Tennessee transcended mortal man by possessing the patience and coolness to not chomp down on the pick.

Almost everyone seemed to chew tobacco, a real bestseller at Carmon's. One of Carmon's teenage helpers would alternate turning burgers on the grill and spitting into the waste basket. Yummy. "Could you pass the salt, please?"

I couldn't get over how names change to reflect the locale. Bogota was pronounced "BA-GO-DA", not BO-GA-TA like the Columbian city. Bogota was once called Burnt Mills Ferry but the mill burned down sometime after 1864. The people who owned the mill renamed the town after their hometown, Bogota, Columbia. So why did the locals here (and in Cairo, Illinois; New Madrid, Missouri; St. Jacques, Michigan; and others) pronounce their town's name in its unique way? Pride? Wanting their own identity? To say that they're Americans and not bound by traditions of Europe and the past? Reverse condescension? They even went one better in Bogota, Tennessee by pronouncing the capital city of Columbia, "BA-GO-DA."

After an hour and a half of breakfast and conversation I decided to go. I still needed water and told Carmon that I would stop back.

"Don't let your horse eat any milo suckers," Carmon yelled after me. "They make 'em sick if its after the first frost."

As I walked back to the untended Carter and buggy I thought that Bogota was a nice little town. A curious mixture of 1985 and 1955. There was a rehearsal that night for the town play, a spoof this year on the "Farm Aid" concert. Everyone in Bogota was affected by what happened to the farmer. For such a small and isolated place, issues of the working place and foreign policy directly affected the people around Bogota.

Lots was happening and how energy was handled was determining people's futures. A nearby aluminum plant was going to close if people didn't settle for a cut in pay—electric bills were making business as usual untenable. Many of the employees exercised their independence and stubbornness, and said that they'd sooner take a loss of job than a cut in pay. The people hung onto a certain amount of distrust for the people running the aluminum business and the electric company.

Viewed historically, maybe they had good reason to doubt the company's claims. Still, with push already to shove, people were thinking short term. Like the person who develops a heart condition because of their lifestyle but refuses to change their damaging diet and exercise patterns. The diet needed to change. The world was changing fast.

Carter was eating grass. I checked to make sure that no milo was around. He seemed friendlier than usual and came up to me several times, probably looking for oats, but I figured he was meaning, "What's happening buddy?!"

I got the buggy cleaned and straightened while Carter ate. It was sunny the morning of November 7 but also 45 degrees. My hands were cold from the northwest wind. It was quiet and I was in no hurry. I warmed my hands by caressing the spot around Carter's big eyes and ears, so soft and tender and warm. We were in west Tennessee and I hugged him.

As I enjoyed my company, a truck rolled up. It was Prentiss Johnson, a director of 16 years with the Forked Deer (pronounced Four-ka-deer) electric cooperative in Halls, Tennessee. Carmon had told him where I was at and though he had milo to get out of the fields, he wanted to say hi. Prentiss was in his fifties and sat in his truck with the motor running and the door open. We talked and picked our teeth.

While we talked co-op and farm and buggy talk, Carter walked over to us several times, each time returning to eat more grass. Once I heard a bottle pop under Carter's feet. I cleaned the grass and manure from each foot but saw no sign of any cut.

Prentiss said that most of the electricity in Tennessee came from federally generated hydropower of TVA. Since such power was still considered public power, the cooperatives were able to offer reasonably priced juice. In Tennessee's case, people preferred to be on co-op lines. Not only was the electricity democratic, but it was cheaper. As the Statue of Liberty prepared to turn 100 years old, I wasn't sure that people wouldn't choose cheap over democratic.

By 9:45 I began to harness Carter and Prentiss remembered that he was busy and left. Everything seemed in order. Back down the deserted road we went.

We were out of water. To water him that first night in Tennessee, I had climbed over a barbed wire fence and fetched about three gallons at a time from a cattle trough. Each time I had to skim some slime from the top. The cattle drank from it and Fat Boy didn't seem to mind, though he would slosh the water a bit with his lips so he could avoid sucking down any slime. He drank about ten gallons that night. Rather than repeat the step-n'-fetchit act and to avoid the slime, I planned to refill the two six gallon jugs at Carmon's place.

When we arrived at Carmon's, four men playing cards interrupted their game to take a look. I had to draw the water from the bathroom and while I carried the water jugs in and out, Carmon insisted I take a breakfast roll and bag of chips with me. He offered another paper bag to fill with candy. I declined the candy. I thanked Carmon and friends again and drove Carter next door to Lanea's.

I wanted to thank Lanea for offering her corral for Carter the night before and knocked on the front door. I knocked a second time. Finally I knocked on the window but still no answer. We began our second day in Tennessee.

We didn't get far when Carmon and Brenda drove up and Brenda wished me luck. The school play rehearsal had gone well enough, though there were some fussy musicians that were getting short of temper. As we talked, Carter began stomping his rear feet. Again I checked for cuts but there were none.

We headed for Kentucky. The sun was out of the south and behind us, so that Carter could see a distinct horse head shadow directly on the pavement in front of him. He broke into a trot on his own. I figured he was getting excited from the other horse and thought it was cute. I slowed him to a walk.

He then stopped to unload. That was predictable enough. Every day for the first hour, he would dump three times. The exercise stimulated his bowels. But today the load was just a couple of small droppings. And after 100 yards, he did it again. We resumed travel and Carter again broke into an unasked for trot. Either he was just feeling exceptionally healthy, or something wasn't right.

Then I saw his rear legs begin to buckle and I knew something was wrong. We were only about a mile north of town and I decided to turn back and seek advice. The rear legs buckled and were drawn spasmodically up to his gut. Carter went down!

Carter was on the pavement, in his harness and between the fills. He groaned painfully and I was shocked. This couldn't be happening! I talked to him and rubbed his favorite spot between the eyes and ears, trying to coax him to normalcy. He groaned again and his head went flat onto the pavement. I thought of the nightmare I had a week or so earlier when Carter had a heart attack. Could it be?! I felt helpless.

We were in the middle of northbound Tennessee 78. I reached into the buggy to turn on the emergency flashers. A man drove by on a tractor. He said he knew nothing about horses but would call a vet.

I took the bit out of Carter's mouth and desperately tried to remember some of the stories I had been told. Vaguely I thought of colic. "Oh, Carter, please get up! What's wrong babe?"

Three minutes after it all began, I looked up and saw Lanea's face. My knockings had woken her up and she was looking for us to say goodbye. She recognized colic right away. When she said colic I asked her if it wasn't important to make him walk. She agreed. As I tried pulling his halter and coaxing him, Lanea tried pushing his rear. It was hopeless, we couldn't budge this heap. Then Carter stood up on his own. I unhitched him as fast as I could but again a muscle spasm hit, and his rear legs buckled. Again he went down.

The stories I had been told related how a horse with colic would roll on the ground, trying to alleviate the acute stomach pain. In the process they could "twist a gut" and unless immediate surgery was performed, they would die. Carter couldn't roll because even though he was unhitched from the buggy, he was still between the fills. Lanea and I prodded him to his feet. This time we were able to walk him twenty feet and off the road. He went down for a third time.

Things looked bad. Lanea ran to her truck to call her vet in Dyersburg, twenty miles away, saying that she would come back as soon as possible. I pushed the buggy off the road and grabbed the lead rope and whip from the buggy. Seconds later I was turning back to Carter and he was again on his feet.

"Oh, please, Carter. Stay up. You've got to fight this, boy!"

I couldn't let him go down again. I made Carter walk back and forth on a path off the road. I held my left hand outstretched, pulling the lead rope and giving Carter direction, while whipping the upper part of his rear legs with the whip in my right hand. Sometimes, whenever he had a muscle spasm, I would have to hit him as hard and as fast as I could. My arms got tired and I looked toward the road, hoping to see Lanea. I knew I couldn't keep this up, but I couldn't stop or Carter might die. While we walked, I held the whip in my mouth and undid the harness with one hand, taking the weight of the harness off of him and strewing the side of the path with leather.

Lanea returned after about 15 minutes and took the lead rope from my left hand. I walked behind with the whip. Many times Carter's rear legs pulled up in constricting abdominal spasms and I'd try to make the pain from the whip greater than that from the stomach. I hated it but it worked.

As Lanea, Carter and I walked in the sun, a car drove up to the buggy on the road and shouted, "Is this the buggy from Michigan?"

"Yes, it is, but you'll have to come down here. Carter's sick."

It was Mark Christ, a reporter for the *Memphis Commercial Appeal*. While we continued to walk, Mark interviewed us. I surprised myself by declaring the trip officially at an end. We were in Tennessee, only four days short of our intended finish date, so why not? And I sure didn't want to jeopardize Carter's well being. I couldn't believe the entire chain of events, but our trip was over!

Lanea's vet arrived after an hour and a half of walking. He administered mineral oil via a stomach tube through Carter's nostril and gave Carter a muscle relaxant shot. A four-year veteran out of vet school, he spent an hour with us and charged $59.50 for the life saving "housecall." He prescribed some medicine to give Carter to help prevent foundering and wished us luck.

Alone in Bogota, Tennessee. Stranded with a solar powered and computerized Mennonite buggy and a disabled horse. Now what? Lanea offered to help and while she held Carter, I tied the buggy to her truck. She slowly drove the buggy back to her house. I walked Carter back.

It was a sentimental walk along the side of Tennessee 78. Carter seemed to walk okay and I was happy that Carter seemed to be all right. It was strange to think that the trip was over. I felt some remorse that we had traveled 1350 miles and not 1400, and I was disappointed that we wouldn't make it to Kentucky. But all things considered, I was counting my blessings . . . and wondering what had caused the colic. I never learned.

Lanea and I put Carter in with Daisy, her pregnant mare. Lanea was as gracious as Superwoman could be, first saving the life of my horse and then opening her home to me. I spent the next two nights at Lanea's, sleeping in her spare bedroom, playing cards with Homer, Vickie and Lanea until 3 a.m., and making phone calls.

The next day I called Eugene Kluesner and told him what had happened and where we were. He said that he would come down in two days to pick Carter up. Then I called Weldon Schramp in Perryville, Missouri and he offered to drive down the very next day and pick me and the buggy up.

Carmon invited me to breakfast in the morning and I moaned out of bed at 7:30. I said good morning to Lanea's six-year-old daughter, Tessia, who was up and at the Saturday morning cartoons. Fifteen minutes after I walked next door for breakfast, Tessia came over and hung around. She was as likable as her mother.

Carmon lit up when he heard I would be in town that night, because now I could go to the play at the school. Prentiss dropped in and said he couldn't go to the play and gave me a front row ticket to the sold out gig. Then he told me that the manager of Four-ka-deer electric cooperative, Russell Jacocks, had invited us to lunch that day.

At noon I met Prentiss and Russell at Carmon's place and we drove north to Reelfoot Lake. Russell had worked as a lineman before climbing to his current position. He was a good ol' boy, nearing retirement, with Popeye sized forearms. He knew every inch of electric line in the area. Russell was from an old school that didn't accept too much outside criticism. His way or the highway.

The lunch was a feast.

We returned to Bogota and Lanea gave me a ride with Tessia to Dyersburg to pick up Carter's bute medicine to prevent foundering. I spent the afternoon making notes, writing postcards, and watching Carter. I walked to the paddock and crawled inside with Carter. It was good to see him standing and healthy. I put my hand on his stomach and softly touched it to see if it was still sore. Ouch! Carter had reached around and nipped me hard on the butt. It was.

That night I attended the town's play called "Farm Aid," sitting in the front row. The country music was excellent. The actors did a good job and had a good time. Several people came up to me to say they thought my trip was a good thing and wished me luck. Most were farmers. All were country.

The next morning I again had breakfast with Carmon and his crew. Then I unloaded the buggy of most of its weight so that when Weldon arrived, we would be able to load it on the back of his pickup more easily.

Weldon arrived. He liked Carter and walked over to say hi.

"Don't touch his stomach," I said. Weldon smiled and probably wondered what I was talking about.

I walked back into the store. The domino table was full with eight or nine players. "Can I get a couple of volunteers from this volunteer state to help me load the buggy onto the pickup?" I asked.

In a flash, before I had a chance to ask twice, the entire store emptied. Nine of us pushed and pulled the buggy up a ramp of 2″ × 12″'s. I was reminded of the Iwo Jima statue. Cooperation. Friends and common purpose.

We made short work of loading all the paraphernalia and there was nothing left to do except leave. Weldon and I walked back to Carter. He would be picked up the next day by Gene and Evelyn and I wouldn't see him again until next April. I was careful not to touch his belly and a couple of tears came to my eyes.

"You be good, Carter. I'll see you later."

Carter's large head pushed up against my chest and he nudged me. He wasn't after oats this time. Horses love, too.

The Commercial Appeal, Memphis, Friday, November 8, 1985. By Mark Christ

Lanea Clark and Scott Hudson walk Carter as they await the veterinarian.

Horse-buggy trip is tribute to REA

By MARK CHRIST
From The Commercial Appeal
Dyersburg, Tenn., Bureau

BOGOTA, Tenn. — A 1,350-mile trip marked by the kindness of strangers ended yesterday, appropriately with a helping hand.

Scott Hudson, 36, of Williamsburg, Mich., has gone through six states since he left his Northern home in May for a horse-and-buggy ride to commemorate the 50th anniversary of the Rural Electrification Administration, which brought power and light to areas urban power companies would not supply.

During his trip, Hudson and his 6-year-old Belgian gelding, Carter, have been helped time after time by people offering a place to sleep, a bite to eat for man and beast or, at an Amish community in Iowa, new rubber for a broken buggy wheel.

"It's not me, it's the horse," Hudson said yesterday. "Everyone loves Carter."

Perhaps the most frightening part of the trek occurred yesterday morning when Carter suddenly collapsed on Tennessee 78 as Hudson headed for Kentucky. But help was soon on the way.

A passing farmer sent for a veterinarian. Lanea Clark of Bogota stopped and, diagnosing cholic, helped Hudson get Carter on his feet and walked the horse until the doctor arrived. Carter was treated and should be OK, but Hudson said yesterday he will end his trek a few days earlier than the planned Nov. 11 date.

The six-month journey through Michigan, Wisconsin, Iowa, Illinois, Missouri and Tennessee was undertaken by the former air traffic controller to help keep alive the warmth and cooperation that marked REA's beginning 50 years ago.

A member of the board of directors of the Cherryland Rural Electric Cooperative, Hudson has visited about 30 cooperatives during his journey. He will visit Rochdale, England — home of the cooperative movement — and Egypt, India and Nepal, where "they're doing today what REA did 50 years ago."

The end result of the international trip will be a book on REA and cooperatives Hudson plans to finish by next spring and, hopefully, backing for a proposed cooperative senior citizens' housing complex in his native Michigan.

Carter pulled Hudson through the American portion of the trip in an unusual buggy built last winter by Canadian Mennonites. The buggy features two solar "photovoltaic panels" that provide power for his word processor and other electric equipment.

"It's the world's first electrified, computerized buggy," Hudson said.

Carter and the buggy will not be going overseas with Hudson. The buggy will be returned to Michigan and the horse will stay at a Missouri farm until his owner returns.

For now, they both plan to spend a few days resting in Bogota.

15

International Cooperation

He that can travel well afoot, keeps a good horse.

—Ben Franklin

The trip was over, yet only half over. Or, so I thought. Carter and I had taken our solarized carriage 1350 miles to Tennessee, and in the process traversed the areas of 28 rural electric cooperatives. With approximately 1000 such cooperatives we had only touched the surface of people, places, and possibilities.

Carter would spend the winter with a good looking filly in Missouri but now it was time for me to travel overseas. I wasn't organized. I hoped to travel to Great Britain, Egypt, India and Nepal so that I could begin to learn what role cooperatives played internationally and better understand the changing realities that an international economy was bringing. Any meaningful commemoration needed to look not only backward but to the future, both inside and out.

I felt that it was important to immerse myself in a reality found only outside of the U.S.A. To see the disease, to experience living conditions that are seldom tolerated in the United States, to hear the coughing, to see the aspirations in the children's eyes, to travel at a slower pace—these things and more were necessary for an understanding of some of the forces that were impacting daily change throughout the world . .

Weldon had had my old third-gear-only 1969 Ford pickup fixed and it took me and the buggy to an early winter and a foot of snow in northern Michigan. The drive from eastern Missouri took 15 hours and included high headwinds for much of the trip. Still, we traversed the distance with incomparable speed and comfort compared to the trip west and south.

It took a week to get unpacked, my cold barn warmed, packed, reservations to fly, the barn winterized and on the road again. I was in the go mode. I drove to TWA in Detroit to pay $2173 for my airfare from New York to England to Cairo to Bombay and from New Delhi to Kathmandu to New Delhi to London to New York. I intended to travel overland from Egypt to Israel and back for Christmas, and from Bombay to New Delhi. Most of the travel in Nepal would be by foot.

I spent the night with my parents in southeast Michigan and was reminded of the song "Cats in the Cradle" by Harry Chapin. As a kid, the song goes, the dad was always busy and didn't have time to spend with his son. As the child grew to manhood, the father now asked time from the son, but the son was too busy. My father gave me basically the same talk, telling me that I was selfish. He said that there was little reason for me to be in such a big hurry and that after following a horse's ass for six months, I should spent some time with those who loved me. I didn't disagree with him, but my journey's first deadline was Cairo by November 30.

I left early in the morning of November 20 and drove to Solon, Ohio, to return my borrowed photovoltaic panels to Jack Kondos of Sovonics, Inc. While visiting Sovonics, Jack showed me some of their latest developments, with possible applications to the electrical realities in the world today. Jack took the two panels I had been using and loaned me a new, portable and foldable PV panel that could be easily carried and stowed and that would operate my 6 volt tape player. I dreamed of getting a picture of the unit operating my player in Nepal, a million miles from nowhere, with a pack-donkey and the Himalayas in the background.

From Ohio I drove to Washington, D.C., to get required visas. The plane from New York was scheduled to depart November 22. There wasn't much time. In fact, not enough time. I only managed one visa, for Nepal.

From Washington I drove to Connecticut to spend the night with my sister and her family. I would leave my car at their place. When I stepped into the limo to ride to the airport, I found myself feeling very free. My load was light. I felt strong and excited. For the first time in a long time, I rode and didn't drive. There was no horse to take care of. As the limo sped along New York's tollways, I relaxed.

Travel was a stimulating form of education yet things were so much easier in our own backyards. I didn't know what surprised me most—why so many people traveled and were involved with international affairs, or that so few were.

Landing in London I took a four hour bus ride to northern England to the town called Rochdale (pronounced Raa-CH-dale). When I boarded the bus the driver took my ticket and asked why I was going to Rochdale.

Before I could answer he said, "You're going to see the cooperatives."

I asked what made him think so.

"Lot of people do. Me great grandmother, me father, me wife's folks, we were all in the co-op. You're registered at birth. Me great grandfather was in it when it started," he said.

There had been cooperatives before the co-op in Rochdale, but few had lasted. On August 11, 1844, 28 people met formally for the first time to band together to provide themselves with goods that they could otherwise not afford. They named themselves the Rochdale Equitable Pioneers' Society.

By December of the same year they had organized to the extent that they had their first retail store open, selling simply sugar, butter, flour, oatmeal and a few tallow candles. Curiously, the few candles that were intended for sale were never sold because they had to be used to light the small shop. The "powers that be"—the gas company—would not serve these upstarts. Exactly like what happened in the United States and exactly why electrical cooperatives formed in rural America. Furthermore, the shop was located on a road called Old Lane. The city fathers renamed it Toad Lane, not exactly endearing.

Rochdale was a cotton and textile community that found itself in the midst of a changing world economy and by 1844 England no longer controlled the world market. Cooperatives were formed to better serve people. The thing that set this cooperative apart from its predecessors was a written set of principles. Six such principles continue to guide any true cooperative:

1) Voluntary and open membership;
2) Democratic control—one member, one vote;
3) Payment of fixed interest on capital. This eliminated the likelihood of speculation in cooperative stock and emphasized service rather than profit;
4) Surplus monies returned to members in proportion to purchases—the dividend, or "divis," or patronage capital;
5) Education for members and workers. This recognized that cooperative owners would not value and support something they did not understand.
6) Cooperation with other cooperatives.

The bus arrived in Rochdale after dark and I learned that Toad Lane was nearby. The first thing I did was to walk to the first co-op.

With time it had been swallowed up by bigger co-ops and the only thing on Toad Lane was a small museum, housed in the same building where the co-op sold its first goods. Not impressive in physical appearance, the brick building was three stories high, 30' × 50' in size. The museum was closed.

After talking with several bobbies at the bobbie station and a number of people on the street, I found a pub that rented rooms. After months of rural hospitality I now had to pay for a place to stay. I paid $16.60 (U.S.) for a bare room with a single bed. There was no weather stripping and probably no insulation, and it was heated by an electric space heater 2' × 3' × 8". There was a community bathroom that provided hot water via a small electric "point of use" water heater mounted on the wall in the shower.

Water pressure was low. The good news was that breakfast came with the price.

The people were friendly and I enjoyed being in a new culture, however similar, especially since English was the language. Of course my slanged up Americanese wasn't English but basically the language was the same and communication was free and easy. I appreciated fluency. To be able to express a thought or an idea in words, without having to think how to say it, was a big deal.

While coming out of a bakery in downtown Rochdale, I heard a passerby mention the words "terrorists" and "Egypt." Great! Such timing, I thought. That night I was at a pub and news of the latest hijacking came on the telly. A flight originating in Athens and bound for Cairo, wound up in Malta with the pilot axing one of the terrorists to death. In four days I was scheduled to fly to Cairo.

For the sake of a better understanding of the situation, I asked the bartender, "If you were going to fly to Cairo tomorrow, what would you do?"

"I'd go to Cairo. What will be, will be," he replied, without hesitation.

I ordered another pint of beer. I had a cousin the same age as me in California who had just run the Pike's Peak marathon and was as healthy as one could hope to be. He learned that he had terminal cancer. Life was a question of fate and odds didn't exist. Hosni Mubarak, president of Egypt, appeared on the screen. I learned firsthand about the events and decided there was no reason not to go.

When Monday rolled around I walked to the museum and the curator, Mr. Bert Millington, gave me a personalized tour. He was a distinguished looking man, near 60, and it felt sorta' cool to sign the register only pages after the queen.

I left Toad Lane and boarded a bus for England's second largest city, Manchester. Barbara Deverick of North Carolina's Blue Ridge electric cooperative was very active in international cooperation and had given me the names and addresses of people I should contact when I arrived in the various countries.

I arrived in Manchester and found myself in the city's tallest building—the co-op building. I went to the office of the #1 co-op man in England, but to no avail. Having a letter of introduction, so to speak, had its advantages, but also disadvantages. In this case Lloyd Wilkenson was too big and at an international cooperative meeting in Brussels.

I spoke with others in the building, including the librarian and lovely assistant librarian. We talked for awhile and then they made a phone call for me to Loughborough, south of Nottingham Forest. The co-ops had a college there and these librarians thought that I could learn a lot in a short period by visiting the college. An appointment was made for me to meet the college people at lunchtime the next day.

I left the monolithic looking skyscraper and wondered how big a role the cooperative played in England. I learned that half of the families in England belonged to some cooperative while it was closer to one in six families in the U.S. Were the co-ops remaining genuinely democratic and truly competitive? I had watched the British motorcycle industry fall to the Japanese. Historically, I knew that 1897 had been the year that marked the peak of the British empire. In 1850 England possessed fully one half of the world's industrial production capability. By 1910 that capability had dropped to one-fifteenth!

If rural electric cooperatives were maturing at 50 years of age, I wondered if there might be some correlation between the rise and fall of Great Britain in the international economy and the role played by the United States. Just as Great Britain was a mere shadow of its once mighty empire, the U.S. had come into its mighty own after WWI. By the end of WWII the U.S. possessed 34% of the world's industrial capability. By 2000, at the rate things were going in 1985, the U.S. would be down to 20%.

I looked for a place to spend the cold night, carrying my 40 pounds of luggage. While I walked, I thought.

Some people told me that the prices in the many retail cooperative stores were "dear," and that there really was no advantage any more to being a member. I heard that the "divi's" were seldom returned, supposedly one of the basic tenants of cooperative society. I turned around to look at the tall steel and glass building rising above the others and thought that perhaps the cooperative had built too many defenses into its organization in order to protect its "leaders," and in the process had isolated the people at the top and lost its democratic roots. I didn't know, but when buildings become tall and represent an organization known for its grass roots, I become skeptical.

I found a room at Miller's Motel, even less luxurious than the pub had been. Same price but this time when I looked for heat in the small, dingy room, I found a meter and a slot for a coin to turn on the electric space heater. In addition, there was a sign in the bathroom reading, "Due to high cost of electricity all baths and showers must be paid for in advance—30 pence."

The next morning I took a cab to the train station. It was snowing lightly. The train offered a nice view of the English countryside. It seemed very ordered after my months with Carter in America's farmland. Very old. Egypt would be even older. Only three more days! My two year goal and dream of being in Cairo was awfully close! I thought about what I was doing and accepted fate, trying to think realistically.

My plans were to do the international portion of the trip and then return home to write a commemorative book. Except for numerous reports in newspapers and cooperative magazines, and a few printings of my Electric Burro Travel Series columns, I remained basically unpublished and unpaid. If I was to actually do what I was trying to do, I would need a lot of luck and as much money as possible since I planned to publish the book on my own.

I couldn't rely on finding a publisher willing to take a risk with me. If the odds were against a greenhorn surviving 1350 miles, the odds for a new writer getting a first book printed and distributed by a publisher were even greater. I didn't believe in odds, but sometimes allowed them consideration.

I began to think that my international trip would serve mainly to make me more broke and less able to accomplish what I hoped for. It was relevant, but it complicated the story I hoped to tell. As much as anything else, I'd probably need the money already invested in airfare. Again I thought, "Why Cairo?"

My train of thought was interrupted when my train of travel pulled into Loughborough. I grabbed a taxi and headed for the co-op college. The driver knew all about the college. Stanford Hall was a mansion on 300 acres of magnificent country estate which dated back to 1558 and Queen Mary. The grounds were immaculately manicured and included a flamingo pond, a seal pit, and cricket grounds. The mansion was complete with an indoor badminton court. In 1945 the English national cooperative organization acquired the place for the price of "an old song" and continued to provide cooperative instruction for students from all around the world (since 1919).

When I arrived, Miss Molly Bury was expecting me, and she proceeded to give me a tour. She asked my plans and I replied that I would like to spend a few days at the school. The cooperative spirit prevailed and she told me that one of the college's dormitory rooms was available, so I signed up for two days at $26 (U.S.) per day, which included three meals and heat. The modern room was clean and bright. There was still a community bathroom arrangement, but the showers had unlimited hot water. Very American.

Approximately 25 countries were represented at the college while I was there. The programs included graduate studies as well as nine month courses and covered most any aspect of cooperative involvement. Subjects included cooperative principles and practice, law and regulation, marketing, retailing and distribution, computer studies, national development policy, fundamentals of management, and, of course, accounting. Facilities included a complete television studio which allowed for hands-on learning and cooperative television program development. Also a wonderful cooperative oriented library.

One particularly interesting course was for "mature students." Among these students was a readily apparent cooperative espirit de corps. Eligibility for this course was determined by an age greater than 23, and an interview which ascertained if a person possessed sufficient determination to continue along in their career path with a cooperative slant, or to change career directions. This program provided a very real way to address the rapidly changing international economy and worker displacement. Cooperative education. Cooperative re-training. The cooperative principles established in Rochdale were more than a bunch of words in Loughborough.

By my second day at the college, the lone American was a bit of a curiosity. Seems not too many Americans attend the cooperative college.

After several rousing games of badminton with some students and staff, including a striking "education officer," Claire Bishop, and a Nigerian student who looked a lot like Jesse Jackson, all gathered in the dining room to eat. Staff sat with students.

I sat next to an Indian instructor and we talked about the college and my planned trip. With the wisdom of ancient India, he thought that I needed better organization and that I would benefit more from my travels if I took the time to make the necessary arrangements before traveling further. I didn't try to explain how I had been approaching every day and night with some abandon. But I thought about what he said.

That night I sat in on a council meeting of the students. One problem that continually arose was one of linguistics. Some students complained of other languages being used too often, contrary to the rules, and insisted on English being used in mixed groups. Those whose first language was not English insisted on their right to occasionally use their own language so they could better communicate ideas and feelings.

At breakfast on the second day I sat down with students from England and Nigeria. I wasn't aware that the long table where I sat was divided between types of menus. There were meals prepared for Moslems, Hindus and Christians. I was sitting in the Moslem section of the table and was served a meal fitting for a Moslem. An adjustment was made and we shared a laugh at my expense.

I realized that all of the countries of my intended travel were represented here at the college. My plane to Cairo was scheduled to leave the next day. My mind was busy.

After breakfast I walked the three or four miles into town and had good time to reflect. I appreciated the different culture and felt that there was much objectivity to be gained by seeing things from a new angle. There was a red English phone booth. Double decked busses passed me, driving on the "wrong" side of the road. I got a particular kick from a sign on the building of an

"Approved Riding Establishment" that offered horse manure droppings for 30 pence, or five pounds per load! Very British.

As I walked along I heard gun shots ahead. The shot from the guns was falling all around me and as they fell through the leaves I wondered if I was in some sort of restricted area. I came to a field with three well dressed men spaced evenly apart, all facing the same direction with shotguns in their hands. I exposed my western Yankee upbringing and went up to the nearest of the three. I asked if it was safe to be walking where I was.

"Yes," the gentleman replied tersely.

Another pheasant was released from the next field. The man in the middle shot, and missed. I felt my prejudice and preferred my crude Michigan hunting style.

Downtown Loughborough featured outdoor markets on November 28 and as I came to the center, or centre, I saw a stand with a dozen or so unplucked pheasants hanging from a food stand. It'd never play in Peoria.

After visiting several bakeries I decided to put it off no longer. I walked to a travel agency. I asked about Cairo, ticket availability, and possible refund policies. I anguished and turned to leave, saying I might be back. I walked some more. What to do? After I had passed the hanging pheasants several times, I returned to the travel people.

"I'd like to cancel these tickets," I said, and handed the agent my entire collection of paid air tickets. I didn't like it.

epilogue

On November 30, 1985 I was over the Atlantic, flying to the United States, away from my intended destination of two years. I felt regret.

For two full years I had wondered why I had picked Cairo as a goal. Finally I understood. Cairo had given me direction. It served as a goal to get me off dead center. By declaring Cairo I had to put myself in a stance where I could change my life. The changes had happened, and they were good and positive.

I gazed out the window of the jumbo jet. I thought of the children who had smiled and waved and jumped and laughed and said, "Hi, horsey." I had waved back for Carter, thinking that a horse and buggy traveling down the road was something special to these children. In rural America, the days of the horse and buggy were pretty much gone.

In the next instant, some older people would drive by and wave and smile. They didn't have to jump or say "Hi, horsey," because the sparkle in their eyes said it all. These people remembered days gone by and many probably hadn't even seen me because they had been taken back to times past.

I had enjoyed being a part of the world's first solar powered and computerized buggy and had grown to love a beast of unflagging strength and willingness. I thought of how much comfort I received from listening to a three-quarter ton horse breathe deeply as he recovered from climbing a long and steep hill.

I had become used to the many questions as we traveled along the highways and byways. The road had become my home and many people had opened their homes to me. If I had spread a message of cooperation in some small way, I had received the same.

There was a time in Wisconsin when a preacher had stopped in the middle of a rural road to ask, "What are you?" What a question! Was the man asking about my light? Far below I saw the tiny lights of an oceangoing freighter and wondered what stories were behind those quiet lights.

DID YOU BORROW THIS COPY?

If so, NOW is the time to order your own personal copy of "**NEIGHBORS, Electric Burro on the Road to Bogota**".

Please enclose check or money order payable to "Breakaw a y Publishing"

☐ Quality Hardbound—$16.95

☐ Quality Paperback—$4.95

☒ Please add $2.00 postage and handling for one book, $1.00 for each additional book. Michigan residents add 4% sales tax.

PURCHASE ORDER:

Please send _____ copies of "**NEIGHBORS, Electric Burro on the Road to Bogota**" to:

Name _____

Address _____

City _____ State _____ Zip _____

Comments: _____

_____

_____

_____

"**NEIGHBORS, Electric Burro on the Road to Bogota**" is available at special quantity discounts for bulk purchases for gifts, educational purposes, and other promotions—inquiries invited.

TO: Breakaw a y Publications
    8344 Old M–72
    P.O. Box 169
    Williamsburg, Michigan 49690

Use separate piece of paper, or cut along this line to use this page as order form